FAMILY VALUES

FAMILY VALUES

The Ethics of Parent-Child Relationships

Harry Brighouse and Adam Swift

PRINCETON UNIVERSITY PRESS

Princeton & Oxford

Copyright © 2014 by Princeton University Press
Published by Princeton University Press, 41 William Street,
Princeton, New Jersey 08540
In the United Kingdom: Princeton University Press, 6 Oxford Street,
Woodstock, Oxfordshire OX20 1TW

press.princeton.edu

Jacket image: *Freedom from Want*, illustration, *Saturday Evening Post*, March 1943.
Norman Rockwell Museum Collections. Printed by permission of the Norman
Rockwell Family Agency. Copyright © 2014 the Norman Rockwell Family Entities.

"On Children" from *The Prophet* by Kahlil Gibran, copyright © 1923
by Kahlil Gibran and renewed 1951 by Administrators C.T.A. of Kahlil Gibran
Estate and Mary G. Gibran. Used by permission of Alfred A. Knopf, an imprint of
the Knopf Doubleday Publishing Group, a division of Random House LLC.
All rights reserved. Any third party use of this material, outside of this publication,
is prohibited. Interested parties must apply directly
to Random House LLC for permission.

LIBRARY OF CONGRESS CATALOGING-IN-PUBLICATION DATA

Brighouse, Harry.
Family values : the ethics of parent-child relationships / Harry Brighouse and
Adam Swift.
pages cm
Includes bibliographical references and index.
ISBN 978–0–691–12691–3 (hardcover : alk. paper) 1. Families. 2. Values. I. Swift,
Adam, 1961- II. Title.
HQ728.B7385 2014   306.85—dc23
2013044237

British Library Cataloging-in-Publication Data is available

This book has been composed in Minion Pro and John Sans Pro

Printed on acid-free paper ∞

Printed in the United States of America

1 3 5 7 9 10 8 6 4 2

On Children

Your children are not your children.
They are the sons and daughters of Life's longing for itself.
They come through you but not from you,
And though they are with you yet they belong not to you.

You may give them your love but not your thoughts,
For they have their own thoughts.
You may house their bodies but not their souls,
For their souls dwell in the house of tomorrow,
which you cannot visit, not even in your dreams.
You may strive to be like them,
but seek not to make them like you.
For life goes not backward nor tarries with yesterday.

You are the bows from which your children
as living arrows are sent forth.
The archer sees the mark upon the path of the infinite,
and He bends you with His might
that His arrows may go swift and far.
Let your bending in the archer's hand be for gladness;
For even as He loves the arrow that flies,
so He loves also the bow that is stable.

—Kahlil Gibran

CONTENTS

PREFACE

This book offers an account of why families are valuable. Or rather, since some families are, alas, dreadful, it offers an account of why "the family" is valuable—why it is generally a good thing that children are raised by parents. Some may regard this as a pointless exercise. Even to ask such a fundamental question may seem to betray not merely an ignorance of evolutionary biology but a kind of emotional blindness, an insensitivity to the stuff of human relationships, a deafness to the strains of love.

There is something right about that response. Our account will indeed appeal to some rather elementary observations about the value of intimate loving relationships within the family. Where some, most famously Plato, have argued for the superiority of collective child-rearing institutions, we will come down on the side of the conventional wisdom—and the wisdom of the ages—rejecting this and related suggestions as failing to understand the very special things that parents and children can do for one another.[1] But, traditional and reassuring though our views may be in that respect, we are confident that readers will find much of what follows rather more disconcerting.

Identifying the proper content of "family values" is, for us, the first step toward working out a normative theory of the family. Only by thinking carefully about why it is good for children to be raised by parents, and good for parents to raise children, can we derive a satisfying and appropriately detailed understanding of the morality of family life. We want to know what parents should be required to do for their children, what they should be permitted but not required to do for their children, what rights (if any) they have to exercise control over their children's upbringing, what rights (if any) those children have to be treated (or not to be treated) in certain ways, and so on. These are questions of moral and political philosophy—questions about the proper division of responsibility for child rearing as between parents and society. The state decides what parents should be free to do to, with, and for their children; indeed, it sometimes decides who should be permitted to become parents in the first place. We set out a theory that aims to guide the state in its deliberations. In a democracy, it is the citizenry who determine how the state acts, so another way of putting this is to say that our theory aims to guide us in our deliberations as citizens. Moreover, since we believe that reasons of state are essentially continuous with reasons that apply to people in their personal lives, that theory can also guide individual parents in their day-to-day dealings with their children.

It is here that our approach will reveal its true colors. Our analysis of the family's value focuses on the goods distinctively made possible by familial relationships; that's why we call it the "relationship goods" account. But if it is the relationships—and the good things that they produce—that are valuable, then our answer to these normative questions must focus very specifically on the content of those relationships, and on the conditions necessary for the goods to be realized by those engaging in them. This leads to some rather controversial conclusions. We will argue, for example, that parents are not required to pursue their children's "best interests," that they have no right to confer their wealth on their children, and that they have only very limited rights to transmit their values or religious convictions to their children. Indeed, our account of "family values" lends little support to the normativity of the two-parent heterosexual family, nor does it imply that adults have a fundamental right to parent their biological children.

For some readers, these conclusions will be enough to put us firmly among the forces of darkness, and immediately reveal as disingenuous our attempt, in our title, to present ourselves as articulators and defenders of "family values." To suggest that the state may properly regulate parent-child interactions so as to restrict parents' freedom to educate (or not to educate) their children as they wish, or may significantly limit parents' freedom to transmit values or property to their children, is already to deny the status of "the family" as a private institution that should be immune from political interference. And to entertain the possibility that "family values" can be realized in single-parent families or by same-sex parents, or without regard to the biological connection between parents and children, is to miss those features of the family that explain quite why it is such an important social institution—and why it is in such a state of crisis. For traditional advocates of "family values," we will doubtless seem to be more the problem than the solution. With friends like us, it might be thought, the family hardly needs enemies.

We hope that those inclined to this attitude will bear with us. It's true that our use of "family values" represents an attempt to rescue that term from its traditional context and significance, to outline an account of those values that sits more easily with other, liberal and egalitarian, commitments. But our theory really *is* a theory about why families are valuable. And we share with conservatives a sense that familial relationships have sometimes been undervalued by those committed to a progressive or leftist political agenda.

Whether or not one thinks the family is in crisis, the little we have said so far is already enough to show that "the family" is. Those words mean different things to different people; the content of the concept varies across the disputants in this particular battle in the culture wars. Must a family include children, or can a childless couple constitute a family? Must the children in a family be biologically connected to "their" parents? The term "parent" is similarly contested. For some, a parent just is a child's biological progenitor; for others, that term refers more properly to the person who "parents" the child, the person who does the "parenting," irrespective of biological connection. This variation in usage reflects the fact that we are living through huge changes in the way we understand, and experience, the relationships between children and the adults who create and/or raise them. Developments in reproductive technology have forced a rethinking of the boundary between the "natural" and the "social"—we now face and make procreative choices in contexts where until recently we simply faced the givens of nature. (A child can now have several *biological* parents—as well as being "parented" by an indeterminate number of adults.)[2] Social trends such as the growth of divorce, single parenthood, and same-sex relationships have similarly challenged long-held assumptions and raised deep questions about what families are and why exactly we should care about them.

For us, this flux, and the conceptual confusion it generates, call for the philosophical enterprise undertaken here: a fundamental, "back-to-basics," analysis of the values at stake in the raising of children, and an investigation of the institutions and practices that those values justify. Still, some readers may be so hostile to our account that they are not willing to accept it as an account of "the family" at all,[3] so it may be helpful to say something about our method, and to explain why, despite its being so far removed from much existing familial practice, we nonetheless present what we offer as a defense of the family—as an articulation of "family values properly understood." Our project is the construction, from first principles or elementary considerations of value, of a theory about the best way for the raising of children to be organized. Social institutions are justified mainly by their tendency to promote, and to distribute in a just way, well-being, where "well-being" includes all the things that make people's lives go well. So the basic question is this: what arrangements for the raising of children tend to make people's lives go well? We are interested not only in what is good for children, though their interests are surely very important, but also in what is good for adults, both parents themselves and those who are not themselves involved in the raising of children.

It should be clear how, conceptually speaking, the answer to that question might not be "the family" at all. It might not be good that children should be raised by a small number of particular adults. Perhaps more collective child-rearing arrangements would raise children to be happier, more productive, and more altruistic adults. If it is good that children be raised by a small number of adults, it might be bad that those adults should have much discretion over how the children are raised. Perhaps a common regime for child rearing, executed by particular adults but decided collectively by the community as a whole, would make for more well-being, or for its fairer distribution.

We regard what we offer as a defense of "the family," rather than as an argument against it, because our answer to the question of how the raising of children should be organized is an institution that is rather similar to the family as that is conventionally understood. We argue that intimate but authoritative relationships between children and a small number of particular adults, relationships in which the adults have considerable discretion over the details of how the children are raised, *is* the best arrangement for raising children, taking into account all the interests at stake. We derive something that closely resembles the conventional family from first principles, by arguing that it is the arrangement for raising children that is most conducive to making human beings' lives go well. But close resemblance is not identity. The arrangement that does most for well-being departs in significant respects from conventional conceptions of the family. The extent to which parents may exercise discretion over their children's lives is considerably smaller, and the ways in which they may act to promote their children's interests are considerably more limited. And, perhaps most controversially, adults have no fundamental right to parent their own biological children. For us, then, this "back-to-basics" exercise yields complex and provocative fruit. It partly defends, and partly challenges, currently dominant understandings of the family.

If the family did not exist, it would be necessary to invent it; its invention would be morally required. But the family that it would be necessary to invent would not be that celebrated by traditionalists. To be sure, it would be a place of love, the crucial site of emotional development for children and important also for the flourishing of many adults. And we accept the traditional view that the parent's authority over the child is indeed a key feature. The family is properly a locus of intimate-yet-authoritative relationships between adults and the children they parent.[4] But it is also one in which parents' rights over their children, their authority to act on their judgments about how their children's lives should go, are strictly limited, conditional on parents' discharging their duties to their children at quite a high level, and quite properly subject to scrutiny and, where necessary, regulation by the state.

The family is a hot, often controversial, topic in many academic disciplines, and it is currently high up the political agenda in many countries. Sociologists, bioethicists, analysts of social policy, political scientists, economists, legal scholars, students of gender studies, anthropologists, historians, and policymakers all come at the issue with their own perspectives and interests. Although this is an exercise in political philosophy, we have tried to write it in a way that is accessible to nonspecialists. Hence, in particular, part 1's attempt to locate the family in its philosophical contexts, some of which may seem familiar to—and could perhaps be skipped by—those already steeped in liberal or egalitarian theory. We believe that this foundational normative enterprise can helpfully inform the thinking of those engaging with the family from a range of disciplinary perspectives.

Our theory also meshes nicely with recent attempts to develop a "politics of well-being"—to move beyond the rather narrow focus on GDP and material prosperity that has dominated political and economic thinking for so long.[5] Happiness is not everything, by any means, but it is certainly something, and there is considerable evidence that good relationships make people happy.[6] Parent-child relationships can be crucial components of flourishing for adults, and, for children, they can lay (or fail to lay) the foundations for healthy and happy relationships as adults. Of course, there are serious questions about whether the state can in practice, and may legitimately, promote individual well-being, especially in its emotional dimensions. There is something paradoxical about the idea of harnessing the coercive power of the state in the pursuit of better personal relationships, and many are understandably suspicious of attempts by politicians to jump on the well-being bandwagon. When the UK government adds parenting classes, in some circumstances compulsory ones, to its arsenal of policies, there are bound to be fears that the "nanny state" has gone too far.[7] We hope that our concept of "relationship goods," and our account of what families need to be like in order to realize them, will prove useful contributions to these important debates.

Until recently, the normative aspects of the family were primarily explored by feminist theorists, nearly all of them women. The focus, for many, was the justice (or, rather, the injustice) of gender relationships within the family. The way that the conventional domestic division of labor interacts with prevalent labor-market practices to produce inequalities of opportunity as between men and women, the associated unequal distribution of bargaining power, and hence effective freedom of exit, within the household: these were, and still are, the stuff of a substantial and important literature in political philosophy.[8]

We should be clear from the outset, then, that we are interested specifically in familial relationships between adults and children. We do not doubt that the family as it actually exists has been, and continues to be, a crucial site of gender injustice, but its gendered aspect is not our topic here. The theory we develop makes no assumptions about how the job of caring for children is, or should be, divided between men and women, nor about how any such division should impact on the distribution of goods more generally. Indeed, as we've already said, our theory does not in itself require that the family should contain two parents at all, let alone that they be a man and a woman. The theory might, in combination with empirical evidence about child development, have more specific implications for family structure, including the gendered division of parental labor, but these are derivative; they emerge, if they do, from consideration of what is needed for flourishing parent-child relationships. And even if a gendered division of parenting responsibilities is indeed implied, nothing to justify gender *inequality* follows from it.[9]

Not all feminists present themselves as critics of gender injustice. Some reject the concept of justice itself. For them, the "ethic of justice" is an unhelpful, and distinctively male, frame through which to view the obligations that attend personal relationships. Even if appropriate to public or political matters, where impartiality and objectivity might indeed have a lot going for them, the extension of "justice" into the domain of such relationships represents an unhelpful, and fundamentally alien, intrusion. It would be better to conceptualize that domain in terms of an "ethic of care," which begins in and develops out of the lived experience of women's attachments to the children they mother.[10]

In focusing on the goods that can be realized in parent-child relationships, our theory attempts to combine the insights offered by advocates of an ethic of care with an attention to distributive justice that we regard as morally inescapable. We seek to incorporate within the distributive paradigm (some of) those relationship-based aspects of human well-being that have usually been regarded as beyond its ken. Whether the attempt succeeds, whether it is possible to bring about such a reconciliation without doing injustice to either (or both) of the two perspectives, it must of course be for our readers to judge.

We are among the first cohorts of fathers to take on anything approaching an equal share of child-care responsibilities, and we detect among our generation a greater willingness of men to write about the family and parenting. We should not overstate the case. Many canonical political theorists had clear views about the family, however distasteful or anachronistic those views may seem to us now. And, of course, some of the most sensitive writers and theorists about parent-child relationships have been men, such as Winnicott, Bettelheim, and Bowlby.[11] But it is only relatively recently that significant numbers of men have themselves started to play a full role in the day-to-day rearing of their children—whether out of a concern for gender justice or an appreciation of the joys of parenting (or both). One side effect of the trend toward the "New Fatherhood" is men's increasing confidence that they can think and write about parenting without feeling that they are pronouncing on matters that are fundamentally alien to them, or not really their business. We see ourselves as double beneficiaries of feminism: personally enabled to play a larger role in raising our children, professionally enabled to work in the intellectual space opened up by feminist theorists.

There is a real question as to whether recent cultural shifts toward gender-neutral parenting—indeed toward the gender-neutral concept of "parent" rather than "mother" and "father"—constitute unambiguously positive developments. Some view them rather as attempting to deny fundamental facts of gender difference, some of which are crucially significant for children's emotional development, and even as the latest (albeit perhaps unconscious) attempt by men to dominate women, a colonizing of terrain previously identified as distinctively female.[12] For the most part, we do indeed frame our discussion in gender-neutral terms, reflecting our belief that, relative to current norms, women, men, and children would all benefit from a more equal division of child care between men and women. Certainly our own lives have been hugely enriched by our experience of parenting. We hope that the benefit to us has not come at undue, or even any, cost to our children and their mothers.

ACKNOWLEDGMENTS

This book is the offspring of a sixteen-year relationship and has been gestating for a very long time. Harry met Adam in Madison, in 1998, with Erik Olin Wright and the Havens Center for the Study of Social Structure and Social Change acting as unwitting matchmakers. Our first few dates were spent discussing the first draft of what was eventually to become Swift's *How Not to Be a Hypocrite: School Choice for the Morally Perplexed Parent*. The liaison was cemented between 2000 and 2002, when Brighouse lived in Oxford while working at London's Institute of Education and Swift held a British Academy Research Readership at Nuffield College. Since that honeymoon period, things have evolved into something like a transatlantic marriage. Though not monogamous—each of us has dallied with various others from time to time— the relationship has been committed enough for us to have (at last) produced this progeny.

Given that we've been at it for so long, it's not surprising that we owe a huge amount to many institutions and individuals. We are grateful to audiences at the American Political Science Association, Bowling Green State University, Cornell University, the Philosophy of Education Society of Great Britain, the London School of Economics, the Nuffield Political Theory Workshop, Queen's University Kingston, Roehampton University, University College, Dublin, the Graduate Conference on Political Theory at the University of Warwick, the Universities of Birmingham, Bristol, East Anglia, Essex, Kobe, Lisbon, Montreal, Pennsylvania, Reading, Rochester, South Carolina, and Toronto, Massachusetts Institute of Technology, the Oxford Political Thought Conference, UCLA, the University of Wisconsin's Institute of the Humanities and Center for the Humanities, ECPR workshop Granada, Oxford's Centre for the Study of Social Justice, Princeton's Center for Human Values, the Stanford Political Theory Workshop, the Society for Applied Philosophy, Warwick's Centre for Ethics, Law and Public Affairs, Erasmus University Rotterdam, the Institute of Advanced Study in Princeton, the September ("No Bullshit Marxism") Group, and Pompeu Fabra University, Barcelona. Special thanks are due to Stephen Macedo, Richard Holton, Ingrid Robeyns, and Matthew Clayton for organizing workshops and conferences that were particularly valuable staging posts along the way.

We have surely forgotten valuable corrections and suggestions received since the book's conception, but we do remember at least some of those from Jaime Ahlberg, Danielle Allen, Richard Arneson, John Baker, Christopher Bertram, Larry Blum, Paul Bou-Habib, Sam Bowles, Andrea Bueschel, Tania Burchardt, Eamonn Callan, Simon Caney, Paula Casal, Dario Castiglione, Clare Chambers, Lindsey Chambers, the late Jim Childs, Matthew Clayton, the late Jerry Cohen, Joshua Cohen, David Copp, Randall Curren, Marissa Daniels, Geert Demuijnck, Cecile Fabre, Tim Fowler, Anca Gheaus, Diane Gereluk, Sue Gerhardt, Pablo Gilabert, Herbert Gintis, Lynn Glueck, Sarah Hannan, Sally Haslanger, Dan Hausman, Barbara Herman, Richard Holton, Adam Hosein, Donald Hubin, Tom Hurka, Sandy Jencks, A. J. Julius, Eva Feder Kittay, Tony Laden, Hugh Lazenby, Lewis Leavitt, Meira Levinson, Loren Lomasky, Kathleen Lynch, Kenneth Macdonald, Stephen Macedo, Colin Macleod, Dan McDermott, Mike McPherson, Emily McRae, David Miller, John Miller, Serena Olsaretti, Marina Oshana, Philip Pettit, Anne Phillips, Mark Philp, Rob Reich, Fiona Reid, Arthur Ripstein, Ingrid Robeyns, Miriam Ronzoni, Michael Rossington, Debra Satz, Tamar Schapiro, Gina Schouten, Francis Schrag, Victor Seidler, Liam Shields, Seana Shiffrin, Anna-Marie Smith, Hillel Steiner, Zofia Stemplowska, Sarah Stroud, Judith Suissa, Christine Sypnowich, Victor Tadros, John Tasioulas, Simon Thompson, James Tooley, Joan Tronto, Peter Vallentyne, Philippe Van Parijs, Leigh Vicens, Matt Waldren, Brynn Welch, Andrew Williams, Bekka Williams, and Erik Olin Wright. Emma Marston, Gina Schouten, and Shanna Slank have provided valuable research assistance. Some of the ideas in the book have been aired at CrookedTimber.org, where we have often received helpful comments. We are grateful also to three anonymous readers of two previous drafts for Princeton University Press, and to many more anonymous readers for various academic journals.

With all that help there shouldn't be any, but all remaining errors are Brighouse's.

Harry Brighouse is grateful to the Carnegie Corporation of New York, the Wisconsin Alumni Research Foundation, UW-Madison's Institute for Research in the Humanities, and, especially, to the Spencer Foundation and his colleagues there. Adam Swift thanks the British Academy and Nuffield College for granting and hosting the Research Readership during which he began work on this project, the Arts and Humanities Research Council for awarding him a Research Fellowship to bring it closer to fruition, Balliol College and Oxford's Department of Politics and International Relations, and Warwick's Department of Politics and International Studies, for various stints of sabbatical leave.

Ian Malcolm, who commissioned the book, Rob Tempio, who inherited it, and Lauren Lepow, who copyedited it, have been wonderfully supportive and patient. We were supposed to deliver the manuscript in 2007, so they have had a lot to be patient about.

We are grateful to the University of Chicago Press, John Wiley and Sons, and Oxford University Press for permission to incorporate material (some of it substantially revised) from "Parents' Rights and the Value of the Family," *Ethics* 117, no. 1 (2006): 80–108; "Legitimate Parental Partiality," *Philosophy & Public Affairs* 37, no. 1 (2009): 43–80; and "The Goods of Parenting," in *Family-Making: Contemporary Ethical Challenges*, ed. Françoise Baylis and Carolyn Macleod (Oxford: Oxford University Press, 2014), pp. 11–28.

In a book about families it's particularly nice to acknowledge our children and our parents, who have taught us so much about familial relationship goods. So far, Danny, Lillie, Madeline, Maisy, and Oliver have provided us with seventy-eight parenting-years between us. Without them we might have done lots of other things, but we certainly wouldn't have written this book.

Part One

Liberty, Equality, Family

Introduction

The family poses two challenges to any theory of social justice. The egalitarian challenge focuses on the distribution of goods and opportunities between children born into different families. We can conceive those goods in a variety of ways. Economists tend to focus on expected income over the life-course; sociologists investigate chances of social mobility; philosophers typically think in more abstract terms such as resources or opportunities for well-being. But however we frame or measure the inequality, it is clear that children born into different families face unequal prospects.[1] Similarly, there is disagreement about how much, or what aspects, of that inequality count as unjust. For some, all inequalities that are not the result of individuals' choices are failures of justice. Others adopt the more conventional view that justice requires equality of opportunity in the limited sense that people's chances of achieving desirable jobs should reflect their own merits rather than their family background. But whatever the categories, and however radical the conception of social justice, the concern that children's prospects should not be too dependent on their social origins is familiar. The egalitarian challenge demands an account of why families should be permitted to create inequalities between children, and what kinds of familial interactions, creating what kinds of inequalities, are indeed justified.

The liberal challenge concerns the distribution of freedom and authority between parents, children, and the state. Liberals think it valuable that individuals be free to make and act on their own judgments about how they are to live their lives; justifying authority requires an account of how anybody can have the right to decide for others. Children are born helpless and incapable of judgment, so somebody else must have the job of deciding what happens to them. Should that be the child's parents, or does the state have the right to determine what the child eats or drinks, where she sleeps, what television programs she watches, what school she attends? From the parent's point of view, any attempt by the state to regulate her dealings with her children may look like a denial of her freedom to live the life of her choice. But children are separate people, with their own lives to live, and it is one of the state's tasks to protect its citizens, and its prospective citizens, from undue interference by others, including their parents. As they develop, children quickly become capable of forming their own views. What justifies anybody else—parent *or* state—in retaining authority over them then? The liberal challenge demands an account of who—child, parent, state—should have the right to decide what in relation to children's lives.

As egalitarian liberals, we take both challenges seriously. Our egalitarianism leads us to condemn the inequalities that arise between children born into different families. Our liberalism makes us worry about the rights that parents and children have over their own lives, and with respect to each other, and about the proper limits of state authority with regard to both parents and children. The two challenges intersect. If parents should be free to act in ways that confer advantage on their children, without regard to any resulting inequalities between those children and others, then we have a deep incompatibility between egalitarian justice and parents' rights. If the only way to ensure equality between children is to abolish the family altogether and raise children in state institutions, then we can achieve full satisfaction of egalitarian principles only by wholly rejecting the right of adults to parent children. What is needed, and what we offer, is an account of the family's value—an account of "family values"—that gives it its proper place. One that responds adequately to the egalitarian objection to the family while also providing a coherent account of who—children themselves, parents, and the state—has the right to decide what about children's lives.

Egalitarian liberals are concerned to strike the right balance between equality and liberty. For us, social justice requires that the state treat its citizens as equals, and that requirement has serious distributive implications, demanding much more equal distributions, of a variety of goods, than exist in any contemporary societies. But, as liberals, we recognize that it is valuable for people to make and act on their own judgments about how they should live, and important that they be accorded the freedoms necessary for them to live well. The problem, of course, is that the freedoms liberals value tend to disrupt the equality egalitarians value. Those freedoms include not only the freedom to pursue their own interests to some extent but also the freedom to engage in relationships that depend on treating particular others as special—to act partially in favor of themselves and their loved ones. A world in which we were required to treat everybody the same—friend, lover, child, stranger—would be a dystopic nightmare, a world where nobody enjoyed the relationships that make us human. Some of the most valuable elements in human lives depend precisely on our treating particular others as special. The family, the natural home of such relationships, is a particularly stark locus of the tensions embodied in the view that people should enjoy equal freedom, or have equal opportunity to live valuable lives.

A completely harmonious reconciliation may not be possible. We do not show that plausible understandings of the family, equality, and liberty can be constructed in a way that eliminates all conflicts between the family and equality, or resolves all difficulties concerning authority over children. Our more modest aim is to offer an account of "family values properly understood" that shows the possibility of child-rearing practices and institutions that realize the values distinctively made available by familial relationships, that respects those individual liberties that are indeed worthy of respect, and that mitigates—massively mitigates—the conflict with equality.

The family has only recently begun to receive the careful attention needed to provide satisfactory responses to these two challenges. Public declarations of human rights, devised specifically to provide a consensual focal point, can hardly be expected to venture into controversial matters, so we should not be surprised if their pronouncements are rather vague. Thus, for example, the Universal Declaration of Human Rights tells us that "the family is the natural and fundamental group unit of society and is entitled to protection by society and the State" (Article 16.3), while the European Convention on Human Rights announces that "everyone has the right to respect for his private and family life" (Article 8) and that "men and women of marriageable age have the right to marry and found a family" (Article 12).[2]

Previous work by philosophers has taken us a good deal further,[3] but in our view none has yet engaged with the full range of issues at stake with the necessary degree of specificity. Taking the challenges seriously requires us to ask why it would be a bad idea to abolish the family. If the family is valuable, then it must be possible to identify the good things that it contributes to human lives. What exactly would be lost, and by whom, if children were to be raised by the state? Our answer to that question, developed in part 2, focuses on a distinctive set of goods, which we call "familial relationship goods"; that answer provides an account of the value of the family that is detailed enough to furnish appropriately nuanced responses to both challenges. Part 1 sets out those challenges in more detail.

CHAPTER 1

Liberalism and the Family

The liberal challenge to a normative theory of the family demands an account of who should have the right to decide what with regard to children's upbringing. Children are individuals distinct from their parents, individuals whose interests it is the state's job to protect and promote. Yet, we will argue, children have a crucial interest in a relationship in which they are subject to their parents' authority, and many adults have an important interest in participating in the kind of relationship where they get to exercise that authority. How to think about the allocation of rights, and what rights—rights to do *what* exactly?— should be held by whom, is thus a complex issue.

By the end of part 2, we will have presented our basic justification of the family, understood as a way of raising children that gives parents an important sphere of discretion over their children's lives—albeit one that is limited by the duty to provide what children need (what *they* have a right to). This is our account of the basis of adults' right *to* parent (and the child's right to be parented). In part 3, we will go on to explore in greater detail the proper content of parents' rights over their children, focusing particularly on the ways in which parents may (and may not) legitimately confer advantage on their children (chapter 5) and shape their values (chapter 6). This is our explication of the rights *of* parents: what it is exactly that the right to parent gives you a right to do to, with, and for your children. To determine whether parents have rights, and, if so, what they are, a substantive investigation of the goods at stake in the parent-child relationship is needed. What is it about the value of the family, and the parent-child relationship in particular, that makes it so important to protect it with rights, and what rights are needed to protect it?

All this talk of rights may alarm some readers. Never mind the liberal challenge to the family: what about the family's challenge to liberalism? Isn't it a crucial feature of loving familial relationships that they resist liberal categories?

For some, the very project of developing a liberal theory of the family, and of conceiving parent-child relationships in terms of rights and duties, is misguided. We disagree. This chapter sets out the ways in which the family might be thought to pose problems for the liberal framework, and defends our adoption of that framework from the objection that it simply cannot do justice to—or, perhaps, fails adequately to care about—the ethically significant phenomena attending parent-child relationships.

Liberalism and Communitarianism

We should start by clearing the decks. Liberalism is widely misunderstood and much maligned, so in order to get to the real issues we need to deal with a red herring. According to some critics, liberalism neglects the significance of attachments, relationships, and communities for human beings, positing people as atomistic, rational, autonomous, self-interested individuals. If that were an accurate picture, then it is not hard to see how liberalism and the family would be at loggerheads. The family is where we experience our most important attachments and relationships, a realm not of rationality but of emotion and intimacy, a sphere of commitment and self-sacrifice.

If liberalism were the problem, communitarianism might seem like the solution. Certainly many of those advocating family values, and those most concerned about the social pressures that threaten them, have identified themselves as "communitarian." The Communitarian Network website announces that "communitarians have been in the forefront of efforts to strengthen and rebuild the family and to restore a child-centered focus to both our marriage culture and our public policy."[1] The Responsive Communitarian Platform urges us to "start with the family," claiming that "fathers and mothers, consumed by 'making it' and consumerism, or preoccupied with personal advancement, who come home too late and too tired to attend to the needs of their children, cannot discharge their most elementary duty to their children and their fellow citizens," and claims that "child-raising is important, valuable work, work that must be honored rather than denigrated by both parents and the community."[2] Over twenty years ago, an influential group of communitarian thinkers claimed that "society *is not fostering a family-friendly environment and has a responsibility to do so*; economic pressures on parents, especially mothers, are mounting and the popular culture is making the raising of children an ever more challenging task."[3] David Popenoe tells us that "communitarians believe that the highest social value should be placed on parent-child relationships and the fostering of a child-centered society."[4]

If one has to be a "communitarian" in order to see that relationships and at-tachments are valuable for human beings, or to acknowledge the significance of commitment and self-restraint, then we are communitarians. Much of our argument, indeed our very category of "relationship goods," may well strike the reader as "communitarian" in spirit, and we have no wish to deny the sub-stantial overlap between our position and the "pro-family" concerns of com-munitarians.[5] But this appreciation of "community" neither conflicts nor even contrasts with our liberalism.[6]

That caricature set aside, we can move on to two of the more serious objec-tions to our—indeed any—attempt to construct a liberal theory of the fam-ily. Both start from the observation that liberalism is fundamentally a political philosophy, a theory about the proper role of the state, specifically concerned with the proper regulation of a political community's public life or collective ar-rangements. If that is the right way to think about liberalism—which it is—then the idea of a liberal theory of the family might immediately look confused. The family, it might seem, belongs to the private, not the public or political, sphere. What goes on within it must then be beyond liberalism's remit, a matter for people to decide in their capacity as private individuals, not for citizens col-lectively to determine. And insofar as philosophers *do* attempt to conceptualize relations within the family in terms developed to deal with interactions be-tween citizens in the public sphere—in terms of rights and duties, with a focus on autonomy and rationality—they must be failing to capture the true nature, and distinctive value, of familial relationships. To apply liberal categories to re-lations within the family is incoherent (because, for liberals, the family must be private) or inappropriate (because the family is properly conceived as a realm of intimacy, love, and emotion, not rights, duties, and autonomy or rational-ity) or both. Either way, liberalism is not the right place to look for a theory of family values.

Both these objections have mainly been articulated by feminists concerned primarily with relationships between adult men and women in the family, but they are at least as pertinent to parent-child relationships, in some ways more so.[7] For even if, as we shall argue, it is a mistake to think that liberalism regards the family as private, the idea that children in some sense belong to their par-ents continues to influence many who reject the once-common view that wives belong to their husbands. Similarly, the inapplicability of liberal concepts such as rights, duty, rationality, and autonomy seems plainer in the case of familial relationships between parents and children than it does in the case of familial relationships between adults. To be sure, the feminist critique of the "ethic of justice" developed in large part via a claim that women's moral experience dif-fers from men's precisely because of their more direct involvement in caring, nurturing relationships with their children. In that sense, the parent-child relationship, and the inappropriateness of applying justice categories to it, were indeed a crucial part of that story. Still, even those doubtful about the more general case for an "ethic of care" over an "ethic of justice" may feel that liberal categories are particularly unhelpful for our understanding of the moral relationship between parents and children.

The Family and the Private Sphere

Let us start with the suggestion that liberals regard the family as part of the private sphere, and so can have little or nothing to say about it. For some, of course, this is all to the good. On this view, what liberalism gets right is precisely that the state has no business meddling with people's personal lives—and what could be more personal than their relationships with their children? For others, those for whom "the personal is political," this inability to engage with matters within the family is a crucial weakness, since it renders liberalism inert in an area of life where individuals—typically women and children—are highly vulnerable to oppression, exploitation, and injustice. We think that both responses, approving and disapproving, are misconceived. Both misunderstand the sense in which liberal political philosophy argues for a distinction between the public and the private, and both are wrong to think that liberals regard the family as on the "private" side of that distinction. It is true that, as a matter of historical fact, liberals—along with other political philosophers—have tended to argue that the domestic or familial sphere lies beyond, or prior to, politics. Indeed, we can plausibly trace the origins of political philosophy to Aristotle's distinction, in his *Politics*, between the *oikos*, or household, and the *polis*, or political community.[8] So the suggestion that politics should not extend into family matters does indeed have a long, and in some ways distinguished, history. Still, we should not confuse the general idea that some matters should be "private," in the sense of being properly beyond the authority of the state and subject only to the judgment of the individual, with any particular view about what those matters are. Liberals' belief in the value of individuals' autonomously choosing their own way of life does indeed commit them to some version of the public-private distinction. Its content is a separate question.[9]

We cannot simply posit "the family" as belonging to the private sphere and therefore immune from legislation. What should be left free from legislation is precisely what we need to decide. If there are any familial matters where individuals' judgments should be regarded as authoritative, they will emerge from careful consideration of what is valuable about the family, not by taking for granted that it is a private institution. As David Archard puts it: "We cannot say that the family is, as a matter of fact, a private institution and therefore ought not to be subject to state supervision and control. Rather, we must show that the nature of familial life and activity is such that these are properly beyond the scope of legal and political governance."[10]

The point of the idea of a private sphere is to specify a range within which individuals are, or should be, free from political regulation. Families are made up of more than one individual, so the very idea of the family as "private" can involve confusion—the misconception that an individual can claim that his (or her) relations with family members are a matter to be determined by him (or her) alone. The idea of the family as private *might* make sense if all family members were there as a matter of choice. In that case we could think of it as a voluntary association, and it could be that the terms of that association were indeed something in which others had no legitimate interest, something that should be a matter entirely for the voluntarily associating individuals to decide. Even in associations formed by adults, though, we need to think carefully about the context and terms of the association. Is the choice to associate genuinely voluntary or are some parties effectively constrained—by social norms, by lack of alternatives—to accept unfair or exploitative terms? Do parties retain an effective, and not merely a formal, exit option if they decide that they no longer wish to continue the association?

Feminists have rightly drawn our attention to worries of this kind, and cast serious doubt on the view that familial arrangements between adults are an exclusively private matter.[11] But with a focus on parent-child relationships things are surely more straightforward. We cannot regard children as participants in a voluntary association. They are nonconsenting nonadults. The claim that how parents treat their children is no business of the state makes sense only when understood as asserting that children are somehow extensions of, part of, or perhaps the possession of, their parents. Only then can parents' claim to a private sphere be thought to cover their treatment of their children.

Such views must surely be rejected. The doctrine of *patria potestas* gave Roman fathers absolute property rights over their children, including the right to dispose of them as property and to kill them, and Lockean arguments about the acquisition of property through labor might seem to support the idea that children should count among their parents' possessions.[12] But children are separate human beings. To regard them as owned by their parents, and so properly subject only to parental power, is to fail to recognize the important role the state can and must play in protecting children from their parents.

The same applies to less fully proprietarian accounts that might be invoked to justify giving parents extensive rights to control their children's lives by assimilating those rights to the parent's own proper sphere of individual freedom. Robert Nozick regards children as "part of one's substance . . . part of a wider identity you have";[13] Charles Fried believes that "the right to form one's child's values, one's child's life plan and the right to lavish attention on the child are extensions of the basic right not to be interfered with in doing these things for oneself."[14] For William Galston, "the ability of parents to raise their children in a manner consistent with their deepest commitments is an essential element of expressive liberty."[15] For Eammon Callan, 'the freedom to rear our children according to the dictates of conscience is for most of us as important as any other expression of conscience, and the freedom to organize and sustain the life of the family in keeping with our own values is as significant as our liberty to associate outside the family for any purpose whatsoever."[16] Such perspectives do not distinguish sharply enough between one's rights over one's own life and one's rights over other people's. Our account will not reject the idea that parents have some rights over their children, nor that there are important aspects of the parent-child relationship that must be treated as private. There are indeed places within the family where the state cannot properly go, where it is important that it is parents who have authority over their children. But, for us, those rights and that authority are quite strictly specified, limited, and conditional. They are not grounded in any general claim about the family's being part of a private sphere.

Talk of the private sphere invites us to conceive that which should be private in spatial terms, as if there were some places—such as the home—that the state does not have the authority to enter. It can easily seem as if the mere physical location, being at home with one's family, puts one in a place where one is—or should be—beyond the reach of the state, as if one's front door marked the boundary between the public and the private. But this conceptualization of "the private" as designating a literal space is misleading. What is private is just what is not properly subject to political authority. Its content is given by a range of activities—paradigmatically concerning sex and religion—that are judged to be areas of life where the individual must have the freedom to decide for herself, free from political interference. These are not literally spatial "areas," though they may often coincide with them. Thus, for example, we are inclined to think of the bedroom or church as private spaces because they are the typical location for activities where the state has no legitimate role. But the reasoning does not identify a particular place as private and judge that whatever goes on there is no business of the state. Rather, it identifies activities concerning which individuals should be left free from regulation to make and act on their own judgments, and, sometimes, derives from that claims about places where the state's monitoring or surveilling presence would be inappropriate.

We can distinguish two different reasons to regard parent-child relationships, or, more plausibly, aspects of those relationships, as beyond the proper reach of state action, and the spaces within which they are normally conducted—such as the home—as not normally subject to inspection by state authorities. Parents may have the right to decide for themselves how they treat their children. In that case, the state would simply have no legitimate interest in those aspects of the relationships. But one might reach that conclusion simply because one recognized the high cost of any attempt to enforce particular views about how those affairs should be conducted. The kind of monitoring and policing that would be needed for such a policy to succeed might be so intrusive as to destroy that which is indeed valuable about the family—its intimacy and spontaneity. In this second case, we would be leaving the family free from regulation because regulation would bring its own moral costs, not because the state lacks the authority to make and act on judgments about proper conduct in parent-child relationships.

The idea of the family as private sometimes rests on a confusion between these two quite distinct cases. To see them come apart, think about official attempts to devise unobtrusive or discreet ways of monitoring what goes on between parents and children, as when teachers and health visitors are trained to look out for signs that all is not as it should be. In some areas of parent-child relationships, those where we accept that the state has legitimate authority but worry that a heavy-handed approach would destroy the family's valuable spontaneity and intimacy, this seems quite appropriate. Although all would object to dystopic scenarios where parents are required to report systematically on their child-handling techniques and the state engages in random and unannounced inspections, we have no problem with more subtle or inconspicuous attempts to monitor relations between parents and children, or to infer them from more readily observable contexts. In other areas, though, the issue is not the subtlety of the state's regulatory instruments, and whether properly regulable interactions can be monitored without excessive and spontaneity-destroying intrusiveness. It is the impropriety of the state's taking any interest whatsoever.

Few think the state has *no* role to play in regulating the treatment of children by their parents. Even the most ardent advocate of family privacy usually accepts that it is proper for state agencies to attempt to protect children from abuse and negligence. In practice, then, the issue is how to strike the right balance between child protection and respect for the integrity of the family (which in effect means respect for the parents' preferred way of raising their children). This involves very difficult practical judgments about when state intervention is indeed in children's interests, given that it can be valuable for children to maintain relationships even with abusive or neglectful parents, and taking into account realistic judgments about the alternative forms of care that await them if they are taken into the state's custody.

Asking whether the state can legitimately intervene in parent-child relationships frames things too crudely. The real questions are finer grained: Which interests of children are worthy of protection by the state? Which interests of parents ground which rights of theirs not to be interfered with in their child-raising endeavors? Where some defenders of parents' rights would see the state's role as limited to that of preventing the neglect and abuse of children, giving parents a very wide sphere of authority over their children subject only to that constraint, the liberalism that we endorse is concerned with the protection of children's interests in a thicker sense. For us, children have a vital interest in developing the capacity for autonomy, and parents harm children—in ways that the state may legitimately seek to prevent—when they deny them the kind of upbringing that develops that capacity. This thicker conception of children's interests, and of what counts as harm, obviously opens up a greater role for the state. It sets up greater scope for conflict between parents' views about how their children should be raised and children's own interests; to insist that children be allowed to develop their capacity for autonomy is to refuse to tolerate parenting practices that obstruct that development. But this can be conceived as a difference of degree, between people with different views about what interests of children are important enough to warrant state protection. It is not a difference of kind, between those who accept and those who reject the claim that the family is "private."

Although doubtless more statist than many readers will find congenial, our view by no means implies that the state has authority over all aspects of children's upbringing. In some areas it is important that parents exercise authority over their children. That exercise is valuable for parents; having the discretion to decide for oneself certain things about how one's children are raised is a key component of what makes parent-child relationships valuable for those doing the parenting. Imagine what it would be like to parent children in a society where an official manual prescribed every detail that it was one's job simply to execute, or where one was required, at the end of each day, to submit a log detailing one's interactions with one's children for official approval (or disapproval). But parents' exercising discretion is valuable also for children; it is important for children to experience their parents as authoritative, as free to make and act on their own choices about their children's lives rather than simply as functionaries of a nanny state. So parents should have some freedom not only with respect to their own lives but also with respect to those of their children.

Still, it is true that, for us, the area of discretion for parents is considerably more limited, and more easily forfeited, than on other liberal accounts, and the state is given a correspondingly greater role in regulating the upbringing of children. Some will object to this not because they insist that parents have the right to raise their children however they wish—they might accept that in principle the polity may legitimately judge that certain child-rearing practices are harmful, and has the authority to seek to protect children from them. The objection may rather be that in practice the state is not going to do any better than parents. Parents can raise children badly, to be sure, but isn't the state likely to do no better, and perhaps a great deal worse?

We share these worries. There are indeed good reasons why it is generally better to leave the raising of children to parents, and although some of these are principled (we will argue that adults have a right to a certain kind of intimate relationship with children), and some of them appeal to children's interests that parents are distinctively well placed to promote (such as their interest in being loved), some of them are much more practical. Even affluent well-intentioned societies have not been very good at creating state institutions that provide children with the kind of stable attachments they need not simply to develop their capacity for autonomy but also to become adults with the emotional resources to sustain healthy relationships. Keeping in mind these practical limitations will often lead to the conclusion that children whose parenting is far from ideal are better off with their parents than they would be in the care of public authorities. So we are by no means advocating a massively interventionist state, ready to tear children away from the bosom of their families as soon as it detects any suboptimal, or even inadequate, parenting. The state must act wisely and with due modesty, being realistic about its own capacities and the likely consequences of any actions it might take. But it may legitimately act to promote children's autonomy, and various other interests that we will identify in due course, to the extent that it can do that without its actions being counterproductive.

Liberal Categories and Parent-Child Relationships

Having argued that the family is not "private" in the sense that makes it beyond the reach of politics, we now turn to the second objection: that the concepts and categories that form the core of liberalism are simply inappropriate as ways of approaching relationships within the family. Those concepts and categories were developed specifically to elucidate the moral aspects of people's political relationships—the relationships between adult citizens, or between such citizens and their state. To focus on people's interest in autonomy and rationality, and to conceive their needs and obligations in terms of rights and duties, may be helpful in that context, but applying those categories to parent-child relationships, to what should be a realm of intimacy, love, and affection, is misleading and misguided. Even if the family is not beyond politics, does it not disfigure and distort our understanding of the value of familial relationships to conceive them in such terms?

Yes and no. We accept that some versions of liberalism have discussed parent-child relationships in a rather narrow way. But while the value of loving, intimate-but-authoritative parent-child relationships has been underexplored or underemphasized, liberalism can accommodate a more nuanced perspective. More, we believe that liberalism provides the right framework for understanding that value. Our "relationship goods" account is, among other things, an attempt to incorporate within a liberal framework a more sensitive appreciation of the significance of parent-child relationships that, at the theoretical or philosophical level, is owed mainly to feminists, many of whom took themselves to be writing in opposition to liberalism.

It is important to distinguish between those matters on which a political theory is silent, those that constitute blind spots, and those that genuinely cannot be accommodated or incorporated within it. The fact that a theory is silent about something is sometimes presented as an objection to it. The assumption seems to be that a theory is valid only if it explicitly covers everything that comes within its domain. We reject that assumption. It may indeed be desirable for a theory explicitly to explore its implications for all the (important) issues that it touches. But the mere fact that a theory does not say anything about a relevant issue, or even about a range of relevant issues, is not evidence that that theory is mistaken or should be rejected. It does not even imply that those developing the theory should have said something about which they were silent. To point out a silence is merely to invite advocates of the theory to speak to matters that they have hitherto refrained from addressing, perhaps for the sake of focus.

Blind spots are different from silences. A blind spot is an area where a political theory has not taken proper account of something that it should have—where, for example, it fails to see that the things it is explicitly concerned to promote depend for their realization on others that it has not noticed, or where, too focused on the beneficial impact of its proposed policies, it neglects their unintended consequences. Unlike mere silence, this is indeed a fault. Something is not being seen that needs to be seen, within the theory's own terms. Even so, a blind spot is still not a reason to reject a theory. Having had a blind spot brought to their attention, a theory's advocates may quite appropriately seek to make good the defect by explaining how their theory can in fact acknowledge and give proper place to that which it had failed to in the past. There are indeed grounds for rejecting a theory when it cannot adequately acknowledge and accommodate those matters on which it has been silent, or that have been its blind spots. But we hope to show that liberalism can speak to matters on which it has been silent, and that a clear view of what were previously its blind spots does not require abandonment of the liberal framework.

The book as a whole will allow the reader to judge whether that hope has been realized. In this chapter we can only sketch our responses to two influential variants of the charge that it is distorting to apply liberal categories to parent-child relationships. The first focuses on the capacities of individuals that liberals value. We have suggested that it is important that children be raised in such a way that they are able to develop their capacity for autonomy, and that the state may legitimately regulate the family to achieve this aim. This objection claims that the liberal focus on autonomy yields an impoverished understanding of children's developmental needs and leads to a one-sided account of the value of the parent-child relationships. The second focuses on liberalism's way of framing the content of those relationships. We will present much of our argument in terms of the rights, and duties, that family members have against, and to, one another. This objection claims that conceiving familial relationships in such terms reveals liberalism's inability to understand the true nature of the family as a site of love and care.

Autonomy

Our response to the first objection is simple. It is important that children develop the capacity for autonomy. The capacity to reflect on one's life-choices, to be aware that it is possible to live one's life in many different ways, to make a reasoned judgment about which way is right for one, and to act on that judgment—that is indeed extremely valuable, and parents who raise their children in such a way that they lack autonomy do them wrong. But autonomy is not the *only* capacity that liberals care about, and there is no need to abandon liberalism to acknowledge that children have other developmental interests too. Moreover, many of those other interests are themselves preconditions of autonomy. An individual who is incapable of forming healthy relationships with others, for example, or of exercising the self-restraint needed to conquer those short-term desires that conflict with her more considered goals, is not able to lead an autonomous life.

The idea that liberals are preoccupied with children's developing intellectual capacities, with education in a rather narrow sense, owes a good deal to John Locke. According to Barbara Arneil, Locke's influential theory of parental authority "transforms 'taking care of children' to 'informing the mind'. . . . [For Locke,] 'The first part then of Parental Power, or rather duty . . . is Education . . . [but] a Man may put the Tuition of his Son in other hands' (ii.69)."[17] As Shelley Burtt puts it, Locke holds that "what separates children from adults and justifies their quite comprehensive subordination is . . . simply an undeveloped reasoning faculty."[18] Both commentators see this tunnel vision focusing on "a narrowly intellectual version of maturity"[19] as deriving from a preoccupation with children as future citizens. In Burtt's view: "The question of how to care for children (beyond educational needs) is lost to liberal theory from this point onwards. The development of children beyond the intellectual dimension (namely physical, social or emotional development), or the extent to which the state might be concerned with their care, is simply written out of liberal theory at its inception. It is not that Locke is unaware of the broader caring and development needs of children. Rather, given that the singular objective is to produce 'rational citizens', the process of producing such creatures makes such questions simply, but utterly, irrelevant to liberal political theory."[20]

It's true that liberal theory has tended to focus on children's interest in developing rationality and autonomy, and this owes a good deal to liberalism's understanding of itself as concerned specifically that children be prepared for citizenship. But liberals should not be concerned only with that aspect of their development. To regard liberalism as a political philosophy that cares only about people's interests qua citizens is to confuse two issues. Liberals need to provide an account of how and why it is legitimate for people qua citizens, as members of a polity, to use the coercive apparatus of the state to promote the interests of their fellow citizens, including their future citizens. But that is not to say that the interests that it promotes can only be those that people have qua citizens, or those needed for the proper exercise of the rights and duties of citizenship. We will see later that members of a state may indeed have some interest in children's becoming adults with qualities, such as trustworthiness or the capacity to cooperate, that are valuable to their fellow citizens. But it is wrong to think that the state's role in regulating the family must be limited to ensuring the production of good citizens.

Indeed, we agree with Burtt's own view that "authority over other human beings should extend only so far as making up the deficits that legitimate their subordination. . . . Children are adult 'works in progress'. The reason we exclude them from the community of social and political equals is that they lack a range of social, emotional, and cognitive capacities that cannot be developed apart from their subordination to caring adults. . . . this more expansive picture of children's needs brings with it a different understanding of the nature and extent of parental power."[21] For us, as for Burtt, "the way we think of children and their needs determines the sort of authority we think it is appropriate to exercise over them."[22] Children's developmental needs are not exclusively, or even primarily, cognitive. Liberalism's neglect of this should be thought of as a blind spot, and one that our theory attempts to bring clearly into view.

Rights and Duties

The second objection worries about liberalism's tendency to conceive familial relationships in terms of the rights and duties that individual family members have with respect to one another. If the family is the realm of intimacy and affection, these concepts are inappropriate. It is essential to intimate loving relationships that participants are not doing what they do for one another out of duty, that they do not claim the right to be treated in particular ways. Conceiving familial relationships in such terms misses the point. It models them in ways that may be apt for thinking about the moral relationships between independent adults, but that fail to capture what is special about the family. Indeed, if one grants, as we do, that the loving relationship between parents and children plays a role in justifying the family as the best way to raise children, then all mention of rights and duties might seem to run into a fundamental conceptual incoherence, for nobody can have a duty to love another person, and nobody can have a right to be loved.

Before getting on to the more challenging versions of this objection, we must again insist on the importance of seeing children as separate individuals from their parents. That may seem banal, but some critics of liberalism query even this elementary proposition. Thus, for example, Barbara Arneil objects to John Eekelaar's innocuous observation that, in order to conceive them as having rights, "children's interests must be capable of isolation from the interests of others."[23] For Arneil, "This analytical separation of the child from his/her community, while necessary to a rights theory based on interests, is difficult to reconcile with the dependent nature of children and the symbiotic character of their relationship to their care-givers."[24] This is surely a non sequitur. One can acknowledge children's dependence on, and even their "symbiotic" relationship with, their parents (though we would not ourselves endorse that metaphor) without denying that they are separate people, with interests of their own. To think otherwise is simply to assimilate parents and children into a single entity, denying even the conceptual possibility that parents may fail to act in their children's interests (or vice versa), or that parents and children's interests may sometimes conflict.

The real issue is whether, granted that parents and children are separate individuals with separate interests, a discourse of rights and duties is an appropriate way to talk and think about their relationship. We accept that that relationship is (or should be) an intimate and loving one, and we accept also that it is problematic to think in terms of someone's having a duty to love, or a right to be loved. One's emotions are not directly amenable to the will—one cannot always be held responsible for them—in the way that ascribing such rights and duties would imply. As Kant put it: "Love is a matter of feeling, not of willing, and I cannot love because I will to, still less because I ought to (I cannot be constrained to love); so a duty to love is an absurdity."[25] Nonetheless, it is again possible to assimilate this apparently antiliberal perspective into an avowedly liberal framework. As long we tread carefully, a proper appreciation of the value of loving, intimate, and caring relationships can, and should, be combined with an approach that insists on thinking about rights and duties as relevant to parent-child relationships. The two are not incompatible.

We can distinguish two variants of the objection. The general worry is that applying such categories to any aspect of the parent-child relationship postulates an unduly separate or even antagonistic relationship between family members, missing out on the peculiar and special nature of the family. The more specific version objects only to the idea that family members can have duties to love one another. Let us take each in turn.

On our view, parents' rights over their children are justified by appeal to children's rather than parents' interests. If parents have the right to decide when their children go to bed, or where they are to go on holiday, that is because children's interests will be better served by their parents' having the relevant forms of authority than by that authority's being in the hands of some other agent (such as the state), or than by children's making those decisions for themselves. Although, on our account, parents are not required to promote their children's interests at all costs, without regard to the effects on their own interests or those of others outside the parent-child relationship, parental rights over children are justified precisely because the children will fare better in a situation where it is parents who have the authority to take the decisions than one in which children themselves, or anybody else, has that authority. We adopt what Joseph Raz calls the "service" conception of authority, under which "the role and primary normal function" of authorities is "to serve the governed."[26] Conceiving the authority relation between parents and children in this way should go some way toward dispelling the worry about antagonism.

Moreover, holding that individual members of families have rights against one another, and duties to treat one another in certain ways, does not imply that family life goes well when family members conceive their relations in such terms. Relationships in which people act out of love for one another are surely better than those in which they are motivated only by an awareness of their duties or the other's rights. Indeed, a family whose members are continually, or even frequently, motivated by a sense of their duties to one another is a family whose members are not enjoying the spontaneous, intimate loving relationship that plays the key role in justifying the family as the best social arrangement for raising children. But how family members are typically motivated, or how they need to be motivated in order to provide relationship goods for one another, is a separate issue from that of whether they do in fact have rights and duties with respect to one another.[27] We believe that they do, and articulate the detailed content of those rights and duties later in the book.

Why deny that parents have duties not to abuse or neglect their children, that their children have a right not to be abused or neglected, or, hardly more controversially, that parents have the right to direct their children's behavior within certain specified limits? Our own account of parental rights and duties, and of children's rights, will in fact go beyond these minimal suggestions, but they are enough to expose the implausibility of denying that "rights talk" can properly be applied within the family. The idea that parents can fail to do what parents are morally required to do for the children in their care, or what those children have a right to expect from their parents, is surely uncontroversial.

Thinking in terms of rights and duties within the family is important partly because it helps us understand when the state may legitimately intervene. If parents fail to discharge their "duty of care" to their children, then they forfeit the right to parent those children. It is children's right to be cared for that justifies the state's stepping in when the parent fails in that task. As we have said, the state may not be able to do better for the child even than neglectful parents, so we do not claim that the state is right to intervene wherever parents fail to discharge their parental duties. Nonetheless, framing familial obligations and expectations in terms of rights and duties clarifies the proper role of the state, and it is appropriate for those who are not themselves involved in the relationship to adopt such a perspective.

We would go further. Something has surely gone wrong if parents and children primarily conceive their relationship in terms of their separate interests, and the rights and duties that they generate. But a loving parent, one who is indeed motivated by the reasons and emotions appropriate to the parent-child relationship, may *sometimes* find it helpful to formulate his or her understanding of that relationship in that way. Perhaps a perfectly loving parent would never need recourse to reflection of that kind. But for many of us what it *is* to be a loving parent is partly to be willing, when the need arises, to see things in such terms. A parent who always does what she does for her child out of duty is not a good parent. She lacks the capacity to act spontaneously from love and thereby deprives her child, and herself, of something special and valuable. But a parent who never reflects on what she owes her children as people separate from herself is either a saint or worryingly unreflective—and unlikely to parent her children very well. To suggest that a rights discourse has no place in the heads of family members is dangerously to romanticize and idealize the family.

What of the more specific charge that it makes no sense to posit a right to be loved because the idea of a duty to love is, as Kant put it, "an absurdity"? Our justification of the family puts a good deal of weight on the value of intimate loving relationships between parents and children. The family is the child-rearing arrangement in which people are most likely to experience such relationships, and this fact—its tendency to generate relationship goods that we claim to be hugely valuable for many adults and all children—plays a key role in our argument. Children need love if they are to realize their potential for flourishing, and many adults fully flourish only if they experience, and act on, parental love for a child. Given our general aim of showing how liberalism can accommodate matters often regarded as beyond its domain, it would be convenient if we could argue that parents do indeed have a duty to love their children. Even for us, that is a bridge too far.

Parents have a duty of care for their children, which includes the duty *to* care for them, but the "care" they have a duty to provide must be articulated in terms that render it amenable to the will. For some people, the love that children need—a distinctive kind of attentiveness, an emotional availability, an experience of being (experienced as) special, or of unconditional love—is not, we believe, amenable to the will in the required sense. It is not something that it makes sense morally to demand of all parents, or to regard as morally required of them. Ought implies can. Parents lacking the capacity to love their children in this way cannot coherently be said to have a duty to do so. Some parents have so little experience of being loved themselves that they simply cannot love children in the necessary way. Such parents have no duty to love their children—and their children have no right to their love.

This might be thought a serious weakness in our approach. Loving relationships are central to our account, yet we deny that all children have a right to be loved because we don't think it coherent to regard parents as having a duty to love their children. Doesn't this show that the liberal framework cannot, after all, cope with the sphere of emotion and intimacy? No. Other associated rights and duties, pertaining to the child's developmental need to be loved, go a long way toward making good the deficit.

In the first place, only some parents lack the emotional capacity to love, rather than merely to care for, their children. Where parents possess that capacity, then there is nothing incoherent in thinking that they have a duty to exercise it. It may be confused to think that this kind of spontaneous intimacy and emotional attentiveness can directly be summoned as a matter of will. A parent struggling hard to love her children, directly motivated by a sense of duty, does not provide what they need. But that is just a specific case of the general issue we discussed. It is, moreover, perfectly coherent for a parent who finds it hard to love her children to try to cultivate her capacity to do just that. Although not directly amenable to the will, emotions are not entirely beyond our control either. By attending to the reasons one has to love, including the great importance of that love to one's children, and by creating situations likely to foster it—such as spending time with them when one is at one's most emotionally available and least tired or preoccupied with other things—one can deliberately encourage it. Parents may not all have a duty to love their children, but given the crucial importance of love to the child's healthy emotional development, they all have a duty to try to develop the capacity to love them. And those who have the capacity have a duty to exercise it.[28]

Indeed, adults who believe themselves, for whatever reason, to lack not only the capacity but also the potential to develop it, may have a duty not to become parents. Adults who discover they lack the capacity, or find that they have lost it, may have a duty to try to find others who can do so—in the extreme case by giving their child up for adoption. There are good reasons not to make this a legal duty. We do not want the state to get involved in the business of deciding which adults are and are not able to provide the love that children need. And adults who judge themselves unable to love their children may still have reason to procreate—if there are others who want to be parents, who possess and wish to exercise their capacity to love but are not themselves able to procreate. Still, there is nothing odd about the idea of adults recognizing the responsibilities that attend the role of parent, judging themselves simply incapable of discharging them adequately, and deciding that they have a duty not to assume, or continue in, that role.[29]

Conclusion

On the one hand, liberalism takes individuals to be the fundamental objects of moral concern, and the rights it claims people have are primarily rights of individuals over their own lives: the core liberal idea is that it is important for individuals to exercise their own judgment about how they are to live. One of the things that many choose to do with their lives, and that many regard as among their most important life projects, is to raise children—and to exercise their own judgments about how to raise them. On the other hand, parental rights are rights over others, they are rights over others who have no realistic exit option, and they are rights over others whose capacity to make their own judgments about how they are to live their lives is no less important than that of the adults raising them. Suppose the latter implies—as we will argue it does—that parents' rights are limited by their duty to do what they can to ensure that their children develop the capacity for autonomy. That still leaves big questions about what it is that gives any particular adult the moral standing to subject a child to *her* judgments about how that child should be raised, and about the range of matters within which her judgments should indeed be decisive.

This chapter has not attempted to make any headway on those big questions. Its aim has been rather to disarm those who regard liberal theory as ill-equipped to provide answers—or perhaps regard the questions themselves as misconceived. Whether or not our particular answers convince, we hope at least to have persuaded skeptical readers of the case for framing the issues in liberal terms.[30]

CHAPTER 2

Equality and the Family

Much moral and political philosophy is concerned to identify the proper balance between the individual's pursuit of her own interests and that concern and respect for the interests of others required by the recognition that all are of equal moral worth. As individuals, we are constantly and inevitably making choices about the extent to which we further our own well-being or restrain its pursuit for the sake of others. When it comes to politics, in our role as citizens making the rules that govern us, we have to consider the extent to which the state may properly limit individuals' pursuit of their own interests and constrain their actions in ways that will contribute to the good of others.

Compared to the unbridled pursuit of egoistic satisfaction, the family appears as a realm of altruism and self-sacrifice. Familial relationships are constituted by responsibilities and obligations. To parent a child is to be committed to supporting her at considerable cost to oneself. All parents who are doing their job properly surrender huge amounts of freedom and devote to their children substantial resources—time, energy, money—that they could have spent on themselves.[1] Where necessary, parents are often willing to risk serious harms for the sake of their children, sometimes to accept certain death. It seems hard to see how these phenomena can be captured in terms of the individual's prudence or self-interest. From this perspective, as Laurence Thomas puts it, "the project of having children can only be understood as a remarkably altruistic endeavor."[2]

But from another perspective, the family looks more like an obstacle to altruism than the locus of its realization. Even if it were entirely selfless, parents' concern for their children's well-being is hardly inspired by a standpoint that treats all as equally valuable. It may be admirable to put others' well-being ahead of one's own, but when those being favored are one's own children, and that is why they are being favored, then that seems partial rather than impartial.

One is favoring particular others, and one is doing so because of their relationship to oneself. We might think of the individual as at the center of a series of concentric circles.[3] As the objects of our concern move outward from the self—through immediate family, extended family, friends, fellow citizens or fellow nationals, perhaps coreligionists, to humankind as a whole (and, for some, to nonhuman animals also)—we become less partial, more sensitive to others who are increasingly distant from ourselves. Seen this way, a parent's acting to promote her own children's interests when she could be doing more to further the good of others, especially the good of others worse off than her children, seems to involve a failure of altruism.

And of course parents' concern for their children's well-being is not entirely selfless. On the whole, people have children because they want to, and believe—we think rightly—that doing so will make their own lives go better. Just three pages before his claim that "the project of having children can only be understood as a remarkably altruistic endeavor," Thomas says, again we think rightly, that "parenting a child is generally seen as an extraordinarily marvellous experience."[4] If the project of parenting a child contributes to the value of one's own life, why isn't it properly conceived as furthering one's own interests rather than limiting their pursuit for the sake of others? There is certainly something distinctive about a project the content of which involves furthering the interests of other people—even where those others are one's own children. But if doing that also contributes to one's own well-being, then it takes on a doubly partial aspect: one is favoring particular others, with whom one has a particular relationship, rather than equally considering the interests of all; and favoring them makes one's own life go better—not better for others, better for oneself.

Together, these observations suggest that the altruism sometimes regarded as the core of "family values" acquires a genuinely moral character only when it transcends the family. For the Russian revolutionary Alexandra Kollontai, "the narrow and exclusive affection of the mother for her own children must expand until it extends to all the children of the great proletarian family. . . . In place of the individual and egoistic family, a great universal family of workers will develop, in which all the workers, men and women, will above all be comrades."[5] Indeed, the idea that the altruism and mutual concern characteristic of familial relationships could and should be extended to wider communities—to fellow citizens, perhaps to humankind as a whole—has played an influential role in egalitarian thinking, as has the suggestion that the family acts as an obstacle to progress by diverting people's energy and attention inward, into the private and away from the public sphere.[6]

We believe that "family values" can indeed serve to distract people from the more morally urgent claims of others. That distraction is all the more effective precisely because the family presents itself as a sphere of altruism. It is easy for parents to persuade themselves that their commitment to family life is not selfish—if they were selfish, they would be out having fun, not sitting at home reading their children bedtime stories. We have no problem with the idea that parents have special moral duties to their children, or that morality permits each of us to favor our own interests over those of others, including our interest in enjoying valuable familial relationships. But in a world where millions die every year for want of basic necessities, much apparently admirable parenting may better be thought of as a self-indulgent retreat, away from the true demands of morality—as, in Samuel Scheffler's words, "the moral equivalent of a tax shelter."[7]

How to balance one's own interests, and those of people with whom one has particular kinds of special relationship, against the interests of others is an extremely difficult issue. For us, the kinds of partiality toward one's children that are indeed justified by appeal to "family values" is a qualitative matter, separate from, and prior to, the quantitative question of the extent to which people may act to realize such values in their own, and their children's, lives. Answers to that second question will be context-specific, depending crucially on the circumstances in which the individual finds herself. By the end of the book, we hope to have supplied the reader with a way of thinking about such matters. At this stage our task is more preliminary: to set out the various kinds of conflict between the value of equality and the value of those parent-child relationships that, for our purposes, constitute the family.

Distributive Equality and Relational Equality

We are treating equality here as a distributive ideal. Some who call themselves egalitarians think this is a mistake. Rather than distributions, these critics insist, social relations are the proper focus of egalitarian concern.[8] Those sympathetic to so-called child liberationism might see this egalitarian hostility to relations of domination or oppression as an apt lens through which to view parent-child relationships.[9] Just as whites, or men, have failed to relate as equals to people of color, or women, so, it is claimed, adults illegitimately treat children as inferior. By regarding children as lacking the capacities that would warrant treatment as independent and responsible agents, adults legitimize their own claim to authority and justify according children dependent and subordinate status in the social and political order. True, from this perspective the fact that it is parents who are accorded rights over children is somewhat incidental. For the child liberationist, things are no better when children are rendered dependent on other adults, and some of the argument, for example on voting rights, is about the proper role of children within the political community and the wider society rather than within the family as such.[10] But just as a key demand of the women's liberation movement required changes to the institution of marriage, so child liberationists often direct their attention to the rights held by children against their parents.

This egalitarian worry is intrafamilial, not interfamilial. It concerns not inequalities between families but inequalities within them. And what is objected to is not the distribution of any type of goods or benefits but the way that intrafamilial relationships are constructed and conducted. The problem is not that families confer unequal benefits and burdens on children raised by different parents. It is that families are sites of inequality that subject children to unjust forms of subordination, domination, and oppression.

We agree that children are often illegitimately subject to the authority of parents; parents do not properly have many of the rights to control their children's lives that they are currently granted. Parents' rights are considerably more limited than is commonly believed, and are conditional on parents' meeting children's interests—including their interest in developing their capacity to become autonomous agents—to a high degree. So we are happy to think of our theory as doing for children what feminist philosophers have done for women. Where feminists reject patriarchy, we reject "parentarchy."

That said, it is obviously sometimes in children's interests to have their lives controlled by adults, in complicated, age-dependent and sphere-of-discretion-dependent ways. What children should be free to decide for themselves will depend on their emotional, physical, and intellectual maturity. Nobody thinks that very young children should be deciding for themselves what to eat, where to cross the road, and the like. But as children get older, the kind of authority over them that is justified changes. One learns autonomy in large part by practicing it, so the duty to help children develop the capacity for autonomy implies careful judgments about when children are ready to start making their own choices, and gradually increasing their discretion over their own lives.

Two further claims may be more interesting. First, we follow so-called child-centered justifications of the family in claiming that it is valuable for children not merely that adults have the authority to decide some matters about what happens to and for children but that the adults in question be those children's parents (rather than, for example, state functionaries working in child-rearing institutions). More distinctively, our approach emphasizes the importance for the child's development of her having a relationship with the parent in which the parent is experienced as authoritative, as making her own judgments (rather than, say, carrying out orders from an official, directive, child-rearing manual). So we defend not merely authority over children but the (limitedly, conditionally) authoritative family. Second, and more controversially, we argue that exercising authoritative control over children's lives is something that it is in adults' interests to do. So we defend the (limitedly, conditionally) authoritative family partly because it is a good institution for those who get to exercise the authority within it. This second thought puts us quite sharply at odds with child liberationists, who tend to focus exclusively on the interests of children.

More generally, we deny the strong version of the relational egalitarian position which claims that distributions matter only if they impact on social relationships. The fact that people's lives are equally important has distributive implications—implications about the distribution of opportunities to flourish or to be authors of their own lives—that go beyond the impact of those distributions on social relationships. To soften the contrast between "relational" and "distributive" approaches, we can frame our insistence on the distinct importance of distributions in ways congenial to the relational egalitarian: for us, a society that permits unjustified or illegitimate inequalities between its members *just is* one whose members are not treating one another, relating to one another, as equals. The distributions themselves *express* inegalitarian relationships. To live with others in an unequal society on terms that cannot be justified to those who have less is not merely a distributive failure; it is also a failure of relationship.[11]

The Family versus Fair Equality of Opportunity

Families are a problem even for a rather mainstream version of the egalitarian ideal. One does not have to favor anything as far-fetched and widely discredited as equality of outcome to be concerned about the unequalizing influence of family background. Nor does one have to appeal to a particularly demanding or controversial conception of equality of opportunity.[12] Families impact on children's opportunities, not merely on their outcomes, and the fact that children are raised in families undermines even a widely shared conception of equality of opportunity: the idea that children's prospects in life should depend on their own merits rather than on their social origins. This view derives much of its appeal from the idea of a fair competition; the thought is that outcome inequalities can be fully justified only if they result from fair procedures, procedures that do not allow (what should be) irrelevant factors to influence how people fare or where they end up. Modern industrial societies are structured so that socially produced rewards—income, wealth, status, positions in the occupational structure, and the opportunities for self-exploration and fulfillment that come with them—are distributed extremely unequally, and people compete with one another to secure more rather than less of them. To be legitimate, that competition must be conducted on fair terms, not skewed in favor of those born to advantage. In the familiar metaphor, the playing field should be level, which means that children with the same abilities, and willingness to use them, should enjoy the same chances of success, irrespective of their family background.

That condition is not satisfied simply by the formal requirement—represented in UK law by what has become known as "Equal Opportunities" legislation—that jobs and the rewards that accompany them go to those best qualified to carry them out. We know, of course, that recruitment practices often fail to meet even that less demanding standard. A person's race, gender, religion, and, sometimes, class background can all influence her chance of success in the labor market in ways that violate even the idea of "careers open to talents."[13] But fair equality of opportunity requires more than that the similarly qualified are treated equally, more than that people get jobs on the basis of what we might call their "relevant competences." It demands also that children born into different families have the same opportunities to develop qualifications and competences in the first place. As Rawls puts it, fair equality of opportunity requires "not merely that public offices and social positions be open in the formal sense, but that all should have a fair chance to attain them. To specify the idea of a fair chance we say: supposing that there is a distribution of native endowments, those who have the same level of talent and ability and the same willingness to use these gifts should have the same prospects of success regardless of their social class of origin."[14]

Which is where the problems start. The idea of fair equality of opportunity is curiously ambivalent. On the one hand, when compared with more radically egalitarian visions of social justice, it can seem somewhat conservative, apparently serving to legitimate a fundamentally inegalitarian and competitive economic system. There will inevitably be winners and losers, it suggests, and the only kind of equality to be pursued is that needed to make sure the right people win (and the "wrong" people lose).[15] It has appeal, moreover, to those with no deep interest in equality whatsoever, since it can be seen rather as a means to economic efficiency. An optimally productive society will not waste the economic potential of any of its members. That potential is best realized by our ensuring that all have equal opportunity, first to acquire useful skills and knowledge, and then to deploy them in the carrying out of appropriate occupational tasks. Inequalities of opportunity, from this perspective, distort not the fair distribution of rewards to people, but the efficient allocation of people to jobs.[16] Much of the popular appeal of fair equality of opportunity, we suspect, derives from its apparent compatibility with other dominant values—inequality, competition, efficiency—and the way in which it seems not to challenge fundamentally the organizing principles of our contemporary affluent Western societies.

On the other hand, taken seriously it is extremely radical. So radical, indeed, that it rarely is taken seriously. A moment's reflection on the myriad ways in which a child's prospects are influenced by her familial circumstances suggests that the vision of a society in which children born to different families enjoy the same opportunities to develop marketable competences and qualifications can only be a chimera. Children of wealthy parents will have access to high-quality schooling, food, health care, housing, and holidays that are bound to foster their development in ways not available to children born into poverty. Suppose we eliminated economic inequalities between parents, or somehow insulated children's developmental opportunities from their influence. Different parents would still be members of different social networks; their friends and colleagues would be different—and unequally valuable as contacts, or sources of information, that could be used to help their children in the competition for jobs and the qualifications helpful to their achievement. Get rid of that cause of inequality in opportunities and parents will still be unequally informed about the choices available to their children and which of them are the best means to their success. And information of that kind will be just a small part of the cultural capital that parents will remain able to convert into competitive advantage for their children—whether intentionally or inadvertently—as the unintended by-product of apparently innocuous interactions like bedtime stories and talk at family meals. Moreover, parents with the same economic and cultural capital, and similar networks, may simply make different choices about what to do with them: some may regard promoting their children's interests as their major life project; others may prefer to spend their time and energy on other things. All of these are mechanisms by which families interrupt, or disrupt, fair equality of opportunity.

So despite its competitive aspect, and its prima facie endorsement of inequalities of outcome that result from fair competition, fair equality of opportunity turns out to be thoroughly subversive. Parents' "outcomes"—how they fare in the competition for jobs and rewards attaching to those jobs—are intimately connected to their children's "opportunities": their prospects for success (or failure) in that competition. (We will discuss later the idea that outcomes for parents just *are* opportunities for their children.) Fully to realize fair equality of opportunity would require drastic measures. Either we would have to eliminate all the relevant inequalities between parents, in which case we'd need equality of outcome with respect to all the things that are helpful to children's development. Or we would have to eliminate all the mechanisms by which inequalities between parents generate unequal developmental opportunities for children. Since those mechanisms extend to the very core of the parent-child relationship, the latter seems to imply the abolition of the family itself as the social institution in which children are raised.

We have a good deal to say about the "abolish relevant inequalities between parents" route, but we don't have anything *new* to say about it. To maintain focus, we will simply put the more general arguments for and against permitting or welcoming certain kinds of inequality between parents to one side. Suppose we did somehow succeed in establishing genuinely fair equality of opportunity between the members of one generation. Legitimate processes—mechanisms and interactions that it would be wrong to prevent—and distributive outcomes of those processes that allow people to take responsibility for their own choices (and not other peoples') would lead to inequalities of outcome.[17] Parents must have some freedom to make their own choices, in line with their own preferences, even though that means that they will end up with somewhat unequal amounts of the various resources—money, education, information, contacts, time—helpful to their children's development. (We say "*some* freedom" and "*somewhat* unequal amounts" because our all-things-considered judgments grant individuals much less freedom, and justify much less unequal outcomes, than are currently accepted.)

Parents' Unequal Outcomes and Children's Unequal Opportunities

We will concentrate instead on the second drastic strategy: eliminating the mechanisms by which inequalities and differences between parents turn into unequal developmental opportunities for children. We will argue that parents are currently allowed to do too much for their children, and in too many ways. Our societies not only permit unjustifiable inequalities between parents; they also grant parents unjustifiable means of converting their own resources into superior prospects for their children. In effect, then, children of disadvantaged parents suffer a double burden, relative to their more advantaged peers: they are competing against children of parents who (a) have access to illegitimately more resources, which (b) they can use to promote their children's interests by illegitimate means. But, just as we do not object to all resource inequalities between parents, so we accept some of the mechanisms by which parents may convert resource advantages into superior opportunities for their children.

That is partly because we understand "resources" broadly. It's tempting to focus on parents' using their wealth to purchase developmental opportunities for their children. It is certainly easy to conceive many ways in which parents' market power is likely to affect their children's development through differential access to better housing and schooling, computers and books at home, mind-broadening holidays, and so on. All of these do indeed happen and all of them disrupt fair equality of opportunity. But recent research suggests that these mechanisms are actually less important explanations of why children raised in different families fare unequally well. It looks as if personality variables, preferences and choices that can be thought of as aspects or expressions of people's identities, and the kinds of cultural capital (or its absence) that result in large part from childhood socialization within the family, are more important. The correlation between parents' and children's economic position results in large part from the transmission, from parents to children, of those characteristics that were conducive to parents' own success (or lack of it) rather than from parents' own economic resources (or lack of them) in procuring (or failing to procure) developmental opportunities for children.[18] The important "resources" that different parents unequally bring to parenting should, it seems, be conceived as features of parents themselves—what they know, how they behave, what they are like—rather than as the material assets at their disposal.

Moreover, not all the *differences* between parents that turn into unequal opportunities for children can properly be conceived as *inequalities*. Some inequalities of opportunity between children arise not because parents have unequal resources available to them but because parents make different choices about what to do with their resources. Children's prospects depend not only on what their parents *can* do for them, but also on what those parents *want* to do for them.

On the one hand, different parents may simply weigh the promotion of their children's interests differently, relative to the other things they care about. Few parents, however loving, regard their children's well-being as the *only* thing that matters in their lives. Some will devote themselves to good causes (Charles Dickens's Mrs. Jellyby in *Bleak House* comes to mind).[19] Some will devote themselves to themselves—to their own professional advancement, or intellectual output, or watching TV. Although parents surely bear onerous responsibilities, they are not morally required to subordinate their own to their children's interests entirely. Variation in the extent to which parents seek to promote their children's interests may lead to children's enjoying (or suffering) unequal opportunities—even when compared to other children whose parents have the same resources at their disposal.

On the other hand, and more importantly, different parents will have different views about what their children's interests *are*. We don't mean simply that different parents will disagree about how best to further their children's prospects of success in the competition for income and status, though that is surely the case. If they agree on the goal, then differences in judgments about how best to achieve it might better be conceived as inequalities in the resources they bring to parenting than as a difference in their preferences. Rather, different parents will disagree about what it *is* for their children's lives to go well. Some may care above all that their children grow up to be devout worshippers of the deity the parents themselves worship; some may encourage their children to eschew the rat race and material success and live a life of abstemious simplicity. The principle we have been discussing requires that, irrespective of their family background, children with the same abilities and willingness to use them should enjoy the same chances of success in the competition for income, wealth, status, positions in the occupational structure, and the opportunities for self-realization and fulfillment that come with them. Parents' different understandings of what would count as success for their children may influence their children's prospects in those terms.

In any case, the conflict between the family and fair equality of opportunity runs deeper than many progressives have wanted to believe. If children's developmental opportunities depended on their parents' economic resources, so that economic (dis)advantage were transmitted from parents to children via the deployment of parents' differential market power, then one could envisage seriously mitigating (if not altogether eliminating) that transmission through tax-transfer policies. For example, state schooling policies might be designed to disconnect the quality of children's education from parents' income, thereby helping to insulate children's opportunities from excessive influence by their parents' outcomes. But that kind of approach does not get to the heart of the problem. The inequalities between children, as far as their developmental opportunities are concerned, stem from processes more central to—one might say constitutive of—family life than egalitarians might have hoped. It seems to be the informal interactions—the bedtime stories, the talk at table, the family culture, the parenting styles, the inculcation of attitudes and values (some conscious, some unconscious)—that make much of the difference to children's prospects.

This suggests that the only way really to deliver fair equality of opportunity would be to get rid of parent-child relationships—to abolish the family—altogether. Like everybody else, we think that would drastically misjudge the weight of the various considerations at stake. Intimate, loving parent-child relationships are hugely valuable—for both children and parents. They are vital for children's cognitive, moral, and emotional development, so are essential for children's well-being when they reach adulthood, but, of course, they also contribute hugely to children's well-being as children. For many adults, those relationships are vital sources of joy, self-realization, and flourishing. Simply put, it's more important that human beings get to enjoy such relationships than that they get a level playing field on which to compete for jobs, money, and status.

That is obvious as well as simple. But clarifying the nature of the conflict between the family and fair equality of opportunity is worthwhile, even if finding in favor of the former is hardly controversial. For nothing we have said rules out policies intended to make the distribution of opportunities more equal between those born to less or more advantaged parents. There remain strategies that leave families intact and seek to mitigate, neutralize, or compensate for their unequalizing effects. Careful explication of the various mechanisms currently producing those effects helps us to identify precisely which aspects of the family are indeed worthy of protection and which are not so important. We have suggested that the moral significance of the family rests on the intimate relationship between parents and children. That suggestion gives us a way of thinking systematically about the kinds of parent-child interaction that should and need not be respected by policy, or engaged in by parents, in particular circumstances. That suggestion will be developed in part 3.

Is Fair Equality of Opportunity Fair?

In the next section we will explore our rather cryptic observation that, for many, parents' outcomes are children's opportunities. Here we consider the somewhat unsettling implications of the empirical findings just discussed for the way we think about the principle of fair equality of opportunity. We presented that principle in Rawls's formulation, as requiring that those with the same abilities and willingness to use them should enjoy the same chances of success, irrespective of their family's social class. What offends fair equality of opportunity is that family background tilts the playing field between children with similar levels of ability and motivation, by providing them with unequal developmental opportunities. But what about the fact that family background itself *causes* inequalities in abilities and motivations? It looks as if fair equality of opportunity has no objection to what, it now seems, is actually the main kind of mechanism by which parents influence their children's prospects. If successful parents tend to raise more able and better-motivated children than disadvantaged parents do, and *that* explains why children tend to end up in the same kind of position in the distribution of income and status as their parents, then fair equality of opportunity seems to be satisfied.

Let's be clear where the problem lies. We should not think of abilities, in this context, as *developed* abilities. Wealthy or educated parents are better placed than poor or uneducated ones to develop their children's abilities, but that inequality in developmental opportunities is precisely what fair equality of opportunity condemns. "Ability," here, means "native ability" or "natural talent."[20] Though the idea that children are born with different levels of "natural talent" has to be handled with great care,[21] its emphasis on what people are born with—or born as—has the merit of directing our attention to the social processes by which whatever that is gets developed into relevant competences. Those developed "abilities" valued by labor markets are to a very great extent endogenous, the outcome of social interactions, rather than exogenous, or simply "given" prior to those interactions. Fair equality of opportunity is disrupted when children's family backgrounds are allowed unequally to influence the development of natural talents into relevant competences.

The problem is with the second half of the formulation, the bit about motivation. It is easy to see its appeal. People have equal opportunity to get (or become) something when they are equally able to get (or become) it *if they try*. Where one person is simply not willing to make the same effort as another, to achieve something she is no less able to achieve, then what she lacks is not equal opportunity but equal motivation. One reason to focus our distributive attention on opportunities rather than outcomes is precisely that we want people to be responsible for how they fare. That is why fair equality of opportunity fits so neatly with the idea of reward according to desert. If those born with the same natural talents have the same opportunities to develop those talents into marketable skills, we can regard any inequalities in their outcomes as deserved—in the sense that they will result from their own choices about how hard to work to develop those talents.

Except, of course, that children's choices, their capacity to make an effort as well as what they choose to exert their effort on, are substantially a function of their upbringing. How hard they work to develop whatever "native endow-ments" they are born with depends hugely on how they are raised. As Rawls says, "the internal life and culture of the family influence, perhaps as much as anything else, a child's motivation and his capacity to gain from education."[22] Suppose that two genetically identical twins, born in the same hospital on the same day but adopted by different parents, go on to enjoy (or suffer) very unequal prospects, and very different lives, simply because of the less or more effort-encouraging familial cultures they will meet when they get home. One is adopted by conscientious, emotionally mature, reliable parents who instill in him valuable character traits such as self-discipline, perseverance in the face of adversity, and the ability to defer gratification. The other is adopted by parents who have never acquired those traits themselves and so lack the capacity to inculcate them. Suppose that adoption by the second couple would be better for either child than any alternative feasible option. We may judge that, all things considered, this inequality in prospects would be acceptable. But it is hard to think that there is nothing unfair about it. What seems to be unfair is precisely that the two children are not going to have equal opportuni-ties in life.

Why object to the ways in which children's different family backgrounds create inequalities in their developmental opportunities—their chances of de-veloping their natural talents into relevant competences—while not objecting to the ways in which those family backgrounds create inequalities in their mo-tivations or willingness to exert effort? Surely one of the main ways by which different sets of parents tend to produce children with less or more marketable skills is precisely by instilling in them a willingness to do what it takes—to make the effort—to acquire those skills. Even more fundamentally, perhaps, these motivational and character traits are themselves marketable skills. Punc-tuality, self-discipline, and perseverance in the face of difficulty are precisely the kind of attributes that employers look for and lenders expect of those wishing to start their own businesses.

There is something very odd about a principle that condemns inequalities in the developmental opportunities enjoyed by children raised in different fami-lies but confines its concern to those who are similarly motivated or willing to make an effort. That is odd partly because motivational factors so strongly influence the extent to which children develop their "native endowments": being raised by parents who teach one habits conducive to success in the labor market *is* a developmental opportunity. But it's odd also because such factors are themselves among the attributes that are rewarded in competitive market economies.

Parents' Outcomes Are Children's Opportunities?

We introduced the idea of equality of opportunity as a somewhat commonsensical and conventional conception of equality, by contrast with the implausibly restrictive idea of equality of outcome. Nonetheless, interrogating what would be required for the realization even of that apparently modest egalitarian goal suggests that it would be wrong for a society to pursue it wholeheartedly. Parents' outcomes are so closely related to children's opportunities that the only way to realize equality of opportunity would be either (a) to deny parents the opportunity to acquire unequal amounts of the wide range of "resources" relevant to children's opportunities or (b) to block all the mechanisms by which those resources might influence children's prospects. Neither strategy can be justified all things considered. We might want to pursue both strategies to some extent—perhaps to a far greater extent than we do at present—but we must accept some disruption of fair equality of opportunity if we are to allow parents and children to enjoy the goods of family life.

This way of setting out the issues, however, misses something important, something that renders the goal of fair equality of opportunity—indeed many variants of equality of opportunity—problematic or suspect in a more fundamental way. So far, the problem has been simply that parents' outcomes are important causes of children's opportunities. That is why the second strategy—preventing parents' resources from influencing children's opportunities—is conceptually coherent. We may not want to pursue it all the way but at least that strategy makes conceptual sense. A deeper worry is that children's opportunities should *count as* parents' outcomes—that parents' outcomes *include* children's opportunities. If so, then allowing parents to achieve that kind of unequal outcome just is to allow their children to enjoy unequal opportunities. And preventing them from promoting their children's prospects just is to deny them that kind of outcome.

Think about what people are trying to achieve when they seek well-rewarded positions in the occupational structure. In the most general terms we could say that they are after better rather than worse lives—they want their lives to go well and they believe that achieving those positions will help with that. But of course they do not, typically, seek better lives only for themselves; they seek them also for their loved ones, including—often most importantly—their children. And, again of course, they do not want those rewards only so that their children can benefit in childhood, while those children are at home or dependent on the parents. They want them also so that they can help to promote their children's well-being in the future. As we discussed earlier, children's well-being is, for many parents, a crucial component of their own well-being. Certainly that is a goal for which they exert effort and make sacrifices, and a goal that provides a guiding orientation for many of their most important decisions. Their children's having the opportunity for a better life than they would otherwise have *is* an outcome—perhaps, for some, *the* outcome—for which they are striving. Preventing parents from using their resources to promote their children's interests would be to deprive them of the very outcome they had worked to achieve.

So it's not simply that parental resource outcomes are causally related to children's opportunities in ways that are morally valuable enough to make us judge it important to leave at least some of them intact. The problem with fair equality of opportunity is not the causal interrelatedness between parents and children so much as deep interconnections at the level of what it means for a person's life to go well. In part, what it *is* for one parent to be better off than another is precisely for her to be better able to promote her children's interests. The only way to give children a fair chance in life is to deny adults the opportunity to achieve—or fail to achieve—what many will regard as a crucial component of their well-being. What many want the opportunity *to do* is precisely to benefit their children, in large part by developing their abilities in such a way that they are well equipped for the competitive processes that distribute important goods. But the extent that we allow people to do that is the extent to which we fail to provide all with a fair chance. It looks as if fair equality of opportunity is conceptually coherent for only a single generation.

Parents have an interest in promoting their children's well-being, but they also have an interest in getting a fair chance to do that. Where two parents did not themselves enjoy fair equality of opportunity as children, promoting *their* children's interests will itself be among the things they lacked equal opportunity to do. Faced with this deep tension, all we can do is seek a considered way of balancing the different interests at stake, forming careful all-things-considered judgments about how to weigh them against each other. This is hard. To highlight just one complication, the very fact that advantaged parents are able to promote their children's well-being obstructs the ability of disadvantaged parents to promote theirs. Because competitive advantage is so important for the distribution of good things in our societies, it is harder for poor parents to benefit their children if rich parents are allowed to benefit theirs. So disadvantaged parents, no less concerned to promote their children's interests than advantaged parents are, can appeal to that shared concern itself as a reason to restrict the means by which parents may act on it.

Beyond Fair Equality of Opportunity?

So far we have discussed the conflict between family values and equality of opportunity by focusing on a specific version of the latter. The family, we have emphasized, is a problem even for a rather conventional or mainstream conception of that ideal. This section broadens the discussion more thoroughly, widening our horizons to raise more fundamental questions about that conception and the concept of equality of opportunity in general.

Notice, first, that the principle we have been considering is concerned only that people with similar levels of talent and motivation should enjoy equal opportunities. It is thus entirely silent on the question of how opportunities should be distributed between people with *dissimilar* levels of talent and motivation. Some problems with the motivational aspect have been touched on, but what about the other aspect, the focus on people with similar levels of talent? We explained earlier that this should be understood to refer to features that people are born with (their "natural endowments"), and mentioned some doubts about this approach. But suppose we put our suspicion to one side, at least to the extent of allowing that different people are born with somewhat different potentials to develop abilities and capacities likely to be rewarded by labor markets. The question then is this: why is it so important that people with similar levels of natural potential should have equal opportunities and, apparently, not at all important that people with *different* levels should have them?

Think again of two babies born in the same hospital on the same day. The previous example made them genetically identical because we wanted to hone in on the differing effects that family background can have on people's motivation. Now imagine babies—make them twins again if you like—who are genetically different: one born with a good deal of potential to develop characteristics valued by labor markets, another born with very little. Fair equality of opportunity has no objection to the idea that those two will enjoy (or suffer) unequal prospects. Many readers will agree.

Equality of opportunity is concerned to equalize people's circumstances—in particular, their developmental opportunities. It does not require us to eliminate inequalities in prospects that are due to differences constitutive of who those people are. It demands only the removal of the social barriers and silver spoons that prevent people from competing on level terms with those constituted like them. This fits with the idea that people can deserve unequal rewards for the exercise of their different constitutions.[23] It's problematic, on this account, if parents provide their children with unequal developmental opportunities, but not if they provide them, via the inheritance of genetic characteristics, with unequal potentials to be developed. The former refers to extrinsic things, circumstances that affect how well off children are likely to be. The latter seem more intrinsic: change those and what you have are different *children*.

A more radical conception of equality of opportunity would wonder why we should think of people's circumstances and their constitutions so differently. Some people will surely regard their genetic constitutions—their natural endowments (or lack of them)—as regrettable circumstances rather than as a constitutive part of their personhood. And even if others, perhaps more fortunate in the natural lottery, do view their own natural endowments as a crucial part of what makes them who they are, it's not obviously fair that their good fortune should give them superior prospects to those not so lucky. A concern with the distribution of opportunities, rather than outcomes, reflects the idea that it's fair for people to bear the consequences of their responsible choices. If so, and if people are not responsible for their genetic makeup (or "constitution"), then restricting one's conception of equality of opportunity to the similarly constituted can start to seem rather blinkered. Why not hold that *all* people, however constituted, should have the same opportunities?

Perhaps the answer to that question depends on what it is that we want people to have equal opportunities *for*.[24] We introduced fair equality of opportunity as concerned with the competition for jobs, or what social scientists call positions in the occupational structure. That's because jobs are the main ways in which our societies distribute many important goods. When we think about jobs directly, it may seem right to limit the idea of equality of opportunity to the similarly constituted. It would be odd to want those born with a tin ear to have the same chance of becoming a concert pianist as the child prodigy. But that might be because we are factoring in efficiency or productivity considerations rather than limiting ourselves to fairness alone. As we noted, fair equality of opportunity is appealing partly because it seems to combine two distinct ideas: inequalities of opportunity distort both the fair distribution of rewards to people and the efficient allocation of people to jobs. Clearly, given the nature of the activities involved, it would be inefficient to organize society so that all had the same prospect of becoming a CEO or brain surgeon (or an office cleaner or supermarket cashier), whatever their natural endowments. But that doesn't show that it is fair for differently endowed people to have unequal chances of achieving the rewards that currently attach to those jobs.

Rather than thinking in terms of the distribution of opportunities for certain kinds of job, which encourages a confounding of fairness and efficiency considerations, we should focus on the benefits (and disbenefits) that those jobs bring to those who do them. "Jobs," or "occupations," turns out to be shorthand for a wide range of goods (and bads): money, status, safety, interestingness, demandingness, degree of self-realization.[25] With jobs understood as constellations of a number of different forms of advantage (and disadvantage), limiting our concern to equality of opportunity between the similarly talented looks less satisfactory. Maybe the talented and the untalented should not have the same prospect of becoming a brain surgeon or a CEO, but does that mean they shouldn't have the same prospect of enjoying the various good and bad things that societies like ours distribute via those occupational positions? From a distributive perspective, it's unclear why we should care about equality of opportunity only between the similarly constituted. Is it fair, for example, that those born with disabilities should have worse prospects, for those aspects of well-being, than others?

We could go further and query such an emphasis on jobs at all. It's true that societies distribute important components of well-being through the occupational structure. But it's not the only way those components get distributed. Why not care about the fair distribution of opportunities for all the things that make people's lives go better or worse? Focusing on jobs (and on the distribution of opportunities to achieve them) makes sense if we want an easily identifiable, readily operationalized, indicator of people's general standing in the distribution of socially distributed rewards (and of the opportunities to acquire them). But from a philosophical perspective it makes sense to broaden our concern to compass other dimensions of well-being too. If, as we believe, familial relationships are, for many, among the most important elements of human well-being, then presumably we should be interested in equality of opportunity to achieve *those*.

Rather than conceive the family as an obstacle to the realization of equality of opportunity, which is how it is commonly regarded, and how we have treated it so far, we could think of familial relationship goods as themselves among the things that people should have equal opportunity *for*. This opens up a whole new agenda. In what ways does our society influence the distribution of opportunities for healthy, loving familial relationships? What can be done to make that distribution fairer? There will still be a conflict with the family, but now the questions will be why, when, how, and to what extent parents should be permitted to favor themselves, and members of their family, when they could be helping others to realize the goods of family life. And, since we are talking now about intimate, affective, personal relationships, there are of course important questions about the role that social policy and political action may properly play in pursuit of a fairer distribution. What may the state legitimately do as regards people's personal lives? What may it do without counterproductivity;

without, that is, interfering with relationships in such a way as to deprive them of the very qualities that make them so valuable?

We have been leaving unchallenged an unspoken assumption about the people whose equal opportunities we might care about—that they are members of the same society. It's been implicit in our discussion so far that the principle of equality of opportunity applies to people who are living under the same social arrangements, who are participants in what Rawls calls a system of social cooperation. Nothing we have actually said warrants that assumption, but so strong is its grip as the default view that we doubt that many readers will have been thinking about the desirability of fair equality of opportunity as between all human beings throughout the world. It's worth wondering why we should think it unfair if children born to different families in the same society have unequal prospects while not similarly objecting to inequalities of opportunity between those born to different families in different societies.

The answer might depend on what the opportunities are for. One might think, for example, that when the issue is the distribution of jobs, it makes some sense to be interested particularly in fair chances as between children born into the society in which those jobs are held—though even that suggests a rather unrealistic and outdated picture, as if those jobs were not the object of global competition. But if, in good philosophical fashion, we abstract to generic "well-being," then it becomes harder to justify the parochial idea that equality of opportunity between one's fellow citizens matters, while the distribution of opportunities to live a good life, as between them and those born elsewhere, does not. Here, again, there will be important questions about the proper role of politics, about the state as the appropriate agent for the pursuit of our distributive ideals, and about what those ideals should be once we broaden our horizons beyond particular societies or political communities. Some philosophers believe that the state has a particular role to play in promoting distributive justice among its citizens, while it is simply not its job to pursue that goal on a wider scale; some that the idea of distributive justice does not apply on the global scale at all; some that it does but not in a way that involves claims about equality of opportunity.[26] Engaging with these issues would make this a very different book. Still, we want to alert the reader to, and our more detailed analyses in subsequent chapters will deliberately leave open, the possibility that, at the foundational level, our distributive concerns should extend, and perhaps extend equally, to all human beings, irrespective of the state or society into which they are born.

So far we have been discussing different specifications of the general idea of equality of opportunity. But one might wonder why our distributive concerns should be couched in terms of *equality* of opportunity at all. Equality of opportunity has most intuitive appeal in competitive contexts.[27] Think about the proverbial level playing field in its literal, sporting use. We want that field to be level because two teams are competing for the same prize. If one wins, the other loses; so anything that benefits one team simultaneously disadvantages the other. If one team is playing downhill, the other is playing uphill. That's not fair (unless they change ends at halftime), and it's not fair in a way that is harmful for one of the competitors. The same applies to equality of opportunity as usually conceived as a distributive ideal for a society. If some children are born into families that give them a head start in the competition for interesting or well-rewarded jobs, then those not so fortunate are not simply worse off than the lucky ones; they are worse off than they would be if all had equal chances. The fact that some have better opportunities is actively harmful to the rest—it reduces their opportunities. That's because, at any given time, there are only so many interesting and well-rewarded jobs to go round. So equalizing opportunities is actually *improving* some people's opportunities; it's improving the opportunities of those who would otherwise have less.

All things considered, we may end up sacrificing some equality of opportunity for the sake of other values—including family values. But our reluctance to do that derives mainly from the realization that we are thereby condemning some people to worse opportunities for jobs and their associated rewards than they would have had under equality of opportunity. But, once we are thinking about opportunities for well-being, then we seem no longer to be assuming a competitive or zero-sum context. Does your having more opportunity for well-being than I do harm me? It does if we assume that you and I are competing for a given stock of well-being, in the way that we tend to assume that children in the same age cohort are competing with each other for a given number of interesting and well-rewarded jobs or places at good universities. In that case your gain would be my loss, and we would indeed be in a zero-sum situation. But there's no reason generally to think of well-being in that way, in which case the idea that equality of opportunity is what matters loses much, some would say all, of its appeal.

To value people's having equal amounts of something, or equal opportunities for that thing, when the total amount is not fixed, is to value equality even when equality brings no benefit anybody. That seems bizarre.[28] Wanting to "level down"—to deny advantages to some people just because others cannot enjoy them too—looks more like envy than morality, a sin rather than a virtue. Better, it seems, to reject equality, strictly understood, and to endorse a different distributive ideal; perhaps a variant of the "prioritarian" idea that, when assessing the value of distributions, we should give priority to the claims of the worse off. The thought that we should care particularly about the prospects of those who have least seems to fit our intuitive views in lots of cases. It does not support leveling down (because by definition that won't help the worse off), but it does support equality in those contexts where a more equal distribution will benefit those on the wrong end of an inequality. That is why some philosophers have argued that those who think of themselves as "egalitarian" do not, in fact, and strictly speaking, favor *equality*. Rather, they value distributions that give proper weight to the interests of the disadvantaged. Sometimes those distributions will be equal; sometimes they won't.[29]

There is, of course, a good deal more to be said. While accepting the case against leveling down, we must bear in mind how many kinds of inequality of opportunity have adverse effects on those with less. If many goods have positional value, in that their value to their possessor derives in part from how much she has relative to others, then there will be many goods where making opportunities more equal will not in fact be leveling down at all. Some goods, like education, are manifestly positional. The competitive context makes it obvious that some parents' buying their children a superior education harms the prospects of others. Other goods we might call latently positional. Health care might seem different from education—it's not obvious how one child's being healthier than another is bad for the latter. But in fact the relation between health and educational achievement means that, in raising your child on a good diet and ensuring that she gets proper exercise, you are damaging the competitive chances of less healthy children. That's not to say you act wrongly when you raise your child to be healthy. All things considered, that is surely the right thing to do. Nonetheless, when we are dealing with positional goods, the case against preventing parents from conferring superior opportunities on their children need not be perverse or envious. We'd be *leveling*, but not leveling *down*.[30]

Many goods have a positional aspect, but few are entirely positional. There is also, nearly always, benefit to having more rather than less in absolute terms, not simply to having more rather than less relative to others. So we must also keep in mind whether the good we are concerned with is in fixed supply, so that people's opportunities for those goods are competitive or zero-sum, or whether it is capable of increase. Even if the supply of jobs, and associated rewards, is fixed at any particular point in time, over time it is far from fixed, so there is plenty of room for unequal distributions of opportunities that benefit the worse off. Your raising your children to be educated and healthy may indeed damage the competitive chances of some other children. But if yours go on to increase the total number of good things in the world—perhaps, in particular, the number of interesting and well-rewarded jobs—and some of those good considered judgments are going to involve a balancing act, and hence the incomplete realization of any one.

That said, if we can present a position that can be justified to all, in the sense that it gets the balance of values right, then there is an important, quite different, sense in which that outcome will be fair. It will not fully realize fair equality of opportunity, so for particular real people, even the right balance will be unfair in its effects. But, if we get the balancing judgment right, all things considered, we can still defend those effects as "fair" in a broader sense: all relevant interests will have been factored in and accorded their proper weight. Abstracting from the particularities of their own situation, thinking about the interests and values at stake from a disinterested perspective, people would have chosen the proposed balance. In that sense, the judgment, and its implications for particular individuals, would be fair. And, because we will be able to offer that kind of justification of the distributive inequalities, our relationships with one another will have an egalitarian cast—they will be justifiable to us as equals.

The idea of fairness invoked here sees it not as one value to be weighed against others but as itself concerned with all-things-considered judgments. While it is important to keep clear on how our preferred balance of values will not guarantee children fair equality of opportunity (our first point), this perspective has the great merit of focusing our attention on what balancings of values really *can* be justified to those affected by them, especially to those who fare badly under them. It thus demands precise specification of the different domains of value at stake and careful consideration of the ways in which they conflict, and of how we should weigh them when and where they do. We need to know which of the mechanisms that currently disrupt fair equality of opportunity are worthy of protection despite their disruptive tendencies. Only with those—and only those—mechanisms protected, would we be able to justify the unfair inequality of opportunities to those on the wrong end of them. And only then would we enjoy the kind of justificatory relationship expressive of our fundamental equality.

Part Two

Justifying the Family

Introduction

This second part of the book seeks to justify the family—to explain why it is good that children be raised by parents. It's obviously good that they be looked after by *adults*, but what would be wrong with a system in which they were under the charge of different adults at different ages—specialists in dealing with young babies being replaced by experts on toddlers, who in turn would cede authority to those with advanced qualifications on the development of four- to five-year-olds, and so on? Or if continuity of care is important, would there be a problem with requiring newborn babies to be handed over to state-run child-rearing institutions staffed by well-qualified professionals? Or would it be bad if groups of twenty or thirty adults lived together in communes and shared the tasks of child rearing, with no particular child being the particular responsibility of any particular adult? In none of these alternatives would children have *parents*, as we will understand that term, and societies that reared their children those ways would not have *families*.

Of course there are other entirely legitimate uses of "family" that, though different from ours, are not metaphorical. Constellations of cousins, grandparents, uncles, and aunts are described as extended families. ("He's family," we say, when explaining to a child why she should devote an otherwise free afternoon to a boring occasion in honor of a, to her, unknown elderly man.) Adults who live together intimately without children, and with no intention of raising any, think of themselves as families. Given some people's insistence that state recognition or support for relationships between adults should be tied to procreation and/or child rearing, it's important to think of our stipulating parent-child relationships as the key element in "family values" as motivated only by a desire for analytical focus on what we take to be particularly theoretically interesting issues. It is by no means an ideological intervention claiming "the family" for the project of bearing and raising children.

Talk of "extended family," by contrast, fits reasonably well with our putting the parent-child relationship center stage. What the members of an extended family share, normally, can be thought of precisely as a set of interconnected and sometimes overlapping parent-child relationships. What is "extended" here is the parenting relationship, which is broadened to compass parents' parents, and their parents, and their children, and their children, and so on. We do not claim that the value of relationships between members of extended families will be captured entirely by analyses that see them in terms of interconnected parent-child relationships. A close relationship between grandparent and grandchild, for example, can be important in ways that do not depend on the chain of parent-child relationships linking the two. Nonetheless, there is usually something special about the fact that one's grandparents are one's parents' parents and one's grandchildren one's children's children. In concentrating on the family conceived in terms of the parent-child dyad, we are evading the question of how to factor in considerations arising from the value of relationships between members of extended families, a question that becomes particularly salient when, for example, the relationship interests of grandparents conflict with those of parents. It is an important feature of our view that adults benefit from exercising authority over their children, a benefit that dissipates if authority is shared with many other adults. Parenting by committee is not really *parenting*, and that remains true even if the committee is composed entirely of extended family members. Further work would be needed for us to have a clear view about how to incorporate the interests of grandparents, uncles, and aunts, and children's interests in relationships with them, into our theory.

There is a strong and straightforward case for the idea that children should have parents, that children and adults should experience relationships of the kind to be described over the next few chapters. But it does not imply that children should be raised by those adults who are causally responsible for bringing them into the world—their biological parents. For us, the fundamental reasons why children should be raised in families, by parents (rather than by a series of experts, or state child-rearing officials, or groups of adults living in communes), have little to do with biology. It is not the biological relationship that yields the distinctive goods that justify children's being raised in families. Anybody willing to accept that adoptive parents and adopted children can enjoy the kind of relationship we shall describe must acknowledge that what's good about it does not depend on any biological connection between parent and child.

Our project, then, is more radical than it might seem. Our initial question, whether children should be raised by parents, is *not* the question of whether children should be raised by those adults widely regarded as already "their" parents. It's whether there should be "parents" at all. It is, on our account, a separate and further question *which* adults should parent *which* children.

The notion of "biological parent" is multiply ambiguous. We can at least distinguish between an adult who shares some genetic material with a child, and an adult related to a child through the process of gestation. Our emphasis on the significance of the emotional, loving relationship leads us to regard the second as more important than the first, since it is possible, perhaps likely, that such a relationship will have begun to develop in utero—more likely than that the mere fact of genetic connection will have fostered such a relationship, especially as an adult and child can be genetically connected without either's knowing of the other's existence. Biological facts are less or more relevant to the question "Who should parent whom?" insofar as they are associated with the parent-child relationship that, we insist, can develop perfectly well in the absence of any biological connection between parent and child.

So though we identify "the family" with a particular way of raising children, one in which children have parents and one that realizes the relationship goods we will set out in the following chapters, it should by now be clear that it is not *that* particular! It involves an intimate-yet-authoritative relationship between children and the adults who parent them. That kind of relationship is available not only to adoptive families but also to single-parent families and to two-parent families (and, perhaps, to three- or four-parent families) in which both (or all) parents are the same gender.

How should one evaluate child-rearing arrangements? Evaluations of social institutions must consider the interests that they serve, and more specifically the contribution that they make to human well-being or, as we will sometimes say, to flourishing. First, and most obviously, there are the interests of children: their vulnerability, the fact that, however they are raised, they cannot be thought to have had any say in the matter, and the impact of their childhood on their lives as a whole make their interests a priority. Second, adults: adults too may flourish less or more depending on their society's rules about how they may and may not be involved in the process of child rearing. Finally, third parties: whether or not an individual is herself directly involved in raising children, how her society goes about that business will surely affect her, since child-rearing arrangements are bound to have what economists call externalities.

Though useful for analytical purposes, this tripartite division is clearly artificial. Not all children become adults, alas, but all adults were once children; and all people, both children and adults, suffer or enjoy the negative or positive externalities of everybody else's child-rearing arrangements. The framework is an intellectual tool for thinking about the distinct ways in which decisions about how children should be raised affect us all. Any individual pursuing just her own interests will seek to combine these different perspectives and come up with an all-things-considered judgment about which child-rearing practices would be, or would have been, best for her overall. We can approach the social decision in essentially the same way.

Chapters 3 and 4 consider children's and adults' interests in turn. We put the case for what we call a "dual interest" theory of the family: that is, a justification that appeals to the interests of both. A separate chapter on third parties would be a distraction, so we shall begin with some comments about those accounts of the family's importance that put its positive externalities center stage.

The claim that how children are raised affects members of the wider society is uncontroversial. Sociologists often see the family in functional terms, regarding it as the social institution charged with the task of socializing naturally egotistical infants into the norms and expectations of society as a whole. When the media talk about the family's being in crisis or breakdown, the concern is often that it is failing to produce well-socialized, emotionally regulated, cooperative, productive, civically minded, morally developed adults. Some of this concern is doubtless directed at the well-being of the children themselves, but some is more interested in the dire effects on the rest of us. If children are running wild, unable to defer gratification, lacking in basic literacy and numeracy, and so on, that puts everyone at risk. We need them to become economically productive in their adult life because we are going to have to tax their future income to provide for our retirements; this generation's long-term financial arrangements depend on the next generation's being willing and able to take on the baton. They must also be prepared to comply with social norms. The society as a whole has an interest in children's being trained to assume their role as citizens of a liberal democracy, with at least a basic capacity for tolerance and respect for the liberties of others with whom they may disagree.

Few think that responsibility for turning children into adults with such qualities falls entirely on those charged with their primary care—all of us, via the state as our collective agent, are likely to be involved in the process too, most obviously through the provision of public education. But children's relationships with their primary caregivers are important for their emotional, moral, and cognitive development. And, so this argument goes, those primary caregivers should be parents; if you want children to become the kind of adult that is good for the rest of us, then raising them in families is the right way to go about it.[1]

Though we focus on the goods that familial relationships provide for those participating in them, we agree with these claims about their benefits for third parties. Many of the considerations typically presented as yielding positive externalities—such as the emotional, moral, and cognitive development of children—are the same as those framed by our arguments as benefiting the children themselves. This happy alignment of the interests of children and third parties should not be taken for granted. It is, for example, contentious in the case of children's moral development, since it is more controversial to claim that it is good for a person that she act morally than that it is good for other people that she do so. In principle some ways of raising children may be good for third parties but not for children or those raising them. Still, we must keep in mind that all those third parties were, or still are, themselves children, and most are now adults, so any all-things-considered assessment of child-rearing arrangements will factor in the impact of such arrangements on them in these other roles, or with these other hats on. Taking that into account, we can set the interests of third parties to one side at this stage of the argument, though they will figure in part 3, when we consider parents' rights to shape their children's values.

We think of a person has having two kinds of interest. She has an interest in anything that contributes to her well-being or flourishing; anything that makes her life go better is an interest of hers. But she also has an interest in having her dignity respected—in being treated in ways that reflect her moral status as an agent, as a being with the capacity for judgment and choice, even where that respect does *not* make her life go better. The question of whether children have this kind of "dignity" or "agency" interest, and what kinds of treatment it implies, will be discussed in chapter 3.

Focusing here on the first kind, the "well-being" interest, we want to stress that, for us, people's interests may be different from their wants or desires or preferences, mainly because they can be wrong about what makes their life go better. Well-being is objective, not subjective; things can be good or bad for people without their realizing it. So someone can have an "interest" in something, in our sense, without her being remotely interested in it. The evidence shows that, subjectively, many people have no interest in taking exercise. But if we're talking about their objective or real interests, about what will in fact contribute to their well-being or flourishing, then, given current levels of obesity and its effects, we are willing to claim that exercise is in their real interests.[2]

That is supposed to be a fairly unproblematic example. It's fairly unproblematic because the idea that people have an interest in good health is relatively uncontroversial; the unhealthy nonexerciser herself may well acknowledge that she's not doing what would be good for her. Our accounts of children's and adults' interests over the next couple of chapters go well beyond this. But of course even this kind of case is perfectly open to challenge. Who can say whether a person's life goes better if she eats less and exercises more? If she is not interested in being healthy, what justifies the judgment that she is making a mistake? An implicit skepticism about objective conceptions of well-being underlies economists' tendency to take people's preferences at face value, as it were—*de gustibus non est disputandum*—and simply equate well-being (or welfare, as they tend to call it) with preference satisfaction. We hope to persuade the skeptical reader of our objective approach to interests and well-being by articulating, as precisely as possible, the content of some putative interests, making claims about what makes people's lives go better, and considering the various reasons for accepting or rejecting them. That is the aim of the next couple of chapters, where we identify those well-being interests of children and adults that bear on the question of how children should be raised.

Those chapters will invoke a further term: "rights." Chapter 1 attempted to defuse the worry that rights talk is inappropriate in the context of family relationships, and that relied on an implicit notion of what rights are. But the relation between interests and rights, on the one hand, and the difference between the right *to* parent and the rights *of* parents, on the other, require a bit more discussion before we can proceed.

For us, people have a right to do something when their interest in doing it is weighty enough that others have a duty to let them do it; they have a right to be given something when their interest in having it is weighty enough that others have a duty to give it to them.[3] People can have interests in doing or receiving all kinds of things without having the corresponding rights. How do we decide whether an interest is sufficient to ground a duty in others? Two variables have to be taken into account. It matters both how important the interest is and how burdensome the implied duties are. Lots of things would make our lives go better but in such trivial ways that it would be ridiculous to claim that others were under the corresponding duties. Some things that are indeed important to people's well-being would nonetheless impose such unreasonable burdens on others, if they were under a duty to respect or provide them, that we should reject the claim that there is a right to them. This is only a framework for assessing rights claims. When deciding whether people have a right to something—to speak freely, to vote, to receive health care, to have children, to choose their children's school, not to be hit by their parents—we should think about whether their interest in it is sufficient to warrant holding others under the duties that would be implied if we granted the rights claim. All the arguments for or against any given claim have still to be heard.

Although normally justified by the interests of the rights-holders themselves, sometimes rights are held by people other than those whose interests they serve. When someone is given power of attorney over an elderly relative, whether by voluntary transfer or by a judicial ruling, *that* person now has some rights over the relative's affairs (for example, she may be given the right to buy and sell his property). But the person holding and exercising the rights, as trustee or fiduciary, possesses them not because they promote her well-being but because her possessing them is instrumental to the well-being of the person for whom she is acting as fiduciary.[4] Many arguments for parents' rights see them this way. Parents' rights over their children—what others have a duty to let them do to, with, or for those children—are justified, at root, by the children's interests, not those of their parents. We offer a variant of this view, but with a crucial twist. The rights that parents have over their children are indeed justified by appeal to children's interests—parents should have just those rights that it is in children's interests for them to have. But parenting relationships—and hence the family itself—are justified in part by the fact that adults have an interest in playing that fiduciary role. The contribution that familial relationship goods make to the well-being of those who get to be parents helps to justify the practice of children's being raised by parents, in families, and it helps to explicate the basis of the adult right to parent, even though the rights that one has qua parent are grounded entirely in children's interests.

Chapter 3 discusses children's interests in being parented, as well as other interests that their parents must respect and promote as they go about that task. Chapter 4 is about the interests that adults have in parenting. Both chapters go beyond discussion of the relevant interests to make claims about children's and adults' rights. Yet it is not until part 3 that we move on to a thorough explication of parents' rights. Distinguishing two questions helps to explain the rationale for this sequence. First, there is the very basic question of whether children should be raised by parents at all. To answer it we consider the interests of both children and adults, and find in favor of the family: "yes," we argue in this part of the book, "children should indeed be raised by parents." Though some of our reasoning may be new, the conclusion is not. The payoff, we hope, comes when we turn to the second question, which asks what rights parents should have over, or with respect to, the children they parent. That issue is a good deal more controversial than that of whether children should have parents in the first place, but in our view it can seriously be addressed only in the light of an answer to that more fundamental question.

The rights *of* parents, then, are the rights that adults have over, or with respect to, the children they parent. Those rights are discussed in part 3. But what about an adult's right *to* parent? Is the interest that adults have in parenting children sufficiently weighty, and the burdens it imposes on others not so heavy, for that relationship to be claimed as a matter of right? If so, might an adult claim a right to parent not just any child but a particular child, such as one to whom she has a biological connection? We can ask analogous questions about children. Do children have a right to *a* parent, the right to be parented? Do they have, as some have argued, a right to *parents*, to a mother and a father? Can they claim a right to be parented by a particular adult, or by particular adults, such as those who procreatively brought them into being? Though we will say something about these big and difficult questions, we cannot provide a comprehensive treatment; they need further specification before they can properly be addressed, and, on receiving that specification, they quickly disaggregate into a variety of different, and difficult, issues.

Consider, just by way of illustration, the right to parent, which is how we interpret the right to found and raise a family inscribed in declarations of human rights. We could think of this as a negative right, on the model of the right to freedom of association; this might be formulated as the right not to be prevented from parenting the children one has procreatively produced, which is how the right is conventionally understood. Even on this construal, the alleged right raises controversial issues. It is unclear, for example, whether it should be taken to involve the right to produce and raise as many children as one likes, even in circumstances, which many take to be our own, where there is a clear collective interest in limiting fertility for ecological reasons; perhaps our duties to future generations require us to interfere with people's procreative freedoms, at least to some extent. China's (recently relaxed) "one-child policy," though not motivated exclusively by environmental concerns, is clearly relevant here. But we could also think of the right to parent as a positive right, on the model of the right to subsistence, education, or health care; here the right is to receive assistance in the business of acquiring children to parent. Suppose we take the latter seriously, as many societies seem to when they grant would-be parents access to fertility treatment. Interesting questions here already on the political agenda include the extent of any right to assistance (most public health services ration the number of attempts granted to any would-be parent) and, more controversially, who is entitled to such assistance (would-be single parents, same-sex couples, etc.). Here, too, though not on the political agenda, the redistribution of children from their biological parents to the involuntarily childless is a philosophically serious scenario. The fact that our approach gives no fundamental significance to biological connection gives us a distinctive take on such issues.

As with all rights, attempts to specify the content of the right to parent must take a view on the question of whether rights can conflict. On one view, all valid rights claims must be compossible or congruent; rights, *stricto sensu*, cannot conflict. From this perspective, the duties implied by rights claims are not merely prima facie duties but conclusive, all things considered, duties. To say that somebody has a right to do something is to say not only that her interest is weighty enough that others have a duty to let her do it, but also that there are no conflicting duties that are yet more weighty. On this view, we cannot specify the content of the right to parent until we have taken into account not only people's interest in parenting, and the prima facie duties on others which that would entail, but also the rights of others and any competing prima facie duties. One implication of this approach is that people's rights will vary with circumstances. For example, the question of how many children a person has a right procreatively to produce and parent will depend on the content of her duties to others, perhaps most significantly her duties to future generations. In a world where overpopulation massively threatened the most basic interests of future generations, which many claim to be our world, people may not have the same rights to parent that they would have in happier circumstances.[5]

Although we share the aspiration to philosophical precision that motivates this first approach, the chapters that follow will talk about rights in the somewhat looser way that allows them to conflict. This better corresponds to ordinary usage. When people couch claims in terms of rights, they don't, typically, take themselves to be asserting an all-things-considered judgment—one that has taken account of all the competing interests that might be at stake in the particular circumstances. They may indeed understand that such judgments will be needed for us to decide who should in fact be allowed or required to do what. But they conceive those judgments as involving the weighing of conflicting prima facie rights claims. The rights of current would-be parents may compete with the rights of future people, just as the right to privacy may conflict with the right to information, or the right to liberty with the right to security. To be clear, even on this looser view, rights still protect or promote particularly weighty interests. Taken on their own, other things equal, those interests are weighty enough to ground duties in others. But, in particular circumstances, they may be outweighed by other considerations, considerations that impose competing, and more morally urgent, duties.

CHAPTER 3

Children

The family is justified because it produces certain goods that would otherwise not be available, or, in some cases, would be much more difficult to produce. These goods—familial relationship goods—are enjoyed by children and by the adults who are their parents. This chapter will focus on the goods it produces for children, arguing that their interests are such as to support the claim that children have a right to be raised by parents—in families. First, we define what we mean by children and childhood. We then explain what interests are, and describe the interests we think children have. Next, we make the argument that children have a right to a parent, which involves three claims: children have rights; children are appropriate objects of paternalistic care; and for a child's vital interests to be met, she must be cared for, consistently, by only a small number of people. We go on to discuss how a biological connection between parent and child relates to our account of children's right to a parent, and conclude the chapter by looking, briefly, at the implied duty to parent.

Children and Childhood

What are children? The English term "child" has at least three meanings. It is sometimes used to specify a relationship: you are your parent's child, just as your parent continues to be your parent, even when you are an adult, and even when you and your parent are both dead. Sometimes it simply designates people who are chronologically young—below the age of eighteen, or sixteen, or perhaps younger. Finally it is used to describe people who lack the capacities that are taken to characterize normal adulthood: children in the chronological sense remain the paradigm here, but it makes sense to say of a middle-aged man who has not developed normal adult capacities that he remains, and may always be, a child.[1]

We simply stipulate that children are people who, because of their age, have yet to develop the capacities that characterize normal adulthood. This excludes adults who lack the capacities that characterize normal adulthood, and chronological children who lack those capacities not because they are young but because they simply do not have the underlying potential (e.g., those with serious cognitive disabilities). Such people may have the same moral standing as adults, or as children, but there is a big difference between rearing a child who can develop into an independent person and rearing one who cannot. Although some of our analysis covers most cases, some invokes developmental needs that apply specifically to children in our stipulated sense.[2]

Developmental psychologists discern several stages of normal development for children. Newborns are entirely dependent on others for their immediate needs and for the resources and conditions needed to develop adult capacities: independent thought and judgment, some degree of self-reliance, emotional self-control, partial control of their environment, and self-conscious communication. In favorable circumstances, children develop in fairly predictable stages. The social smile (by 8 weeks) is followed by flexible reflexes and one-word sentences (1 year), walking, self-feeding, and self-recognition (2 years), symbolic representations, grammatical morphemes, and conjunctions (4 years) and formal operations and rule following (8 years). Although "normal," these developments do not simply happen: they require the right kind of care.

Similarly, children need the right kind of care to develop into emotionally healthy and successful adults. Stanley Greenspan and T. Berry Brazleton distinguish the following key stages of emotional development prior to adolescence, and comment on the kind of care needed to achieve it. A child must be calm and regulated and be interested and engaged in her environment. By 3 or 4 months, infants should be able to focus on what they are touching, seeing, or hearing, without losing control. Nonverbal communication (6–18 months) enables children better to comprehend human interaction and to learn from it; by 18 months, they have developed a sense of self and also begin solving problems with another person. They then gradually learn how to form a mental idea of, identify, and communicate their wants, needs, and emotions. Between 2½ and 3½, children take these emotional ideas and make connections between different categories of ideas and feelings. They begin to connect feelings across time and can recognize if one is causing the other.

From about 4 to 7½ years, children begin to understand that their parents or other carers are not simply substitutes for each other but are different people.

By the end of this stage, if all has gone well, children should have a firmer grasp of reality (though they still have an active fantasy life), are more emotionally stable, and can grasp more complicated relationships and experience a wider range of emotions. By 10–12 they have usually begun to develop a more consistent sense of self, and will usually experience the conflict between the desire for adult-like independence and the desire for security and dependence.[3]

Obviously, the extent to which children need the care and attention of others, and the kind of care and attention they need, change over time. In infancy, if the changes described above are going to develop, they need intensive and attentive care from a more mature person.[4] At 8 they need a fair amount of contact with other children, not necessarily of their own age, who do not have socially sanctioned authority over them; and at 12 they need a good deal of freedom from the intensive care and attention they experienced in infancy. In the discussion of children's interests that follows, we shall sometimes refer to children, sometimes to young children, and sometimes to very young children or to infants. Specifying on every occasion the exact stage at which an interest or need is pertinent would be laborious, and we hope that the reader will be willing to accept occasionally vague formulations.[5]

What Are Interests?

Children come first when it comes to justifying child-rearing arrangements. Unlike most adults, children enter such arrangements involuntarily, and the quality of their lives as a whole, not just their childhoods, depends heavily on how they are raised. When we adopt a child-centered perspective, we are thinking not solely about that part of people's lives that they spend as children but also about how their childhood impacts on their lives overall. The interests that children have in experiencing some forms of child rearing rather than others include developmental interests, interests in how that child rearing will influence their development into adults. So there are substantive as well as chronological reasons for us to discuss the way that children's interests provide reasons to support the family, before we turn to adults' interests. That said, we suspect it will be easier for readers to get hold of the way we invoke "interests," and the specific issues raised by discussion of children's interests in particular, if we first say something about the structure of adults' interests.

Accounts of adults' interests vary with accounts of well-being. While we do appeal to some substantive claims about particular constituents, we do not try to offer a comprehensive theory of well-being. For purposes of illustration, though, here is Martha Nussbaum's influential attempt to capture adults' interests that do not vary (at this level of abstraction) across social contexts. Nussbaum claims that some threshold level of each of the following goods is necessary for someone to have a successful and flourishing life:

Life: being able to live to the end of a human life of normal length;

Bodily Health: being able to have good health, nourishment, and shelter;

Bodily Integrity: being able to move freely about, to have opportunities for sexual satisfaction, reproductive choices, and being able to be secure against physical violations;

Senses, Imagination and Thought: being able to imagine, think, and reason in a "truly human" way, and having the education necessary to exercise these capabilities;

Emotions: "in general, [being able] to love, to grieve, to experience longing, gratitude and justified anger";

Practical Reason: being able to form a conception of the good and engage in critical reflection about the planning of one's life;

Affiliation: being able to live with and toward others, to recognize and show concern for other human beings, and having the social bases of self-respect and nonhumiliation; being able to be treated as a dignified being with equal worth;

Other Species: being able to live with concern for and in relation to animals, plants, and the world of nature;

Play: being able to laugh, play, and recreate;

Control over Environment: being able to participate effectively in political choices that govern one's life and having real opportunities to hold property, seek employment on an equal basis with others, having freedom from unwarranted search and seizure.[6]

We present Nussbaum's list as illustrative, not definitive; it is just one account of adults' interests. It is helpfully abstract: there are, for example, many different ways of playing, and many different ways of fitting play into one's life; similarly, people vary in what they need to be well-nourished: women and men need slightly different vitamins and minerals. Understanding this can help dissolve potential disagreements about what people have an interest in. The claim that all people have an interest in reaching a high level of literacy, for example, may be countered by the correct observation that nomadic tribespeople in sub-Saharan Africa have no such interest. But we can say that both African nomads and U.S. Midwesterners have an interest in attaining the skills necessary for functioning effectively in the economy they will inhabit.

Notice that Nussbaum's list straddles the distinction, outlined in the introduction to this part of the book, between *well-being interests*, which bear directly on how well one's life goes, and *dignity* or *agency interests*, which bear on the extent to which one is able to manage one's own life freely. Some items pertain directly to well-being; if you are undernourished, your life is worse in a vital respect than if you are well-nourished. But others relate also to the choices people are capable of making, and they may have an interest in being able to make those choices even if their life ends up going worse as a result.

Why is agency important? One reason is that people are usually better placed than others to judge what will serve their own well-being. Big decisions (such as whom and whether to marry, when and whether to have children, where to live, which of our talents to develop) and small decisions (such as what to have for breakfast, how many layers of clothing to wear, which novels to take on holiday) affect the quality of our lives. On the whole, people are likely to be the best judges of the decisions that will best promote or protect their well-being, and the occasional mistake can be thought of as a learning opportunity that will make their lives go better in the long run. But, further, in order for projects and activities to make their contribution to our lives' going well, we usually need to endorse them, to identify with them to some extent from the inside.[7] Even when we are not the "best judge," judgment and choice are powerful mechanisms for inducing the endorsement or identification normally required for the execution of a decision to enhance our well-being.[8]

That is not the whole story though. We can acknowledge that someone might have flourished more had she been made to act on the judgments of others, and still think it important that she was able to make and act on her own—because she thereby got to be the author of her own life. Respecting people's mature capacity for demanding reasons of themselves and of others as justifications of their actions demands of us that we accept their judgments about their good as authoritative. This may be so even if it is demonstrably true that they would be better off acting on someone else's judgments. We value human dignity, and it can be an assault on that dignity to be coerced or manipulated into doing things that reflect the judgments of others rather than our own, even if, on balance, what we are coerced or manipulated into doing improves our well-being.

The distinction between well-being and agency matters here for two reasons. First, children's agency interests differ from those of adults. Being treated paternalistically, even when that paternalism successfully identifies one's good, can disrespect an adult's agency interests (which is not to say that paternalism toward adults is never justified). But an infant's being treated paternalistically need involve no disrespect of her agency interests, because those are entirely future-focused; they are interests in becoming an agent in the future. As children develop, gradually acquiring the capacities worthy of respect in adults, the nature of their interests in agency, and what is involved in respecting them, changes. Second, children's interests in their future agency are important for understanding the task of raising a child. Adults are under a duty to raise children so that, eventually, they no longer need the adults' fiduciary attention. More, the duty is to try to ensure that children develop the capacity to make autonomous choices about how they are to live their lives. This makes raising a child very different from having a pet, or caring for an elder or someone who is severely cognitively disabled.

Children's Interests

For our purposes, four features of children are especially significant. First, children are profoundly dependent on others for their well-being. Often they are not the best available judges of what will promote either their own well-being or their interest in future agency, lacking both access to information and the rational and emotional capacities to process and act on whatever information they have. Second, they are profoundly vulnerable to other people's decisions; when something goes wrong, it is likely to affect the whole of their lives, not just their childhoods, and its going wrong is normally because the decisions of another have failed. Third, unlike other people who are dependent and vulnerable, children can yet develop capabilities that enable them to realize their own interests. The combination of these three features—dependence, vulnerability, and the capacity to develop into nonvulnerable and independent adults—makes children unique. Finally, children, when young, lack a well-developed and stable distinctive conception of what is valuable in their life. These four features have consequences for how we should think about their interests.

Liberal theorists have tended to place a premium on adults' agency interests, demanding that they be protected with rights to freedom of action, freedom of conscience and expression, and the like. Such rights are usually understood to require that individuals be permitted, and sometimes helped, to act as they judge best in the circumstances. This is not because liberals always value agency over well-being; it is assumed that respecting their choices is congruent with their well-being. But young children's well-being and agency are not congruent. Infants have few immediate agency interests, if any: they need constant care, supervision, nutrition, interaction with others, and sleep. Toddlers may have some agency interests connected to their immediate welfare; to get immediate enjoyment and fulfillment, they may need to be able to express themselves, and make choices within a restricted range. For teenagers, and even preteens, some of the value of being able to act on their own judgments is related to their dignity and not merely to their well-being and future agency. But even in the best circumstances young children's agency is very limited in its ability to serve even their immediate welfare interests. Unconstrained, young children explore the world in a way that is largely uninformed about the dangers it presents and must constantly be supervised and restricted. They will consume poisons, walk into busy roads, fall through windows, drown in swimming pools, burn themselves on hot ovens, even if warned not to. Securing their future interests requires care and constraint; they have no countervailing interest in being the author of their own actions.

Granting agency rights to adults is also usually taken to have a protective function for their future agency and well-being interests. A young child's agency interest is in becoming an autonomous adult, one who is able to make and act on her own judgments in the informed and reasoned way that commands respect and usually tends to her well-being. She also has an interest in developing the capacity for a sense of justice—the ability to understand and internalize rules about how to treat others properly. Developing either or both of these capacities requires more than the mere indulgence of her immediate choices: she must be taught to empathize and sympathize, reason about principles, think about moral rules, and discipline her own behavior. Young children have limited understanding of the complexities of adult agency and at best a tenuous grasp on what it takes to develop the requisite emotional traits and cognitive skills to exercise it.

Typically, if children are raised in the right way and the right environment, their capacities change over time. They become better judges of their own well-being as they mature. They also become more adult in that their capacity for agency begins to command respect. Within certain areas of decision making, we might extend effective agency to a twelve-year-old or a fifteen-year-old, even though we know that her judgment is poor, in order to help train her to become a better agent; but we might equally extend her effective agency with respect to some parts of her life simply because we think that her dignity commands it.

We have distinguished children's well-being from their agency interests, and their immediate from their future interests, and we have said that their immediate agency interests are quite different from those of adults because, for the most part, they are interests in developing the capacities for agency that they will come to exercise as adults. This is some help to adults charged with supervising and caring for them, but not much. More guidance can be provided by distinguishing five categories of children's interests; four are developmental, while the fifth concerns childhood itself:

1. Children need the health care, nutrition, shelter, and clothing adequate to their healthy *physical* development within the society in which they are raised.
2. Children need education and upbringing that attends to their *cognitive* development sufficiently well that they become capable of the critical reflection necessary for autonomy, and able to operate effectively in the economy of the society in which they are raised.
3. Children need the education and upbringing that enables them to understand their own *emotional* needs and dispositions, regulate their emotional life, and connect emotionally with other people.
4. Children need the education and upbringing that ensures their development into *moral* persons, who understand the basic demands of morality, are capable of regulating their behavior according to those demands, and are disposed to do so.
5. Children need the freedom, support, and environmental conditions to enjoy their *childhood.*

How to meet these interests well is sensitive to context. So, for example, what precise nutrition and shelter are needed depends both on the prevailing level of social and economic development and on geographic conditions; exactly what cognitive skills are valuable depends on the needs of the society and economy in question. There is also bound to be disagreement over what it takes to meet their needs even within a particular context. For example, most societies with any measure of freedom contain controversy about what morality demands, so what constitutes success in moral development will be somewhat controversial, and even given agreement on what constitutes morality there will be debate over what kinds of child rearing and education will yield a moral child.

Whereas the first three categories all primarily concern the individual's own well-being and agency, some might argue that the primary beneficiary of the child's becoming a moral person is not the child herself but the rest of society. There is, in other words, a strong third-party interest in children's becoming effective moral agents, able and inclined to respect the needs and interests of others in line with the demands of morality. Sometimes, in fact, the individual may be made worse off by particular instances of acting morally, especially if the individual's behavior will go undetected. Philosophers disagree about whether being moral enhances one's own life intrinsically. But even if only because social institutions tend to reward moral behavior, children have an interest in moral development.

While the categories are analytically separate, they are connected. Healthy emotional development serves healthy cognitive and moral development. The link with the latter seems obvious: someone who is unable to identify and regulate her own emotions, or to empathize with others, is not in a good position either to identify or to respect and promote their interests. The link with cognitive development is less obvious but, according to Sue Gerhardt, recent developments in neuroscience have confirmed E. E. Cummings's view that "feelings come first": "It is increasingly being recognised that cognitions depend on emotions . . . the rational part of the brain does not work on its own, but only at the same time as the basic regulatory and emotional parts of the brain. . . . The higher parts of the cortex cannot operate independently of the more primitive gut responses. Cognitive processes elaborate emotional processes, but could not exist without them."[9]

Most philosophical discussions treat childhood as a period of life in which the person is waiting and preparing for adulthood. But our fifth category points to the fact that childhood is valuable in its own right. Childhood is not merely preparation for adulthood—if it were, then children who died before reaching adulthood would have lived worthless lives.[10] Moreover, some goods may have value only, or much more readily, in childhood. We do not have a full list, but we think that innocence about sexuality, for example, is good in childhood, even though for most people it would not be valuable for their adulthood. A certain steady sense of being carefree is also valuable in childhood but is a flaw in most adults. These are what Samantha Brennan has called the "intrinsic goods of childhood," and Anca Gheaus terms "special goods of childhood."[11] Other goods are just more readily available in childhood than in adulthood: the capacities to feel spontaneous joy, to be surprised, and to be thrilled seem to diminish a good deal with age; while they are valuable in adulthood as well as in childhood, it may be unrealistic to expect them to be experienced with great intensity much beyond childhood but entirely realistic to think that many children can experience them fully. And, of course, other goods, like happiness, are readily available in both adulthood and childhood, but their value in childhood, as in adulthood, is not entirely dependent on their long-term developmental consequences.

Do these interests justify the family? We think they do: in fact, we think they ground the claim that children have a right to a parent. The next section will explain what we mean by this and why we think it; we argue that children have some rights, and that these include the right to a parent.

The Right to a Parent

The next chapter will argue that adults have the right to be parents, which in our terms is equivalent to the right to raise children in families. Here we are interested in whether children have the right to be raised by parents, that is, the right to be raised in a family.

This is not a question about the content of the law. What rights are formally conferred on children is of course important, even though many governments fail even to comply with the legislation they have signed up to. But our focus is on the normative or philosophical issue of what rights children can properly claim, and what duties can validly be claimed of others, irrespective of what the law happens to say. We read the question "What rights *do* children have?" as "What rights *should* children have?"

Article 7 of the UN Convention on the Rights of the Child states that "children . . . have the right to know and, as far as possible, to be cared for by their parents"; Article 8 talks of "children's right to a name, a nationality and family ties"; while Article 9 says that "children have the right to live with their parent(s), unless it is bad for them. Children whose parents do not live together have the right to stay in contact with both parents, unless this might hurt the child."[12] Those claims may indeed be valid, but they refer to the situation where a child already has parents, or "family ties," and attempt to pin down the child's rights with respect to that particular person or persons. We are asking the more fundamental question of whether children have a right to parents at all, or to be parented, as such. If a society decided to raise its children in state institutions, would it be violating children's rights to be raised in the particular arrangement we call the family?

Children's Rights

It is more controversial whether children have rights than whether adults do, and the distinction between well-being interests and agency interests helps to explain why. Some theories of rights regard them as specifically protecting one's ability to make and act upon one's own judgments, within certain limits, in various areas of one's life. The right to freedom of religion, for example, is supposed to protect individual conscience and preferences for kinds of worship, so that the individual can conduct her religious and spiritual life as she sees fit. But on the account we have given, children lack the capacities for judgment and choice on which the idea that it makes sense to protect their judgments and choices depends. Moreover, the decisions that they do in fact make are typically heavily influenced by the adults raising them. So it seems inappropriate to say that they have the same rights to freedom of religion and expression as adults have.[13]

These considerations, though valid, fail to establish that children cannot be rights-bearers *tout court*. Even if children lack the capacities for agency that are important in adults, they surely possess two interests that are important enough to warrant holding others under relevant duties. Children have the *potential* for those capacities, and the interest in developing them. Children, that is, have a right to experience the kind of upbringing that will realize their potential to exercise the kind of agency characteristic of normally functioning adults. In particular, as we shall argue in chapter 6, they have the right to become autonomous. Children also have interests in the conditions necessary for their lives to go well, and those interests too are weighty enough to warrant ascribing them rights. Rights-bearers need not have well-developed capacities for judgment or choice, but are simply beings whose moral status is such that their well-being matters enough to impose duties on others—beings like ordinary human adults, ordinary human children, and, perhaps, some animals.[14]

None of this tells us the *content* of children's rights. But we shall now argue that they include the right to a parent. The argument proceeds through two claims: their interests are such as to make them appropriate objects of paternalistic treatment, and the most suitable setting for that treatment is the family. Only an arrangement in which some small number of adults is charged with continuing responsibility for paternalistic treatment of a child—in which those adults are granted very considerable authority over her, and discretion in carrying out the tasks associated with raising her—will adequately protect and promote her interests.

Paternalism

Paternalism involves manipulating or coercing another person with the purpose of serving her good.[15] It seems obvious that paternalism toward infants and very young children is justified, since they lack any capacities for judgment and choice. If their interests have moral importance, then somebody other than them must be acting to ensure that those interests are realized. What is more controversial, though, is whether manipulating or coercing older children, who are developing capacities for judgment and choice, is justified.

Given that even older children's judgments are normally less informed and mature than those of adults, the case against paternalism may seem mysterious. Objections to paternalism toward children typically do not deny the moral significance of their interests. But, as mentioned in chapter 1, some advocates of children's liberation reject much paternalistic treatment. In their view, despite the appearance of incompetence, children do, or *could*, have the relevant capacities; if they lack them, that is precisely a result of their being treated paternalistically. Recent developments in the history and sociology of childhood have claimed that childhood, and, more controversially, the differences between adults and children, are socially constructed. Paternalistic treatment creates a kind of self-fulfilling prophecy: society treats children as incompetent, so they are incompetent; adults shackle children, so that they are dependent. Incompetence is not a biologically determined feature of people of a certain age; it results, rather, from the interaction between such people and the social environment that adults have placed them in.

Consider the analogy with women. In many societies, adult women were regarded as vulnerable and dependent—and they often were, because legal restrictions, nonlegal discrimination, and the sexist distribution of investment in human capital made them so.[16] Similarly, black slaves in the antebellum South were widely seen as lazy or ignorant. But, since teaching slaves to read was illegal, blacks frequently *were* ignorant. As they had no claim on the proceeds of and no control over the conditions of their labor, they developed effective strategies for avoiding work. But they were not *intrinsically* lazy and ignorant. Their deficits, though real, were socially constructed. If children's dependency and incompetence were similarly just a response to the social environment, paternalism toward them would lack justification.

Some sociologists question our ordinary assessments of children's competence in making and acting on judgments for themselves about particular issues. Priscilla Alderson has studied children's consent to surgery, and, citing the testimony of surgeons, claims that children are frequently better decisionmakers than adults. One surgeon had "come across a couple of [eight-year-olds] who are able to make decisions remarkably well. . . . If they ask an appropriate question leading on from the information, I think you can assume that you are able to communicate something they've taken in, and understood and can deal with."[17] Others point to the way in which many children across the world have valuable skills and contribute to their own and their families' subsistence.[18] Michael Freeman, invoking such claims, argues that children should have broadly the same rights as adults, and that, contrary to one of the considerations we drew on to support paternalism, "young children can be highly competent, technically, cognitively, socially and morally . . . some can be agents."[19]

Children's capacities certainly vary across societies, and some children's abilities, especially those deploying fine motor skills and abstract reasoning, exceed those of many adults. And the line between adolescence and adulthood is vague and ragged—plenty of sixteen-year-olds are more mature than plenty of twenty-year-olds, and the same is true for any four- to six-year age gap from about fourteen on.

Despite these facts, three observations support paternalism toward children. First, claims about children's competences should not be exaggerated. Although children are as good as adults at some things and even better at others, it does not follow that they can be agents in a more holistic way. Even quite young children can develop one capacity well, enabling them to make reasonably good decisions about a small range of issues, but that does not justify regarding them as authoritative about their own interests, or anyone else's, outside that small realm. Moreover, not all, or even many, children can develop the skills at which some excel.

Second, even for children with highly developed skills, a concern for the special goods of childhood speaks in favor of maintaining a paternalistic structure. Childhood is a period during which it is possible to enjoy being carefree, and not to have to bear responsibility for decisions about others or, to a considerable extent, one's own interaction with the world. Carefreeness is increasingly unavailable in adulthood (and, as our next chapter implies, many adults need to be burdened by certain cares in order to flourish fully). Providing children with agency rights that imply responsibilities, even if they are capable of the agency in question, may not be an unalloyed good for them, because the responsibilities may bear on them in a way that deprives them of a good specific to their stage in life. A child who knows that her participation in the labor market is essential for her family's survival misses out on one of the special goods of childhood; so does the child who is the main carer for his severely epileptic parent.

Finally, the development and exercise of some capacities in childhood can have serious, and irremediable, opportunity costs for the development of other capacities that matter for the future well-being of the child. Children participating full-time in the labor market mending fishing nets, for example, are unlikely to reach the levels of literacy and numeracy that would enable them not only to compete with others for scarce and unequally distributed goods but also to reflect on their life situations to make the best of them. Similarly, too much responsibility too early may be detrimental to the child's healthy emotional development.

The facts do not suffice to warrant abandoning the generally paternalistic stance that we rely on in justifying the family. Appropriate adults are justified in substituting their wills for those of children when doing so is in those children's interests, which it usually is for much of what we conventionally regard as a person's childhood. In fact, children have a *right* to be treated paternalistically. If, as we have claimed, children have weighty interests in both well-being and future agency, interests that depend for their realization on their *not* being free to do as they will (run into the road, eat too much junk food, skip school), then respect for those interests itself demands that others act paternalistically toward them. The scope of justified paternalistic action, and the means by which it is enacted, may vary widely depending on the child's stage of development. But, in broad terms, adults have a duty to manipulate and coerce children into doing what will be good for them, or what will promote the development of their capacity for autonomy.

Why Parents?

But why should *the family* be the setting for the paternalistic oversight of children's interests? After all, there is much truth in the cliché that "it takes a village to raise a child."[20] On any reasonable account of what it takes to achieve healthy physical, cognitive, emotional, and moral development, one, two, or even four, adults are unlikely to be able to provide everything necessary without help from others. Consider what it takes for a person to develop the capacity for close friendship; undoubtedly parents play a vital role, but without substantial interaction with other children and some with adults, some of which is unsupervised by parents, a child cannot develop the independence and the judgment about other people, or the capacity for intimacy, needed. Children certainly need people other than their parents.[21] But do they need a parent at all? Does it take *a family—a parent*—to raise a child?

Here, briefly, are four different possible arrangements for rearing children:

1. State-regulated quasi-orphanages, in which children are raised by trained and specialized employees;
2. Arrangements, such as those associated with kibbutzim, in which child raising is shared between "parents" and designated child-raising specialists. In the case of the kibbutzim, the main carer, or *metapelet* would typically live with other *metaplot* and a group of children, and children would have contact with their "parents" for about three hours a day;
3. Communes in which a large group of adults collectively and jointly raises a group of children, with no adult thinking of herself as having

any special responsibility for any particular child, and no child thinking of herself as the responsibility of any particular adult;
4. Families, in which a small number (no more than four) adults—
"parents"—raise children.

Our claim that children have a right to a parent rests on the view that only the
last of these is able reliably to meet some of children's vital interests—because
only a particular kind of relationship between children and adults is able to deliver what children need. That kind of relationship, and the goods that it makes
possible, can arise only when authority (including the authority to act paternalistically) and care for a child are concentrated in a small number of adults. A
fuller specification of the kind of relationship we have in mind must be deferred
until part 3, where we discuss parents' rights with respect to the children they
parent, and the kinds of parent-child interaction required, permitted, and prohibited by our "relationship goods" account. Here we aim only to explain why
the family is better for children than these alternative arrangements.

A good way in is to identify the variety of roles or functions that adults
play or fulfill with respect to children. Drawing on a range of research on child
development, Shelley Burtt offers the following list, each item on which is sufficiently distinct that, conceptually at least, it could be played by a different person: Lover (Soulmate), Physical Care-Giver, Homemaker, Financial Provider,
Socializer, Moral Educator, Teacher, Gender Role Model.[22]

As Burtt acknowledges, this is not the only way of dividing up the tasks,
and there is a good deal of overlap even at the conceptual level (e.g., socializer,
moral educator, and teacher). Still, her approach allows us to think about the
range of things that children get from adults, and hence about the different
ways of distributing the various roles between them. The "traditional" gendered
division of labor in the home already gives us a model in which there is considerable specialization between different individuals. In the stereotypical 1950s
sitcom family, the mother is lover, physical caregiver, homemaker, and socializer; the father is the financial provider; they share the role of moral educator,
serve as gender role models for the child, and typically outsource much of the
role of teacher for children beyond the age of five.

Some of these roles can be played simultaneously by many people. Most
children in rich countries have numerous teachers attending to their education
and socialization. Many children have several financial providers—children
from wealthy families are often provided for partly by grandparents and other
relatives, and all rich countries have child-oriented state support for all but the
wealthiest families. But one of these roles is vital: that of lover, or soul mate. It

is the key causal factor for many of the child's weighty developmental interests that we identified earlier in the chapter, and, unlike some of these other roles, it cannot be widely distributed, nor played in turn by a series of different adults. For a child's interests reliably to be met, she needs to be cared for by at least one adult who loves her, the loving relationship needs to be sustained over a long period, and the adult who loves her must be able to exercise a good deal of discretionary authority over her.

Especially during the first three years, children's development depends on effective emotional regulation, which takes place through one-to-one communication, most of which (initially all of which) is nonverbal in nature. The child receives visual, aural, and tactile cues from the carer, and comes to learn the world, and herself, by responding to those cues: simultaneously the carer gets to know the child. The carer must be highly receptive to the child's signals and emotional responses, to both the carer and the wider world, and able to respond to her moment by moment. When a carer fails to regulate well, by giving unclear or confusing signals (e.g., by swinging between harshness and sympathy), or by failing to respond appropriately to happiness or sadness in an infant, then the child cannot form a clear regulatory strategy; children cared for in such a way are at higher risk of psychopathology later in life. Attachment theorists have long stressed the importance of intimate attachment between infants and responsive carers. Recent neuroscience concurs, suggesting that loving, responsive, available caregivers are doing two things: reducing stress and anxiety, thus keeping balance in the child's stress response and limiting exposure to the toxic effects of the cortisol triggered by stress, and providing conditions in the brain for synaptic connections to be made, particularly in the "social brain" areas (e.g., in the prefrontal cortex).[23]

For all this to happen, the carer needs to be in touch with the infant's states. But that requires the carer to know the child well, to understand what patterns have been established. Similarly, for the child to learn how to regulate her responses, she needs to get to know the carer well. They must spend a great deal of time with one another, especially in the earliest years, in order to know each other well enough for the process to work. The carer needs to spend more time with her than more than a few adults could spend with her, unless they were all present simultaneously. But even if several were present simultaneously, the capacities of the infant are limited—she can focus on only one or two people at a time, and it is possible for her to get to know, intimately, only a few carers.

The infant needs at least one adult to be extremely attentive; if that attention is shared among too many adults, it cannot have the desired effects. But, and this is where the authoritative aspect of the relationship comes in, she also needs to experience those few attentive carers as her central disciplinary models. In order to learn self-control, empathy, deferred gratification, and other modes of self-regulation—all of which are important for autonomy—the child needs to observe these traits modeled in her immediate environment, and in people with whom she identifies. For children, identification comes through love and admiration, which are themselves responses to loving warmth in the carer. The provider of the discipline, furthermore, has to be attuned to the needs and personality of the child. To give a simple example, disruptive behavior on an empty stomach is different from disruptive behavior animated by the desire for attention, and should usually be responded to differently. An adult attuned to a child often knows the difference intuitively, even if he or she could not describe the difference to a replacement carer. A carer who does not love or is not intimate with the child is less able to respond in the right way, and less able than a loving and intimate carer to elicit the child's right responses. An unloving carer may perhaps command compliance through fear, but the important developmental aim of disciplining a child is not at-the-moment compliance but over-time internalization.

It is not only because the child needs to love her disciplinarian, and can love only a few people in the necessary way, that authority over her must be concentrated in very few adults. There is a more practical reason too. Adults have their own lives to lead, and the more of them there are, the harder it will be for them to coordinate their lives such that they can all remain closely within the child's orbit—in modern societies people move considerable distances for employment and other reasons—and the more likely is conflict over the details of how the child should be treated. It proves difficult, often, even for both halves of a couple raising a child to commit to being on hand in the way required, and to negotiate a common approach to child rearing. As the number of parents increases, the complexity of negotiation and coordination expands geometrically.

It is important also that those adults with authority over the child are experienced by her as acting at least somewhat spontaneously, and as having the discretion to act on their own judgments. Someone who, when deciding what to give for breakfast, or what stories to read at bedtime, robotically executes the detailed instructions contained in an official state-approved child-raising manual will hardly be providing the kind of loving guidance that tends to induce identification with the authority figure, nor herself experiencing the parent-child relationship as a source of joy and satisfaction in the way most helpful to the child's development. The next chapter will discuss the interest that most adults have in a particular kind of relationship with a child—the kind that we are calling a parenting relationship; we will argue there that the interest is weighty enough to give adults a right to such a relationship. But the rights that parents have over the children they parent are, for us, entirely a function of the interests that children have in being parented by adults with those rights. It is valuable *for children* that the adults who raise them enjoy the relationship. Of course, the job of raising children is onerous and costly in many ways, but the parent whose child is entirely a burden to her will not be providing her child with the kind of relationship she needs, however dutifully she bears and discharges that burden. So it's in children's interests that their parents not be their slaves, nor slavish enforcers of an official child-rearing protocol.

The alternatives in our list could attempt to mimic familial arrangements. But it is very unlikely that the quasi-orphanages could do so with much prospect of success. It may indeed be that particular employees of such institutions could develop a genuinely loving relationship with one or more of the children in their charge, and it is just about possible to imagine such an institution granting those employees the kinds of discretionary authority that we have claimed to be important. In such cases, the employee would effectively become a parent. The contractual or professional aspect would not rule out the possibility of healthy familial relationships developing, though there is a question about whether children could develop the requisite level of trust in someone whom they knew to be acting according to a contract. But as a general rule, and if we are right that children need a single person to love them consistently over the course of their childhood, then the restrictions on freedom of contract required would be extreme, and the regulatory oversight very complicated. Employees of these institutions would have to sign up for many years, and not only could they not withdraw from the contract; they could not be fired, except for the most egregious breaches of contract. Regulators would be highly constrained by the fact that once the relationship has reached a certain stage, the child has no realistic second chance of establishing an acceptable alternative. Of course, it is also true of parents in the family as we know it that they effectively sign up for a long-term and unbreakable commitment when they choose to raise a child; that is what being a parent is. But being a parent is not a profession or an occupation; a parent can change her job if she is unsatisfied with it (and lucky enough to have alternatives) without thereby abandoning a child.

Kibbutzim, or similar arrangements, might have better prospects. However, at least some research finds that children raised in these arrangements have more difficulty establishing and maintaining lasting and intimate relationships than do other children. We are reluctant to base a case against the arrangement on the psychological evidence, because although there are several studies, they are not grounded in a theory of emotional well-being that we could defend as correct, they are not conclusive, and, of course, they are studies of a limited number of specific instances of the arrangement, rather than of the arrangement itself; it could be that some variant of the arrangement that was never tried would have had results as good as those produced by family arrangements.[24] Still, one feature of the kibbutzim arrangements is worth noting. The fact that "parents" normally spent three hours a day with their children means the *metaplot* were not sole carers, but were always raising the children in tandem (and, according to some studies, in some tension) with the parents. This makes it unclear exactly how far the arrangements departed from the family (on our definition).

Think, finally, about the commune arrangement we have described. Given the account of the child's needs we have given, and the necessity of a single person's providing continuity, especially in the earliest years, it seems essential that responsibility for children be distributed formally as in the other arrangements. Some children may be, in effect, parented by a single person who informally adopts them, but the risk is that some, or perhaps many, children either will receive insufficient attention, or will not receive it consistently from one person, as seems to be required.

Of course, in addition to dividing the job up between themselves, it is common for those conventionally regarded as "parents" to devolve aspects of the relationship to others, with complex and subtle divisions of responsibilities in relation to the care of, and authority over, children. This includes those aspects that we have claimed to be crucial for children's healthy development. We cannot get into detailed discussion about wet nurses, nannies, au pairs, childminders, babysitters, and so on, though the next chapter will say something about adults' right to parent children, and why that is not satisfied by acting as a nanny, for example, As far as children's rights are concerned, the important point, for our purposes, is that a complex division of authority and caring may be satisfactory for small children, since they are unaware that the people to whom they are attached do not really have authority over them, and may be fired at will, but this is likely to become problematic as they grow up and learn both of the precarious nature of that relationship and that their "parents" are outsourcing care but not authority.

What Kind of Family?

So children have a right to be raised by parents, in families. What kind of family do they have a right to be raised in? Nothing in our argument supports the claim that the two-parent, nuclear, heterosexual, biological family is the only legitimate family form. On the contrary, we believe that familial relationship goods can be well realized in many types of families. But care is needed here. We do not deny that, given currently prevailing social policies and norms, children raised in certain kinds of family are likely to fare better, at least with respect to some dimensions of well-being, than those raised in others. Moreover, we accept that, even though our account of the child's interest in being parented involves no claim about the intrinsic value of the relationship with a biological parent, it may still be that children's being parented by their biological parents will be better, on average, for children, than any other feasible arrangement— and for more universal, noncontextual reasons. If so, that would ground a child-centered justification of the biological family as the default, even though no child has a right to be parented by her biological parent.

Deferring the issue of biology, consider the various mechanisms by which being the child of a single parent might tend to produce worse outcomes for children than having two parents. The stigma in contexts where the norm of the two-parent family is very strong might cause the harm; here the fact that norms have changed so fast (and reflection on the case where single parenthood has resulted from the death of a parent) make very clear the element of cultural construction. Children of single parents also tend to grow up in poorer households. Studies that look at the differential outcomes, in terms of education and jobs, of children raised in different family forms find that some of the measured disadvantage accruing to children of single-parent families is due to their having fewer resources,[25] not merely economic resources but also time, which is scarcer when there is one parent rather than two. Here too, it is not single parenthood in itself that creates the inequality; it is the way social institutions interact with single parenthood. If society wanted to support such parents so that their children had the same money and time devoted to them, it could do that.[26] Perhaps, though, children with two parents tend to do better for additional reasons: it may be more likely that at least one parent will be able to relate to the child in the way that she needs, or it may be that a single primary carer will tend to perform the role better if supported by someone else who cares about the child.

What about the more specific claim that not only do children need two parents, but those parents should be of different genders? The UK organization

Fathers4Justice says that "no child should be denied their human right to a father."[27] Given that organization's focus on custody and access arrangements after parents have separated, that might be understood as a claim about the importance, to the child, of *continuing* a relationship with someone with whom one has already started a parent-child relationship. Our concern here is the prior question of whether it is only two parents, of different genders, that will tend to be better for children, or can provide what children need and have a right to—the interest in emotional development probably being the most controversial. Advocates of same-sex parenting cite studies showing that such children's outcomes are on average no worse, across a range of measures, than those of children raised by opposite-sex parents. As in the case of the kibbutz, we are reluctant to put too much weight on the studies because measures of emotional well-being do not necessarily align with what really makes people's lives go well. Moreover, it is still much more difficult for same-sex (especially male) couples than for opposite-sex couples to acquire children, so there is an element of selection that makes it hard to draw wider conclusions. Still, what evidence there is suggests that children raised by the same-sex couples who do become parents are not worse off than children raised by opposite-sex couples. Even if the evidence *did* show them to be worse off, we could not conclude that same-sex parenting was worse for any deep reason: that may be a consequence of stigmatizing social norms. What would be needed in order to find that opposite-sex parenting was intrinsically superior is evidence that any disadvantages suffered by children of same-sex parents were not due simply to societal reaction and could not readily be avoided by appropriate interaction with nonparental adults of the other sex.[28]

We draw two lessons from this brief analysis, one about children's rights, one about the justification of child-rearing arrangements more generally. First, what children have a right to is a relationship with at least one adult who will provide the child with the relationship goods that we have identified, which include discharging the duty of care to the child. Many single parents are well able to do this, so there is no general right to two parents as such. Where single parents lack the means or capacities properly to discharge the parental role, the proper response could be to provide them with the support they need. Where it is the societal or cultural reaction to single parenthood that deprives children of the kind of upbringing they have a right to, it may be the reaction that should change. The point generalizes: there are many alternative ways in which societies could be organized so that children raised in different kinds of families would receive the kind of upbringing they have a right to.

But, second, quite apart from the question of rights, it could simply be that some types of family tend, on average, to be better for children than other types—they are more likely to produce better outcomes for the children raised in them. If true, this is also relevant to the question of the kind of child-rearing arrangements that will be justified at the level of policy. It might, for example, help to establish some forms of family as the default, or as the kind to be supported or encouraged by state policy, even though the probabilistic considerations in favor of that form might be defeated in particular cases where we have more detailed information about how best to meet the interests of the children at stake. But here again we must be careful to identify the mechanisms that generate the differential outcomes. These may be context-specific—depending on social policies and norms that could be otherwise. For example, not long ago children born out of wedlock were considerably disadvantaged compared to those born to and raised by married parents, partly because of stigma, partly because of the way in which law treated "legitimate" and "illegitimate" children differently. Those mechanisms could not contribute to a child-centered case in favor of the legal status quo of the time rather than to a case for changing norms and the law. To get the former, we would need deeper, less contingent or circumstantial, grounds for thinking that it was better for children to be raised by married parents.

With these points in mind, let's turn to the view that children have an interest in being parented by an adult to whom they are connected by biology—by what we might call their "biological parent." For many people this is the core meaning of "parent"—witness talk about adopted children seeking out their "real" parents—but it is also somewhat vague, since it fails to distinguish between a person who contributed genetic material to the child (her "progenitors") and someone who gestated the child (her "birth parent"). With the advent of surrogacy and artificial reproductive technologies, that distinction has assumed considerable practical significance, but keeping it clearly in mind is in any case helpful for carefully identifying different variants of the claim that the family should be based on biology. Scientific developments have made it possible to separate in the real world aspects of procreation that were always analytically distinct, and distinct in a way that makes a difference to assessment of the (widespread) idea that it is the biological family that constitutes the best way to raise children. The next chapter will consider a range of claims along these lines that appeal to the interests that adults have in parenting a child with whom they are biologically connected. Here we look solely at the child-centered case for biological parents.

Our articulation of the child's interest in a relationship with a parent makes no reference to biological connection. Nothing important need be lacking, from the child's point of view, if she is raised by an adult without that connection, so children raised by adoptive parents have no complaint, no claim against their biological parents that *they* be the adults with whom they have a relationship of the kind we have described. Of course, one might think that those responsible for bringing children into the world must do what they can to ensure that their children have parents. One might think also that children's procreators owe something to whoever takes on the parental role. But neither of those thoughts concerns the *child's* interest in being parented by her procreators.

Perhaps our account of children's interests simply fails to recognize the very important interest that children have in being parented by an adult to whom they are biologically connected. That interest, it might be argued, is weighty enough to ground a right to be parented by the people who brought one into existence. On such a view, someone who deliberately produces a child without intending to parent her is wronging the child, or who, though capable of parenting the child well, chooses instead to give her up for adoption, deprives her of the kind of relationship to which she has a right. On that view, a child whose parents have no biological connection to her is necessarily missing out on something very important. If that were true, it would provide a child-centered case for supporting the biological family. But it is possible, and we will argue also more plausible, to hold a weaker view about the significance of biology: it may be that, other things equal, procreators are more likely to provide children with the kind of relationship that we have described, and perhaps to serve their interests in other ways, than parents who lack any biological connection to their children. Though weaker, that would point us toward a child-centered justification of the biological family as the default child-rearing arrangement.

As in the case of the two-parent family, assessment of any claims in this area requires care about the extent to which children's interest in being parented by their biological progenitors is context-dependent rather than universal. If, for example, one accepted sociobiological ("selfish gene") claims about progenitors' tending to protect and promote the interests of their offspring better than other adults, then that would surely constitute a strong child-centered reason, of the second kind, to endorse the biological family as the norm. One would then be relying on a view of human nature as fixed or given, at least on a relevant timescale. But other claims in this area put greater weight on social or cultural processes that seem more readily imagined otherwise.

Thus, for example, David Velleman has argued that "knowing one's [biological] relatives and especially one's [biological] parents provides a kind of self-knowledge that is of irreplaceable value in the life-task of identity formation."[29] By this he means not merely that it is important for children to know who their procreators are or were, in the sense of having information about them; the issue is "whether there is significant value in being parented by one's biological parents."[30] One could accept the former claim while denying that there is any particular value to being parented by the people one has the relevant information about. For example, it is plausibly in children's interests that they should know about their genetic ancestry on health grounds, so they can better assess the risks of certain medical conditions and make informed judgments about screening and specific preventative measures. Closer to Velleman's view, it may be that, at least for many of us, knowledge of our origins is important if we are to develop an adequate sense of who we are. Further, perhaps it is helpful not merely to know about but to have some contact with our biological parents. For him, one comes to know oneself not through introspection or by looking in the mirror, but by knowing other people like oneself, people with whom one shares a "family resemblance"—and the kind of "literal family resemblance" that comes from biological connection is crucial. "Not knowing any biological relatives must be like wandering in a world without reflective surfaces, permanently self-blind."[31]

But one can know people, in this sense too, without being parented by them. Velleman may well have captured much of what motivates adopted children to seek out their biological parents. Indeed, according to David Howe and Julia Feast: "The need to have a sense of genealogical and genetic connectedness appears strong. It is part of the drive that motivates people to search. Who do I look like? Where do I come from? Whom am I like in terms of temperament and interests, skills and outlook? But," they continue, "although these needs trigger people to search and seek contact, they do not necessarily imply the desire for a relationship. They are information led: they are designed to meet autobiographical and identity needs."[32] One can accept Velleman's view about the significance for a healthy identity of observation of, or contact with, biological relatives, without taking the further step to a claim about the importance of being raised by them.

Should we accept that view? If correct, it would be enough to support a child-centered case for the biological family as the default arrangement, an "other things equal" claim in favor of biological parenting: children should be parented by somebody, and the relevance of biology to the formation of a healthy identity establishes a presumption in favor of that somebody's being their procreator. We do not challenge that presumption, but Velleman makes stronger claims that will be relevant to harder cases, such as where the default has failed and the biological parent(s) are unavailable or inadequate, or donor conception, where adults contribute to the creation of children without any intention of parenting them. In such cases—especially where the adult interest in parenting (discussed in the next chapter) is relevant—it becomes important to think about what kind of relationship, if any, with biological relatives is strictly necessary for a child to develop a healthy identity, and, insofar as biological connection does tend to be helpful, the extent to which the processes that make it so are culturally specific rather than universal. We could agree that children are owed the kind of parenting they need to develop a sense of self and the capacity for agency, while denying that they must be provided with what they need for the particular, biologically informed, identity that is currently culturally dominant. Perhaps, while discharging our obligations to current children seeking a healthy identity in a culture dominated by particular ways of finding it, we should also be challenging "bionormativity."

The question of the nature of the interrelation between biological connectedness and social kinship (how universal? how deep?) is too big and hard for us to say more. For our purposes, it must be enough to point to the possibility—realized by many adoptees in practice—that, even in a culture that puts great store by narratives involving biology, children can develop a sense of identity that will allow them to live flourishing lives without knowing much, perhaps anything, by way of specific information about their biological relations, let alone being parented by them. It may be easier for them if they know, or even have contact with, their biological kin, but arguably that is because "the contemporary cultural context is dominated by the natural nuclear family schema."[33]

The last couple of pages have treated "biological parents" (or "procreators") as equivalent to "progenitors" (or "genetic parents"). It is the genetic rather than the gestatory connection that concerns Velleman, and his argument about the interest in biological parenting applies as much to fathers as to mothers. But considerations about children's identity-based interest in their origins presumably apply also to the—still very rare—cases of surrogacy, where the woman who gestated and gave birth to a child has no genetic connection to it. Children of surrogate mothers often want to know, or know about, the women who gave birth to them, and where genes and gestation coincide it may be the latter as much as the former that is of interest to adopted children. Insofar as we are concerned with the identity-based aspect of the gestatory association, the issues take the same form as those just discussed.

But gestation may be relevant to parenting, from the child-centered perspective, in at least two other, typically mutually supportive, ways. On the one hand, it may be that, other things equal, a woman who has been pregnant with and given birth to a child is more likely to parent that child well than are other adults. Thus, for example, Caroline Whitbeck has suggested that affection for one's biological children, though partly influenced by socialization and acculturation, results also from universal "bodily experiences," experiences that include pregnancy, labor, childbirth, and postpartum recovery.[34] On this account, gestation helps to create the kind of bond of affection between birth mothers and newborns that gives good, child-centered, grounds for treating parenting by birth mothers as the default. This has the same form as the "selfish gene" argument for regarding biological parents as the default arrangement, but here the mechanism at work is gestation rather than genetics.

On the other hand, one might think that the pregnant mother and the child to whom she gives birth have already begun a loving intimate relationship, perhaps the kind that our account regards as valuable. We will discuss that thought from the adult's point of view in the next chapter, but it can obviously be framed in terms of the child's interests too. It might seem arbitrary to treat the parent-child relationship as starting at birth, so if one holds that a child has a strong interest in continuing to be parented by the person who did the job for the first three months after birth, why not think she has a similar interest in being parented by the person who gestated her for the three months before that? As Anca Gheaus puts it: "If the same process which brings babies into the world also generates their first intimate relationships [with] adults, then relationships between birth parents and their babies need no justification: they are already there from the beginning. Adding the perspective of the baby, who also bonds with its mother whose voice, heartbeat and so on it can recognise during the last phase of gestation, gives additional, child-centred justification, to the right to keep one's birth baby."[35] On this view, a child who is not parented by her birth mother suffers the severance of an already-existing relationship. Suppose that is true. Whether that prebirth relationship does indeed have the properties that explain why, on our account, a parent-child relationship is so important from the child's point of view, and whether it is likely to be as harmful, for the child, to disrupt that relationship at birth as it would be to disrupt it, say, three months later, are issues that require further thought.

The Duty to Parent

Suppose we are right that having a parent is indeed very important. Claiming that children have a right to a parent goes beyond that; it claims that adults have a duty to parent children. Not to "parent" them in the procreative sense—to bring them into being (though there might be circumstances in which at least some people would be under that duty too)—but to provide them with the kind of relationship we have described.[36] As we have explained, the rights and duties in question are prima facie rather than absolute, so the duty to parent may in principle conflict with, and be trumped by, other duties that fall on adults in particular circumstances. But even as a prima facie claim, some may find it implausible. We have emphasized the distinctive and intimate character of the parent-child relationship, and clearly parenting a child is a huge commitment for any adult to undertake. Many fail adequately to parent even those children they have themselves brought into the world.[37] Can we really say that, for every child brought into the world, there is some adult who has a duty to undertake the challenging and onerous task of parenting that child? If so, then we are effectively accusing millions of adults of neglecting their duties, for there are surely millions of children in the world today who lack parents.

A couple of points of clarification may avoid misunderstanding—and perhaps make our claim seem less absurd. First, recall, from chapter 1, the nature of the duty to love. Children need love—that is one of the crucial things parents can give them—but that kind of emotional response to another is not wholly susceptible to the will. Some people are not capable of loving others, and even those who can love some people are not capable of loving others. Since duties are moral imperatives, and since "ought implies can," we deny that there can be a duty to love. The duty in question can only be to *try* to love—the duty to parent is the duty to do what one can to provide a child with the loving relationship that she needs.

Second, when understood as a duty that falls on individuals, the duty to parent is best understood as the duty to play one's part in ensuring that children who need parents get them. Some philosophers think that rights can be claimed only where specifiable agents are under the implied duties. On that view, we would need to know *which* adult had the duty to parent a particular child before we could say that that child had a right to a parent. But we claim that children have that right without being able to say who exactly has the duty to parent them; we think that we can know that *somebody* has a duty to parent in advance of knowing who exactly that somebody is. This is like the claim that human beings have a right not to live in poverty—we, like many, are willing to assert such claims without being able to say who exactly has the duty to do what to relieve poverty. In a sense, then, the child's right to a parent could be understood as the right that adults get together and establish an institutional mechanism for assigning the relevant (perfect) duties to adults in such a way that every child gets a parent. We collectively fail in our duties to children when we fail to establish such institutional mechanisms.

Depending on how many children need parents, and how many adults there are willing to parent, such mechanisms may result in particular adults' being assigned a duty to parent a child when they would rather not take on that role. Perhaps, for example, there would have to be a lottery to assign the relevant duties. But that is not an absurd conclusion. Imagine that, after a shipwreck, you are among a group of adults on a desert island, one of whom proceeds to die in childbirth, leaving her newborn baby in need of someone to care for her. If none of you positively wanted to act as her parent, then the proper way forward might well be for you to agree to institute a fair procedure for deciding who should take on that role. True, you would doubtless also set up a support system for whoever was landed with the job, sharing out the various functions to the extent that was compatible with the child's interests—so, for example, others might be expected to contribute to the material needs of the child, and of the adult now occupied with the task of parenting her. (This would be not unlike the way citizens of many states provide economic support to foster parents.) But if we are right that children have a vital interest in having someone to parent them, then it seems that all adults have a duty to do their bit to try to ensure that an adult is willing to play that role, up to and including the duty to take on the role of parent themselves.

If the claims of the next chapter are correct, then that duty is less onerous than it may seem. There, we will argue that many adults have a weighty interest in parenting—indeed, the contribution that the parent-child relationship can make to the well-being of many adults is sufficient to ground a right to parent. In practice, we believe that some adults on the desert island would positively want to take on the role. The challenge is more likely to consist of devising a fair mechanism to assess competing claims to parent the child than coming up with one to pin the parental duties on reluctant adults, especially if an adequate support structure is put in place.

Conclusion

In order to develop into flourishing adults, and to enjoy the goods intrinsic to childhood, children need to have a particular kind of relationship with one or more, but not many more, adults. Of course, what exactly they need from it changes as they develop: an infant and an adolescent will have different needs. And, again of course, any child at any given time needs the relationship to supply a complex mixture of things: a feeling of being special, lessons in self-discipline, paternalistic authority within certain domains, and so on. When we say that children need *parents*—indeed that they have a *right* to a parent—we are saying both that there is an essential core to what they need that is best delivered by particular people who interact with them continuously during the course of their development, and that those particular people are able to provide the combination of things needed at any particular time. Continuity and combination are implied by the idea that what children need is a particular kind of *relationship*. It's not the same if different adults take charge of different stages, as if the task of raising children could be passed from one to another like a baton in a relay race. And it's not the same if the different influences that children need are distributed across different adults, so that, for example, the person who loves the child might be someone different from the person who has the discretion paternalistically to substitute her judgment for the child's own. Some change in who does what at different stages, and some functional specialization between different adults at any given stage, may indeed be compatible with children's healthy development. But there is a particular combination of functions that have to be provided by the same person, or the same few people, for the child's interests reliably to be met.

Formulating the value of parents to children by reference to children's developmental needs can seem reductive. It casts parents as adults who fulfill particular functions for children, delivering or providing goods in a way that seems to turn the parent-child relationship into a machine for producing specific and well-defined outcomes. Our analytical approach perhaps encourages that kind of suspicion, but we hope it will allay such fears if we remind readers that the products in question are flourishing human beings, and human beings with such moral standing or dignity that their judgments about how they are to live their lives commands respect. The languages of developmental psychology and of philosophy may appear to pull in different directions; we aim to bring them together in fruitful dialogue. Similarly, we trust that our discussion has not lost sight of the crucial fact that what children need, above all, is a spontaneous, intimate relationship with an adult who loves them, one who acknowledges the intrinsic goods of childhood while caring about their well-being, and respecting their individuality, enough to give them the huge amounts of attention, and the loving discipline, that are required for them to develop into the adults they are capable of becoming.

CHAPTER 4

Adults

Children have the right to be raised by a parent. But do adults have a right to parent children? The child's right to be parented imposes duties on others, but parenting could simply be something that adults have a duty to (try to) ensure happens—whether by doing it themselves or by contributing their share to collective arrangements that get it done. Many people want to be parents, but that doesn't mean they have a right to do it—perhaps, instead, the activity of parenting should be distributed only to those who would do it best. Would there be anything wrong with a system that distributed children to adults in the way that maximized the realization of children's interests, even if it left out some adults who would be willing, and adequately good, parents?

We think that there would. Where the previous chapter looked at the goods that familial relationships provide for children, this one focuses on those that such relationships produce in the lives of adults. We argue that parenting a child can make a distinctive and weighty contribution to the well-being of the parent. It cannot be substituted by other forms of relationship, and it contributes to the parent's well-being so substantially, and in a manner so congruent with the interests of children, that it grounds a (conditional, limited) right to parent. The goods in question are important enough, and children's interests well enough served, to impose a duty on others to allow, and indeed to enable, adults to enjoy them.

The right to be a parent is a right to a relationship with a child in which one has certain rights with respect to that child. But what *are* the rights that the right to parent is a right to exercise? Does respecting that right require that parents be permitted to pursue their children's material interests in ways that harm the interests of other children? If so, in which ways and to what extent? Does it require that they be permitted to indoctrinate their children into their religious or other views, or are there limits on the ways in which they may transmit their values? Clearly one cannot fully answer the question of whether there is a right to parent without having content for the kind of relationship at stake. We need to know what kind of relationship we are talking about before we can know whether there is a right to that kind of relationship! But we cannot say everything at once, so we are simply going to defer, to part 3, discussion of the question of what rights parents have over their children. Our aim here is to describe the relationship, and the goods it contributes to adult lives, in enough detail to support our claim that adults have a right to it, but without getting into the details of what precisely the relationship consists in.

What's Special about Being a Parent?

Given that children have a right to have parents, those people given the job of parenting a particular child will have a right to parent that child in the weak sense that others will be under a duty not to undermine the relationship. They will be accorded those rights over their children that are needed for them to discharge the parental role. But a right to parent, in that sense, is compatible with society's allocating children to those adults best able to parent them, in which case the rights of adults to parent children would derive entirely from the interests of children. We think that adults have a right to parent in a stronger sense. Their right is fundamental, not derivative, in that it is grounded in their own interest in being a parent. To be clear, adults' interest in being parents can ground a right only as long as its content fits with the interest that children have being parented. That interest, however weighty, could hardly justify the practice of assigning adults authority over children if it were incompatible with children's interest in the relationship we described in the previous chapter. In that sense, children come first, and an adult's right to raise children is conditional on discharging the parental role adequately well. So what, for us, is the interest that grounds that right?

For most people, intimate relationships with others are essential for their lives to have meaning. Rather than being alone in the world, seeking to fulfill their own pleasures, people thrive when they are connected to other human beings with whom they enjoy deep and close relationships. These relationships are challenging—in an intimate relationship one does not fully control the response of the other person, and one has to discern her interests even when she does not necessarily articulate them well, and act to further those interests and come to share some of them as one's own. The love and voluntary compliance of others in a relationship, when recognized, contributes to a sense of well-being and self-worth, as does successful attendance to the well-being of those others. A life without such relationships, or in which they all fail, is usually an unsuccessful life. If there are exceptions, there are not many.

But our intimate relationships are not all the same—they are not substitutable one for another. People need more than one kind. Most need, usually, a romantic lover, someone to whom we can bare our raw emotions and who we are confident will love us anyway, with whom we share sexual love. We need lasting close friendships with people on whom we can rely for support when in need and who we know can rely on us, people with whom we can share our joys and interests. We also need more casual relationships—relationships of trust with people whose lives we do not know intimately but with whom we form bonds around some particular shared interest, project, or adversity. A successful life is a life with a variety of successful relationships, including a variety of successful intimate relationships.

Many, perhaps most, adults need to be involved in an intimate relationship of a very particular kind in order to have a fully flourishing life. The parent-child relationship is not, in our view, just another intimate relationship, valuable to both sides but substitutable for the adult by an additional relationship with a consenting adult. The relationship is, on the contrary, sui generis, a relationship that involves the adult in a unique combination of joys and challenges; experiencing and meeting these makes a distinctive set of demands on him, and produces a distinctive contribution to his well-being. Other intimate relationships have their own value, but they are not substitutes for a parenting relationship with a child.[1]

The parent is charged with responsibility for both the immediate well-being of the child and the development of the child's capacities. As we saw in the previous chapter, the child has immediate interests in being kept safe, enjoying herself, being sheltered and well-nourished, having loving relationships with proximate others, and so on. She has future interests in many of these same things, but also in becoming the kind of person who is not entirely dependent on others for having her interests met, and the kind of person who can make her own judgments about her interests and act on them. The parent's fiduciary duties are to guarantee the child's immediate well-being, including assuring to her the intrinsic goods of childhood, and to oversee her cognitive, emotional, physical, and moral development. Four broad features of this relationship combine to make the joys and challenges of parenting different from those that attend other kinds of relationship, including other kinds of fiduciary relationship.

First, obviously, parents and children do not have equal power or standing. Children are not in the relationship voluntarily, and, unlike adults, they lack the power to exit the relationship, at least until they reach sufficient age to escape—which will be culturally sensitive, since different societies will monitor and enforce parental power with different levels of enthusiasm and effectiveness. Children are vulnerable to the decisions of their primary caretakers, and, initially, wholly dependent on them for their well-being. An adult with supervisory power over a child has the power of life or death; and this is not, at least when the child is young, reciprocated. Less spectacularly, they have the power to make the child's life miserable or enjoyable (within limits, at least at the enjoyable end).

The second difference between this and most other fiduciary relationships concerns the paternalistic aspect discussed in the previous chapter. The parent-child relationship routinely involves coercing the child to act against her own will, or manipulating her will so that it accords with her interests. So, for example, we might lock away the bleach so that she cannot get at it, even though she has displayed great interest in it, or prevent her from having a third helping of ice cream, on the grounds that neither the bleach nor the ice cream will serve her interests. We might persistently serve whole-grain pasta in the face of her frequent (and accurate) complaints that it is tasteless, in order to habituate her to frequent intake of whole grains. We might engineer her social life in order to diminish the significance of a destructive friendship. Although in relationships with other adults we are obliged to take their interests into account, we do not have fiduciary responsibilities of this kind toward them. Indeed, if one saw one's relationship with, say, one's spouse in this way, one could reasonably be accused of being overbearing, disrespectful, or unloving. In intimate relationships with other adults (with friends, or spouses) one might advise and even argue with those people, but one does not routinely coerce and manipulate them, even in their own interests. To do so would be to fail as a spouse or friend, just as to refrain from doing so with one's children would be to fail as a parent—recall our claim that the child has a right to paternalistic treatment. And where we do have distinctively fiduciary relationships with other adults—even with aging parents—coercing or manipulating them may sometimes be required, but it is not itself a key part of the job.

A third difference concerns the relationship of the fiduciary (the parent) to the interests of the principal (the child). When the parent-child relationship begins, the child does not have specific beliefs about her own good. Later, when she does have beliefs, those beliefs have been formed in response to the environment structured by the parent and, if the parent has been caring for the child, by someone whose capacities have been shaped by the parent. The parent has a good deal of latitude in shaping the specific values of the child, values that will guide her in her own life. (We discuss how much and what kind of latitude in chapter 6.) In other fiduciary relationships what the fiduciary should pursue is typically fixed by reference to the principal's own beliefs about what is good for her, sometimes expressed directly to the fiduciary, sometimes (as in the case of advance directives) expressed previously. But the parent does not have and could not have such a standard to guide her. Of course the interests of children we have elaborated in the previous chapter should guide the parent. In particular, the parent has a duty to try to ensure that the child will become an autonomous agent, someone capable of judging, and acting on her judgments about, her own interests. This is a lengthy process, and one that does not just naturally occur but requires active support. For most parents it is emotionally as well as practically challenging to prepare a child who has been entirely dependent, and whom the parent loves deeply, to become her own person, capable of effectively challenging the parent and the parent's values; capable, ultimately, of rejecting the adult if she thinks it appropriate. Three natural inclinations are frequently at odds with trying to ensure the child's genuine independence: the inclination to be protective of the loved child, the inclination to promote her well-being according to one's own view of what that would amount to, and the inclination to hold on to her for one's own sake. To overcome these inclinations successfully, when one really loves one's child, is emotionally demanding. Successful parenting is, in this respect, an exercise in maturation, because while the parent has the control that he needs in order to carry out his caring and fiduciary tasks for the child, he simultaneously learns that one should not control another person in the way he might like, and learns how not to exercise some of the control he does indeed have. For example, the parent must give the child opportunities for emotional and physical independence, putting the child in situations where she is at risk of failing, but in which the stakes of failure are sufficiently low that the child will be able to bear, and learn from, failure if it happens.

The fiduciary responsibilities of parenthood constitute a distinctive moral burden. But, of course, along with the moral burden come distinctive sources of satisfaction of a much less complicated kind. What children need from parents is not simply the judicious exercise of expertise and authority, of the kind one might hope for from a lawyer or doctor or teacher. What's needed is a *relationship*, and the kind of relationship children need from adults—a parent-child relationship—is also the kind that yields good things to the adults doing the parenting. There is the enjoyment of the love (both the child's for oneself and one's own for the child), but also the enjoyment of the observations the child makes about the world; the pleasure (and sometimes dismay) of seeing the world from the child's perspective; enjoyment of her satisfaction in her successes and of consoling her in her disappointments.

The final difference from other relationships concerns the *quality of the intimacy* of the relationship. The love a parent normally receives from his children, again especially in the early years, is spontaneous and unconditional, and, in particular, outside the rational control of the young child. She shares herself unself-consciously with the parent, revealing her enthusiasms and aversions, fears and anxieties, in an uncontrolled manner. She trusts the adult in charge until the trust is betrayed, and trust must be betrayed consistently and frequently for it to be completely undermined. Adults do not share themselves with each other in this way: intimacy requires a considerable act of will on the part of adults interacting together. But things are different between parents and children. The parent is bound by his fiduciary responsibilities for the child's emotional development to try to be spontaneous and authentic a good deal of the time, both because the child needs to see this modeled and because the child needs to be in a loving relationship with a real person. And, of course, the parent will often be inclined to be spontaneously loving. But his fiduciary obligations also often require him to be less than wholly spontaneous and intimate (despite the child's unconditional intimacy with him). The good parent sometimes masks his disappointment with, sometimes his pride in, the child, and often his frustration with other aspects of his life. He may sometimes hide his amusement at some naughtiness of the child, preferring to chide her for the sake of instilling discipline; conversely, he may sometimes control his anger at similar behavior, substituting inauthentic kindness for the sake of ensuring a better end to the child's day, or because she knows that her angry reaction is, though authentic, inappropriate. He does not inflict on the child, as the child does on him, all of his spontaneous reactions, and all of his emotional responses.

These four features combine to make the relationship between parent and child unlike other intimate relationships, and unlike other fiduciary relationships. Children have a weighty interest in the kind of relationship that will meet their needs and promote their vital interests. Given what that involves—given how complex, interesting, and conducive to the adult's own emotional development it is to be the adult in that relationship—adults too have a weighty interest in being in a parenting relationship. The interest is distinctive, because what the relationship requires of the adult, and allows him to experience, is unique. Other intimate relationships, where those are consensual on both sides and in which the parties are symmetrically situated, are not adequate substitutes.

The relationship as a whole, with its particular intimate character, and the responsibility to play the specific fiduciary role for the person with whom one is intimate in that way, is what adults have an interest in.

The fiduciary aspect to the parental relationship with children has been widely acknowledged since Locke, and is given particular emphasis by so-called child-centered justifications of the family.[2] Our claim here is adult-centered: many adults have an interest in being in a relationship of this sort. They have a nonfiduciary interest in being in a relationship in which they act as a child's fiduciary. That relationship enables them to exercise and develop capacities the development and exercise of which are central to their living fully flourishing lives. The parent comes to learn more about herself, she comes to change as a person, and she experiences pleasures and emotions that otherwise would be unavailable.

It should be clear that the adult's interest in playing the fiduciary role is deeply connected to the content of that role. It's because of *what* children need from their parents that adults have such a weighty interest in giving it to them. Imagine a world in which human children didn't need much more looking after than guinea pigs, or Tamagotchi toys. Imagine that they could develop into autonomous, emotionally well-adjusted adults, and enjoy the special goods of childhood, with that kind and level of input from adults. We think that, even in that hypothetical world, there would be *some* value to being the person responsible for ensuring that children's interests were met. One would, after all, be responsible for the development of a human child, which is a weighty responsibility indeed, and it is good for people, it makes *their* lives go better, to take on and discharge that degree of responsibility. So when we say that, in our world, playing the fiduciary role for a child makes a crucial contribution to the flourishing of (most) adults, we do want that sheer fact of being the person responsible for the child to be part of the story.

But only part of it. Properly to see the weight of the adult interest in parenting, we need to keep our eye not on the plain fact of being the fiduciary but on the content of what children need from those who are their fiduciaries. Children have a right to a relationship with an adult in which that adult supplies a complex combination of things to the child. Adults have an interest in being the fiduciary, and parents' serving as fiduciaries affects the significance, and hence the value, of so much else that happens in the relationship. But what's really valuable here is not being the fiduciary per se but having the kind of relationship that, in fact, is in children's interests. It's that kind of relationship which presents a distinctive challenge, and that kind of challenge which gives adults unique opportunities for flourishing.

Adults can be involved in any number of fiduciary relationships. In our professional lives, as lawyers or social workers or doctors or teachers, we take on duties to serve the interests of our clients or patients or students. In our personal lives, too, we may find ourselves acting as fiduciaries for our aging parents, for example, if they cease to be able adequately to protect and promote their own interests. If we think about the difference between these other kinds of fiduciary relationships and the particular case of the parent-child relationship, we can see that some elements in what is special about being a fiduciary for a child concern the fact that what we're talking about here is a *child*. The moral standing of the person for whom one is acting as fiduciary matters: her possessing the capacity to develop into an autonomous adult, her degree of vulnerability to one's judgments, her involuntary dependence on one, and so on. Failing adequately to discharge one's fiduciary duties to a child would be different from failing to discharge those owed to a client or patient, or even to an aging parent, even if what was involved in fulfilling the duties were the same. But of course they are not the same. Other elements in what is special about being a fiduciary for a child concern *what* children need from their fiduciaries. They need a special kind of *relationship*—a relationship in which the adult offers love and authority, a complex and emotionally challenging combination of openness and restraint, of spontaneity and self-monitoring, of sharing and withholding. It's that kind of relationship that adults have an interest in too.

The fiduciary aspect remains central. Grandparents, or parents' friends, or nannies, can have close relationships with children, and when they go well, those relationships will be conducive to the child's interests and valuable to the adults too. Reading bedtime stories, providing meals, and so on, will be contributing to the well-being of both. Still, there's something distinctively valuable about being the person who not only does those things oneself but has the responsibility to make sure they get done, sometimes by others, and the authority to decide quite how they get done. The challenge is different, and the adult who meets that challenge enjoys a special, and especially valuable, kind of human flourishing.[3]

The Right to Be a Parent

We have deferred to part 3 the implications of our theory for what rights parents, qua parents, have over, or with respect to, their children. Those rights, we will argue, are derived, in the sense that they are justified entirely by appeal to children's interests. Parents have just those rights that it's in their children's interests for them to have—the rights that parents need to have if the relationship is to yield its goods to children. But even with our attention focused on the right *to* parent—which by contrast is grounded in adults' own interests, and in that sense fundamental—important issues remain.

To claim that it's very valuable for adults to be able to have a relationship with a child in which they play the fiduciary role with the content we have described is to posit a deep harmony between adults' and children's interests when it comes to the business of child rearing. The kind of relationship that children need from the adults who raise them is the same kind of relationship that it's in adults' interests to have with the children they raise. That is not a mere coincidence—it points to something profound about what it is to be a human being—but without that correspondence we could not infer that the adult interest in parenting is weighty enough to ground a right to parent. However valuable a way of raising children might be for adults, it could hardly yield a right to raise children that way unless it also met children's interests in being well raised.

So the right in question is a right to *parent*. It is the right to have the kind of relationship with a child that we described earlier in the chapter. Adults do not have the right to raise children if they are not going to parent them properly—if they are not going to fulfill adequately the role of parent. To put the same point in its more conventional formulation, the right to parent is conditional. It is conditional on the adult's being a good enough parent, on his discharging his fiduciary duties to an adequate standard. If he fails to protect and promote his child's interests to that standard, then he forfeits the right to parent. Indeed, some have argued that adults wishing to parent should be required to pass a test of prospective proficiency, so that the right to parent would be conditional on formal approval. As a matter of course, conditions of that kind are imposed on those wishing to become parents by adoption, and it is arguably illogical that people are permitted to raise a child they have procreatively produced without any kind of evidence that they possess the capacities needed properly to parent it.[4] Without taking a stand on that suggestion, we should be clear that, for us, the moral right to parent is conditional on one's indeed possessing, and being willing to exercise, the capacities needed properly to play the role of parent.

But an adult can possess and exercise those capacities, and have the right to parent a child, without being a perfect parent. He doesn't even have to be the best available parent. Our emphasis on the fiduciary nature of the interest that adults have in raising children—the fact that we posit a happy correspondence between the kind of relationship that is in children's and adults' interests— may seem to have eliminated the possibility of conflict between the two. If that were so, there would be no difference between our position and the entirely child-centered view that regards the well-being of children as the only criterion relevant to the assessment of child-rearing arrangements. On that view, children should be parented by whichever adults are going to parent them best. Children's interests do come first, and not only because how they are parented affects their lives as a whole. But theirs are not the only interests at stake. The suggestion that an adult need only be "good enough" to qualify for the right to parent attempts to formulate the right balance between children's and adult's interests. Within certain limits, adults' interests in being a parent can trump children's interests in having the best possible parents. No child has a right to be parented by the adult(s) who would do it best, nor do children as a whole have a right to the way of matching up children and parents that would be best for children overall. Both scenarios could leave perfectly competent parents missing out on the goods of parenting.

Claiming that the right to parent a child is conditional on being "good enough" at the task raises a host of difficult questions. Some are conceptual: does "good enough" involve some absolute standard that a prospective parent must meet, or, to render our view plausible, must it be understood in comparative terms? Since the idea is that an adult's claim to parent a child can, at least in principle, outweigh a child's interest in being parented by someone who would do a better job, then it looks as if it might be relevant *how much* better the alternative would be.[5] Some are epistemological: to what extent can we know whether any given adult is going to be (or is likely to be) good enough? There will be clear cases where a parent, or prospective parent, has, alas, proved herself inadequate to the task, and where it is obvious that some other arrangement would be better for the child, but thankfully these will be the exception rather than the rule. In most cases the information that one would need to make such judgments will not be available, so it will doubtless make sense to rely on general rules of thumb (such as assuming that the child's biological parents will satisfy the condition unless or until there is some evidence to the contrary). Others are moral: what means of acquiring relevant information are permissible? Sometimes we *could* acquire better information about the quality of parenting, or prospective parenting, but only at the cost of excessive intrusion into people's personal lives. Others are practical: are there ways of acquiring that information that would not be counterproductive? Too much monitoring of what goes on in families would be inimical to the enjoyment of familial relationship goods themselves.

We cannot engage with all these complexities here, but it is worth noting two reasons why, in practice, the conditions an adult must meet in order to *retain* parental rights over a child are different from those that she must meet in order to be *granted* those rights in the first place. First, it is worse to sever such a relationship than not to allow it to start. How bad it is to break the relationship—the cost of disruption—will of course depend on various considerations, such as how long it has been going on and the age of the child. But, generally speaking, once an adult has begun raising a child, both child and adult have an interest in that relationship's continuing, and the value of continuity of attachment must be factored in to judgments about who is best placed to raise the child. Children of parents who fail to provide what we would normally expect of a "good enough" parent are likely to be particularly vulnerable to bad outcomes, so their interests, rather than those of their parents, and other prospective parents, will usually be decisive. Somewhat paradoxically, then, considerations of continuity may weigh especially heavily in their case and lead to their being left in the care of parents who in other ways fall short of the "good enough" standard. Depending on what alternative arrangements for raising the child are available—and state institutions have generally been very bad at providing children with a decent start in life—it may yet be that a parent who is not "good enough" is nonetheless a child's best hope. In such cases, we might think that the parent's inadequacy means that she has forfeited the *right* to parent, but she nonetheless remains the best person to exercise parental rights over the child she is parenting.

Second, the right to parent is the right to enjoy a relationship that is somewhat resilient; it matters that the relationship with a child one is parenting be secure against circumstances that could be sufficient to defeat a claim to initiate such a relationship. Imagine being a parent in a world where one's child was liable to be removed just because it turned out, or was discovered, that some alternative arrangement would be better for her. The fact that continuity is itself valuable for the child means that this is less likely to happen than it would otherwise be—being the current parent of a child itself makes one a better parent for her than one would otherwise be. But, still, it might become apparent that, even with that taken into account, somebody else would do a better job. The parent-child relationship would be vulnerable to empirical happenstance in a way that would undermine its capacity to produce the goods we have talked about. "Good enough" parents would continually worry that they might lose their relationship with their children. Children would be aware that the familial relationship was vulnerable in this way. Again, there is an element of paradox here: it is better for children—and for adults—if not too much depends on how well children are being parented. Both have rights to a relationship that is robust against fine-tuned comparative judgments about different adults' relative likelihood of parenting children well. Such judgments may indeed be relevant to questions of initial allocation, as it were. Think about an idealized adoption system in which many adults all had the same interest in parenting and there were not enough children to go round. In that case it would make good sense to attend carefully to the question of who is likely to parent which children best. But, once the children had been allocated, the right to parent, and to be parented, is the right to a relationship that is not so directly at the mercy of revised judgments of that kind.

These considerations explain why, in practice, the bar a parent has to meet in order to count as "good enough" to continue parenting a child may not be much higher than the standard "abuse and neglect" condition. Even modern welfare states have been notoriously bad at providing superior child-rearing arrangements for children who are in abusive and neglectful situations. Removing a child from her family home puts the child at risk twice; first by exposing her to the traumatic transition away from the parents, and second by placing her in an alternative environment that, often, is no better, but which would have to be considerably better in order to compensate for the transition costs. Add in the value of the relationship's being secure against disruption, and (what we will emphasize in part 3) the likely cost to familial relationship goods of the kinds of monitoring of the parent-child relationship that would be needed to make finer judgments, and one can see why it would be problematic for state agencies to work with any more demanding condition.

Is This Picture of Parenting Too Rosy?

Arguing for the child's right to have a parent, in chapter 3, we mentioned the worry that the implied duty—the duty to parent—might be implausibly onerous, and offered the hope that this chapter would help to allay that concern. Here we have claimed that, far from being an undue burden, parenting typically contributes weightily and distinctively to the parent's well-being. Is this picture too rosy? Perhaps so, but before the reader reaches that conclusion, we should head off two potential misunderstandings.

First, for many, parenthood is a source of deep anxiety and frustration. It is a vital source of flourishing only if it is carried out in a social environment that renders its challenges superable. So, for example, poverty and the multiple disadvantages that accompany it can easily create an environment in which it is very difficult even to develop, let alone to exercise, the cognitive and emotional skills that successful parenting requires. Meanwhile children raised in poverty are typically at much higher risk of very bad outcomes than more advantaged children, so that parents seeking conscientiously to protect their children from such outcomes require greater internal resources than are needed by the parents of more advantaged children. Adults' interest in the kind of parent-child relationship we have described is an interest in parenting a child in circumstances that will indeed enable them to realize the goods we have identified. This will have important implications for social policy in a society that claims to care about family values.

Second, parenting a child is not all-consuming. It's true that, done properly, raising a child severely limits one's opportunities to do other things. Some people choose not to be parents for precisely that reason. It's true also that raising a child is likely to be one of the most important things one does with one's life. As Eamonn Callan says, "success or failure in the task, as measured by whatever standards we take to be relevant, is likely to affect profoundly our overall sense of how well or badly our lives have gone."[6] But despite the interest in the fiduciary aspect of the role, parents should not be slaves, entirely and continually subordinating their own interests to those of their children, or always putting their children first. We shall explain this more fully in part 3, where we discuss parents' rights over their children in some detail. Any reader skeptical about the next few paragraphs should suspend her disbelief till then. But it will be helpful to set out briefly here two different ways in which parenting is not like slavery.

On the one hand, parents are not *only* parents. Quite how much of one's time and energy parenting demands will vary with the age of the child, but generally speaking it is perfectly possible to parent well while performing other roles and pursuing other interests. It is common to talk about the "best interests" of the child, and that may indeed be an appropriate practical criterion for adjudicating custody disputes where things have gone wrong and the child is likely to be at serious risk of harm. But it is not plausible to expect parents always and single-mindedly to pursue their child's best interests. Adults who parent will also have lives of their own to lead—they will have rights and duties that have nothing to do with the fact that they are parents—and it is quite appropriate for them sometimes to weigh their own interests, and their duties to others, against those of their children. Imagine someone who, as well as being a parent, and accepting our view of the fiduciary duties that attend that role, also believes—let us assume rightly—that he has a moral obligation to take part in a political demonstration. Imagine further that he cannot find alternative child care, so he has to choose between taking his child with him and not going. He accepts that going on the demonstration is not in his child's best interests; those would be better served by their staying home, or going to the zoo instead—the child is not old enough for her accompanying him plausibly to benefit her in any way. As long as going on the demonstration does no harm to the child, bringing or leaving her below some level that is "good enough," he does indeed have the right to take her with him. That is not a right he has qua parent. But it is a right that makes a difference to what he may do with his child.

Further, it is in *children's* interests for their parents to have their own, independent, interests and pursuits, and in children's interests for their relationship with their parents to be one in which their parents are not required always to act with their children's best interests in mind. Someone who was only a parent—someone for whom "parent" was the entire content of his identity—would not be providing the kind of experience that children need, and the parent-child relationship would surely implode in a kind of self-referential black hole. (Of course, that can happen even when the parent *does* have other identities and interests—if he fails to get the balance right—but it looks inevitable if he doesn't.) It is important for children to experience their parents as independent people, with their own lives to lead, not as people whose sole purpose in life is to serve them. So the task of parenting, although indeed extremely demanding, by its very nature allows parents discretionary time and energy: having a life of one's own is, in fact, part of the job description. The point here is not simply that it's good for children if parents get some time off for themselves, or good for children that they have a sense of their parent as having independent interests. The parent's nonparental interests will, and indeed should, manifest themselves, at least sometimes, in the interactions between parent and child. Parents must allow themselves some space, free of self-monitoring, to experience and express to the child their authentic emotions and attitudes. A parent who never said or did anything to or with his child without first asking himself whether it would be in his child's interests would not be spontaneously sharing himself with his child, there would be a lack of genuine intimacy, and he would thus be failing to provide the kind of relationship that *was* in his child's interests. Paradoxically, the kind of parent-child relationship that is good for children is one in which the parent cares about things other than his children, and doesn't spend all his time thinking about, and then trying to deliver, what would be good for his children.

Three Clarifications

Three further points of clarification are important. First, we are not saying that there are many adults who cannot flourish *at all* without relationships of the kind we have described. People do indeed go to great lengths in order to raise children, and some consider the inability to do so as a profound blight on their lives, but few who miss out conclude that their lives are thereby worthless.

Nonetheless, many regard themselves as having missed out on an experience that would have been necessary for them fully to flourish. Our claim is of that kind—about the contribution parent-child relationships make to a fully flourishing human life.

But, second, we do not say that this is true of *all* adults. A significant proportion of people have no desire to have and raise children, and for many of them the absence of this desire is not an epistemic failing—they are not making a mistake. We are not claiming that all adults need to raise children fully to flourish, and we recognize, further, that there are some for whom parenting would make no contribution to their well-being, and some for whom it would make their lives go worse. So the claim that the relevant relationship goods make a powerful contribution to the flourishing of the rights-holder does not imply that those goods are good for everybody. In this respect the contribution of this kind of relationship is like that of a romantic sexual relationship. Most people are such that they could not flourish fully without it: it contributes something to their flourishing that nothing else could contribute. Others, however, have no need for it. Similarly there may be people who do not need to be parents: those who, although they might really enjoy parenting, could indeed flourish fully without it, and those whose lives would actually be diminished by their being parents. In some cases that might be because the person lacks the capacities needed properly to discharge the fiduciary duties.[7] Noting this does not contradict our general claim about the significance of the relationship, or undermine our view that there is a right to parent.

Finally, we have said that the parent-child relationship has certain features such that being involved in this sort of relationship as a parent makes a vital contribution to the flourishing of the adult. But some parent-child relationships lack some of these features, and some other relationships contain many of them. So, for example, the parent of a child with severe cognitive impairments might experience loving intimacy, and the joy in seeing the world reflected through the eyes of someone for whom she acts as fiduciary in some respects, but her fiduciary obligations do not include preparing her child to become an autonomous adult. It may also be that some children, perhaps those on the far end of the autism spectrum, cannot be intimate with the parent in the way that we have described as being so important and rewarding. Pet owners take on fiduciary obligations, and some have emotionally rich relationships with their pets, as do many who care for adults with severe cognitive impairments, and for the infirm elderly. So not only does our account of the relationship at stake fail to capture every parent-child relationship, but the contrast between it and other caring relationships is not always as stark as we might have been taken to think.

We intend our conception of the parent-child relationship to describe something that many adults have a very strong interest in participating in. Other relationships that resemble it to a greater or lesser degree will yield some of the benefits, but not all. (In some cases, those benefits may ground rights of their own. It's plausible, for example, that some who cannot experience the joys of parenthood have a right to a relationship with a pet.) Some of those other relationships will yield benefits for some of the carers that are not made available by our conception of the parent-child relationship. Our claim is that, for many adults, a relationship that lacks the combination of features we have described will not be a full substitute.

Alternative Accounts

This account of the adult interest in raising children is somewhat controversial; it ignores or leaves out of the picture other widely accepted ideas about what adults may legitimately seek to achieve, and in more straightforwardly self-interested fashion, through parenting. In this section we discuss what we might think of as two of the most widely held rivals to our view, one emphasizing the value of parenting as creative self-extension, the other insisting on the significance of biological connection between parent and child.[8]

One or both of these features may add value to parent-child relationships. It may be that parents who aim creatively to extend themselves via, or who are biologically connected to, their children, enjoy distinctive familial relationship goods not otherwise available. If adults can realize these alternative interests while also enjoying a relationship of the kind we have described, we have no objection. But we have yet to see any elaboration of those interests that suggests they have anything like the weight of those at the heart of our account. Provided she has the capacities on which the right is conditioned, an adult who is deprived of the opportunity to experience the goods at the heart of our account has a serious claim against others; she may have a claim to parent a child even though others would do a better job, and she may have a claim to assistance in the project of becoming a parent. We doubt that the goods appealed to by these alternative accounts will support such claims.

Creative Self-Extension

For Colin Macleod, some of the intrinsic value of family relationship rests in what he calls "creative self-extension," which arises out of "the special opportunity . . . parents have to express their own commitment to ideals and ground-projects by passing them on to children. . . . The recognition that valued features of one's own sense of self have been extended to one's children and form part of their sense of self can be a profound sense of satisfaction. We can see ourselves carried forward in another self we played a significant role in creating."[9] There are two, distinct, elements here: one concerning expression of one's own commitment to one's projects and values, the other concerning the carrying forward of one's own self through a creative process.

One can express commitment to projects and values in many ways, and for many projects and values influencing other people to take notice of them, take them seriously, or adopt them, is part of what it is to be committed to them, or a natural accompaniment to being committed to them. One's children are, like other people, potential adopters. As we will see in chapter 6, the kind of relationship that will deliver the goods we have identified is indeed one in which parents will have some scope to influence their child's emerging values: that is an inevitable side effect of the spontaneous sharing of themselves with their children, and in some (in our view very unusual) circumstances some deliberate influencing of values may be required for the relationship to yield its benefits. The parent's concern to promote her child's well-being may also have implications for the ways in which she may act to shape the child's emerging values—for example, where she believes that her child's endorsing a particular project or value will be important for the child's living a successful life. But for a parent to care that her child in particular shares some specific value or project *out of commitment to that value or project* rather than *out of commitment to the child and the relationship* strikes us as a case of using the child as a means to the realization of the parent's own goals in a way that has little or nothing to do with the nonsubstitutable value of relationship. The only sense in which the parent-child relationship plays any distinctive role is in affording the parent a particularly easy vehicle for the realization of her interest in expressing her commitment to her ideals. On that construal, it is hard to see that there is a weighty relationship good at stake.

The second element is that "we can see ourselves carried forward in another self we played a significant role in creating." The claim here needs to be that there is something distinctively and importantly valuable about raising a child as an act of "creative self-extension": only by raising a child can adults realize this particular, and weighty, contribution to human flourishing. On one reading we have no problem with this. Parenting, on our account, is certainly a creative process—giving a child what she needs to develop from a vulnerable newborn into an autonomous adult is about as creative as it gets. And, again, the kind of relationship we have described, and will elaborate more fully in part 3, certainly gives plenty of room for forms of family life that will tend to generate continuities—of personality, of culture, of attitudes, of turns of phrase—between parents and children, whether as unintended by-product, deliberate concern for shared values, or parental concern for the child's well-being. Certainly parents may value the sense in which their influence is manifest in their children—parented by somebody else, those children would surely have turned out very differently. If that is what it means to "see ourselves carried forward in another self we played a significant role in creating," then that does indeed seem to be a familial relationship good, albeit one that does not compete with our account.

But the fact that Macleod combines the two elements suggests that he has in mind something stronger than this, something closer to (though surely not as extreme as) the view of Edgar Page, for whom "the parental aim is not simply the creation of a person, but rather the creation of a person in the parents' own image."[10] For Page, the interest in creative self-extension here is entirely self-regarding:

> We can normally expect parents to pursue their interest in shaping the child's future with a clear regard for its good. But this does not mean that the parental interest in shaping the child can be reduced to this affection. . . . The propensity of parents to exercise control and guidance over their children, the propensity to determine the development of the child, *far from being aimed simply or primarily at the child's good, is the manifestation of a fundamental and unique interest which lies at the heart of human parenthood* and at the foundation of parental rights.[11]

This clarification emphasizes the extent to which the motive in question views the child as a vehicle for the realization of the parent's own selfish, and indeed somewhat narcissistic, interests.[12] The child is seen as a canvas on which the parent may objectify herself, or a block of raw marble from which she may carve a future version of herself.

No doubt, many parents do derive some satisfaction from extending themselves through shaping their children's lives. But this satisfaction cannot bear much justificatory weight when one examines the structure of adult-child relationships, especially relative to the interest we have identified. There are plenty of other routes for creatively extending oneself. One naturally does it in relationships with other people, people who have some sort of choice about whether to adopt one's influence because one is on a more equal footing with them: friends, colleagues, siblings, and extended family members within one's own generation. And compare, as motives for entering a parenting relationship with a child, creative self-extension with seeking to be a fiduciary for a child who will develop to independence. Both motives, it is true, are self-regarding. But the latter has the interests of another person intrinsically built into it, and those interests define the role. Though self-regarding, the motive is intrinsically other-concerned. By contrast, creative self-extension is, well, self-extending.

We can imagine a parent saying to her adult child (perhaps a little self-consciously!): "I know I wasn't the best possible parent for you, that I was selfish enough to pursue my interest in being a parent even though there was somebody else who I knew would probably have done a better job. I'm sorry about that; I hope you will forgive me. But it was wonderful for me to get to have such a loving relationship with you, to be the person who looked after you and successfully brought you to adulthood." Compare that with "I know I wasn't the best possible parent for you . . . But it was wonderful for me to get to express my commitment to my ideals through you," or "wonderful for me to extend myself creatively by sending you into the world in (the broad outline of) my own image."[13]

Biological Connection

The interest in the kind of relationship that we have elaborated can be realized just as well in adoptive families as in those where parents and children are connected by biology. Everything we have argued would apply in a world in which children were produced by storks. But children do not enter the world like that; they are created out of, and by, other human beings. Many readers will think that our account has overlooked the distinctive interest in raising a child to whom one is biologically connected. As in the case of the alleged value to children of being raised by a biological parent (discussed in the previous chapter), it is important to distinguish the genetic from the gestatory aspect of biology— the progenitive role from that of birth mother. The two usually go together, but they may nonetheless play quite different roles in the argument.

The idea that there is something special about raising one's genetic child is widely held. According to Mary Warnock: "As we become more aware of the role of inherited genes in the character of our children, so the bringing up of children in no way genetically connected to us has come to seem a quite different undertaking from that of bringing up a child who shares our own genes. It may be worthwhile, but it is not the same."[14] Similarly, John Robertson claims that a right to have and raise genetically descendant children is part of our general right to reproductive freedom, and emphasizes that some will resist adoption and want to parent a genetic child because that brings with it a different "packet of experiences."[15] Neither elaborates in any detail the content of the interest in rearing one's genetic offspring; that is more or less taken for granted. Nor do they say anything about why that interest, however elaborated, should be regarded as important.

One thought might be that where parent and child are genetically close, raising the child will be easier, and so the relationship will go better. In the previous chapter we considered the analogous claim from the child-centered perspective—that parent-child relationships where there is a genetic connection between the two will tend to serve children's interests better than those where that connection is lacking. As in that case, whether for sociobiological or cultural reasons, and whether via differences in basic parental motivations or the reactions of others, we would not be surprised if adults parenting their genetic children were more likely to experience a familial relationship of the kind we have described, and thus to enjoy the goods we have identified.

To give one example of the kind of mechanism that might be at work, Carson Strong has argued that raising an adopted child differs from raising a genetically related child in such a way that couples would reasonably be deterred from pursuing it. Strong argues that, as a form of "collaborative" or third-party reproduction (like surrogacy or sperm donation), adoption carries with it a unique potential for interpersonal conflict within the family. Parents might question whether, what, and when to tell their nongenetically related children about their origins. Children might feel a tension between loving the parents who have raised them and wanting to find their genetic parents. Consequently, the potential for strife within the family is great enough to give parents good reason to prefer genetic parenting to adoptive parenting.[16] Notice that it's the very fact that children may want to find their genetic parents that creates the difficulty here. One could acknowledge that—and accept that it gives parents a reason to prefer to raise genetic children—while denying that there would be anything worse about a world in which no child was interested in tracing her genetic parent. Notice also that this argument accords no intrinsic value to the genetic link as such; that link is simply instrumental to a less problematic familial relationship—and the way in which it is less problematic could be formulated in terms of the goods in our account.

But Edgar Page offers a genuinely distinct reason, specifically connecting the interest in rearing an immediate genetic descendant with the interest in creative self-extension discussed above. For him, physically producing the child is itself an essential part of the creative process: "The motive, or the end, of parenthood is surely the creation of the whole person, and this takes within its grasp both the begetting and the raising of the child. . . . The two parts—begetting and rearing—are clearly complementary to each other and neither is entirely intelligible, as a form of human activity, without the other."[17]

For Page, then, the creative dimension of parenting would not adequately be acknowledged by child-rearing arrangements that allowed parents to determine the kind of people their children become but allocated children to parents in ways that gave no fundamental importance to any genetic connection between parent and child. An obvious problem for such an account, as for all that attach great significance to biological connection, is that it seems to rule out the possibility that adoptive parents can fully realize the value of parenting. Even if they were indeed engaging in the kind of creative self-extension that comes through raising a child, they would inevitably be denied the aspect that comes from having physically created the child they are raising. His response is worth quoting at length:

> If all parents were in the position of adoptive parents, i.e. if there were no connection between parenthood and generation, as might be imagined in 'science fiction' worlds, parenthood would not have a place of special value in human life, or not the place it now has. Adoptive parenthood is modelled on natural parenthood and the commitment of adoptive parents to the child is parasitic on the special bond characteristic of natural parents. Without this model there would be a question as to the intelligibility of a commitment of adoptive parents' to young babies, particularly in conditions which severely test them, and indeed as to the intelligibility of their desire for parenthood. (Would it be comparable to the desire for pets?) For most people, I suspect, adopting a child falls short of being a perfect substitute for natural parenthood, but when they undertake it they can at least borrow from and follow the established patterns and practice and attitudes of parenthood grounded on the physical relation. It is difficult to know what adoptive parenthood would be without this.[18]

Parenting an adopted child may indeed be different from parenting a genetic descendant. It may be enjoyable to notice "family resemblances" that are due to genes shared with one's child but not many others in one's immediate environment, for example, and Warnock is right that our understanding of how much is indeed in that category may be changing fast. Doubtless sharing the task of parenting with someone who has come together with you to create a child—so that the child is a living symbol, as well as a product, of your sexual union—can be an enriching experience. So there may be special pleasures, more than pleasures, that can attend the process of parenting a genetic descendant—though the last of these applies only in particular circumstances and hardly supports a claim to parent one's genetic child as such. Nonetheless, we doubt that these particular relationship goods are very weighty relative to the interest we have identified, and we doubt that the adult interest in parenting a genetic child can compete with the child's interest in being well parented. Imagine, now, the parent who says: "I know I wasn't the best possible parent for you, that I was selfish enough to pursue my interest in being a parent even though there was somebody else who I knew would probably have done a better job. I'm sorry about that; I hope you will forgive me. But it was wonderful for me to get to raise the person to whose genetic makeup I was a part contributor."

Where Page claims that we can make sense of adoptive parenthood only by thinking of it as parasitic on a parent-child relationship that is grounded in a genetic connection between parent and child, we have tried to explain the value of parenthood in ways that make no reference to that connection. Perhaps in a world where procreation and parenting were entirely separate, parenthood would have a somewhat different significance from that which it has for most people today. But it is hard to believe that, in such a world, raising a child would be like keeping a pet. Our account explains why not. Page's discussion, and Warnock's and Robertson's comments, neglect the profound respects in which raising a child just is the same experience whether the child is a genetic descendant or not—the day-to-day and minute-to-minute burdens and joys of caring for and overseeing her development are most of what child rearing consists in, and most of what gives it value. Adoptive parents need not model themselves on anybody, for what is specially valuable about the practice of parenting does not depend on a genetic connection between parent and child. There may be both child- and adult-centered reasons to treat genetic parenting as the default— and perhaps even to help adults in the process of acquiring genetic children to parent. But, if so, that is because that kind of parenting is more likely to yield relationship goods that can perfectly well be realized in adoptive families. And it's certainly not because the genetic parent has a weighty claim to parent a child even where there is reason to think somebody else would do a better job.

For women, at least, genetics and gestation tend to go together—prior to the development of IVF it was impossible to be pregnant with a child who was not one's genetic descendant. Even then, of course, all biological fathers had immediate genetic descendants whom they had not gestated. So the interests in parenting a genetically connected child and a child one has carried through pregnancy are distinct. Does the latter provide a weighty interest in biological connection that we have denied the former?

The most plausible claim of this kind has been developed by Anca Gheaus. Noting that our argument for the adult right to parent does nothing to establish a right to parent any particular baby—and so provides no principled objection to the redistribution of babies at birth—she offers an analysis of pregnancy that seeks to explain why birth parents have a right to parent the babies they have gestated. That analysis invokes the burdens of pregnancy, so it shares some elements of what we might think of as a claim about desert or entitlement, according to which birth parents earn the right to parent the child they have gestated. But, as she points out, that argument involves a non sequitur: even if such considerations as the physical, psychological, social, and financial costs of being a parent did justify the right to parent *a* child, they cannot ground the right to parent the particular one for whom they were incurred. To explain why birth parents have that right, we need to invoke the way in which bearing the burdens of pregnancy contributes to the creation of a relationship between parent and child in utero. For her,

> in addition to the resources they invest in pregnancy, birth parents, or at least gestating mothers, are typically highly emotionally invested in the pregnancy. An intimate relationship with the future baby starts even before the baby is born, partly *because* birth parents devote significant resources to pregnancy and incur the many kinds of costs it entails. . . . Bonding during pregnancy provides a very solid reason for thinking that redistributing babies would likely destroy already existing intimate relationships between newborns and their bearing parents.[19]

Earlier in this chapter, we discussed the difference between retaining parental rights and being granted those rights in the first place—the difference between retention and initial allocation. Both adult and child have an interest in continuing an already-existing intimate relationship that is weightier than the interest in starting one, and both have an interest in that relationship's being somewhat resilient against interruption. On Gheaus's view, such a relationship is very likely to have started during pregnancy, in which case redistributing children at birth should be conceived as a matter not of initial allocation but of severing already-existing relationships.

The structure of Gheaus's argument is quite different from the others that we have been discussing in this section. We have considered the views that creative self-extension, and rearing a genetic descendant, are things that adults have an interest in experiencing as part of parenting. Gheaus does not make the parallel claim about gestation; indeed, her case partly depends on the claim that gestation involves actual costs and risks of other harms and is not an intrinsically desirable experience. Whereas, for example, Page implies that a counterfactual world in which different generations were not at all genetically connected would be substantially worse, other things being equal, than ours, Gheaus does not have to say the same about a hypothetical world in which fetuses developed like the person-plants embedded in Judith Thomson's carpet and upholstery.[20] In that respect, her position is closer in spirit to our own. The fundamental interest at stake is an interest in an intimate emotional relationship with the child one is raising; gestation comes into the story because it already establishes such a relationship.

Still, some problematic aspects of the argument are worth emphasis. First, giving a key role to gestation inevitably creates an asymmetry between men and women. Because it is so common for genetics and gestation to go together, it is easy to talk about "birth parents" without being clear that, in this particular context, one is referring not to both genetic parents but to those who carry and give birth to the baby: birth mothers. It is of course possible to bite the bullet on that issue, and accept the logic of the argument: that those who are (almost always) genetic *and* gestatory mothers have rights to parent that are lacked by (merely genetic) fathers. But Gheaus is reluctant to make that move, insisting instead that partners of pregnant women typically share many of the costs. Moreover, she says, by seeing a scan, hearing a heartbeat, feeling and talking to it, as well as experiencing the "fears, hopes and fantasies triggered by the growing fetus," such partners "are capable of being direct participants in the process of creating a relationship with the baby during pregnancy." These attempts to include the partners of pregnant women in the category of "bearing parents" seem a bit of a stretch, and somewhat at odds with that aspect of the argument which insists on the emotional significance of the "bodily connection between fetus and gestating mother."[21]

Second, the nature of the "relationship" in question is not wholly clear. What exactly is it that the gestating mother has an intimate, emotional relationship with? Suppose that, unbeknownst to her, the mother is deliberately handed a different baby from the one to which she has just given birth—perhaps because, in the kind of thought experiment philosophers go in for, an all-knowing midwife has been able to judge that both babies will be better parented if they are switched. Provided the changeling is the same sex as the one she was expecting, and similar with respect to other visible characteristics, it may be that she will simply transfer onto the "new" baby whatever feelings she had for the as-yet-unborn child she was bringing to term. This calls into question the specificity of the "relationship" that was established in utero. The pregnant mother knows very little about the object of her emotional attachment; much of that relationship, perhaps all of it, operates through projection and fantasy. Of course, the mother in question would have been wronged; she would have been deliberately deceived. But would any of the wrong be accurately characterized as the violation of a right to continue, postpartum, an intimate emotional relationship with a particular baby that had begun during pregnancy? The changeling babies seem to us more likely than the mothers to experience a sense of severance, disruption, or interruption, and, as mentioned in the previous chapter, that consideration might point in the direction of a right to be parented by one's gestatory parent. But that is a different argument.

Conclusion

This chapter has set out the adult interest that grounds the right to parent. Children come first, and child-rearing arrangements must meet their needs well. But the kind of relationship with particular adults that they do in fact need—a relationship with "parents"—is something that is also very valuable, and nonsubstitutable, for adults. Indeed, it is valuable enough for us to resist the suggestion that children's interests are the only ones that should be taken into account, even after factoring in that how children are raised affects their whole lives.

Some regard the right to parent the child one has procreated as an application of the more general right to own that which one has produced with one's own body. The only relationship that matters here is the ownership relationship, which gives the procreative parent certain control rights over the child that in some sense "belongs" to the parent. Another view points rather to the investment that biological parents make in "their" children. There might not be a general right to parent as such, but bearing the costs and labor of pregnancy gives one a right to parent the child one has worked so hard to produce. Neither approach gives any special weight to the kind or quality of the relationship between parent and child.

But, as we have seen, it is also possible to accept the structure of our argument, and our emphasis on "familial relationship goods," while giving it and them different content. For example, some believe that there is a particular value to an adult in having a relationship with a child in which one is able to pass on some aspects of oneself to that child—perhaps one's genes, perhaps one's values, perhaps one's property. The adult interest in parenting, on such a view, does derive from something about the value of a distinctive connection between parent and child; there is something important that one is able to achieve by parenting a child that would not otherwise be available. These alternative groundings of the right *to* parent generate different views about the rights *of* parents. In the next part of the book we discuss what our view about why it's good for children to have parents, and for adults to parent children, implies for the question of what rights parents have with respect to children they parent.

Part Three

Parents' Rights

Introduction

Part 2 was supposed to justify the family, which for us means explaining why it's a good thing that children be raised by parents. Here, in part 3, our back-to-philosophical-basics approach starts to yield more controversial claims. Attention shifts from the question of why it matters that children be raised in families to more familiar, and more contested, questions about what rights parents should have over, or with respect to, their children. What does our theory about why there should indeed be parents imply about the rights of parents? On the proprietarian picture, children belong to their parents, "their" parents are assumed to be their biological progenitors, and those parents are assumed to have extensive rights to control the upbringing of "their" children. By abandoning that picture, and thinking more seriously about the values realized by the institution of the family, we hope to have acquired the intellectual resources needed to approach the topic of parents' rights in a more nuanced and critical way. Our familial relationship goods account will have implications across a wide range of such questions, but we will focus on two: parents' rights with respect to the conferral of advantage on their children (in chapter 5) and the shaping of their children's values (in chapter 6).

Because it is a key battleground in debates over liberalism and multiculturalism, the second of these has received a good deal of scholarly attention, especially in the United States. Books with titles such as *Democratic Education, Creating Citizens, The Demands of Liberal Education, Religious Schools v. Children's Rights,* and *Bridging Liberalism and Multiculturalism in Education*[1] discuss the theoretical issues at stake in well-known judicial decisions concerning parents' rights to determine the content of their children's schooling, the state's interest in ensuring that children are raised to take their place as citizens of a liberal democracy, and the different regulatory frameworks appropriate to the curriculum of public schools, private schools, and homeschooling. In the United Kingdom, though the constitutional and institutional contexts are very different, and the theoretical literature correspondingly less developed, political debate over "faith schools" covers some of the same terrain. The focal point of that debate is religion. Do parents have the right to raise their children within their religion or, if they are antireligious, to influence them against religion? It seems obvious to many that they do indeed have such rights, and our argument will not deny such claims altogether. But our view that parents' rights are conditional on their adequately protecting their children's interest in becoming autonomous, and that such rights must be justified by appeal to familial relationship goods, gives us a distinctive take on the issues.

In terms of our introductory framing, parents' role in influencing their children's values arises as an issue within the liberal challenge to the family, set out in chapter 1. Given that children are separate people from their parents, and given that we have rejected the proprietarian account of the relationship between the two, the core question is why parents should have any special authority with respect to the processes that will shape their children's values. Our theory offers an answer. More, it provides a criterion by which to assess, with some degree of precision, not only the various mechanisms by which parents might seek to influence their children's values but also those that may have that effect as an unintended by-product. Those mechanisms certainly include the formal education or schooling of children, which is the topic discussed by much of the literature. But this focus on schooling risks collusion in the view that what goes on in the home is private, as if it is only when children are sent to school (and, for some, only when they are sent to public or state schools) that parents' rights with respect to children's values become a legitimate topic for political debate. Schooling is certainly important; regulation of formal education is a crucial lever, an area where state policy can hope to protect children's interests without too much disruption of family life. But formal education is only one area in which the more elementary or fundamental issues concerning parents' rights to shape their children's values are played out.

Parents' rights to confer advantage on their children, by contrast, are called into question by the egalitarian challenge to the family, set out in chapter 2. We have seen that parents owe a special duty of care to their children, and that the value of their having it is part of what justifies the family. But to allow parents to confer advantage on their children is to permit unfair inequalities between those raised in different families, and nobody, on reflection, believes that parents have the right to promote their children's interests as much as possible, or by any means. Though opinions differ about nepotism in varying contexts, few would endorse a parent's attempts to bribe a jury to find in favor of her child, and none, surely, approve the sentiment of Wanda Holloway, who, found guilty of attempting to murder the mother of her daughter's rival for a place on a cheerleading team (hoping the rival would be so devastated by her loss as to be unable to perform), is reputed to have said, "The things we do for our kids."[2] This topic has received much less philosophical attention than the right to shape values, and liberal theorists, even egalitarian liberal theorists, are noticeably less critical of parental efforts to benefit their children than they are of attempts to influence their values; the liberal critique of value-shaping parents has been pursued with considerably more vigor than the egalitarian critique of advantage-conferring parents. We, by contrast, are more critical. Our theory offers a criterion for assessing benefit-bestowing mechanisms: which can and which cannot be justified by appeal to the value of the family? Such attention as the issue has received has focused on formal education, on the inequality-generating effects of parents' choices of schools for their children. (There has been more of this in the United Kingdom where, unlike the United States, the legitimacy of elite private education has occasionally been subject to serious political debate.) We delve deeper into family life—all the way to bedtime stories and helping with homework.

Another broad-brush way to contrast the conferral of advantage and the shaping of values is that the former primarily concerns conflicts *between* families whereas the latter arises *within* the family. Our theory addresses both in an integrated way. We aim, that is, to shed light both on interfamilial issues, colloquially formulated in terms of parents' rights *on behalf of* their children, and on intrafamilial issues, captured more naturally by talk of parents' rights *over* their children. Taking the individual family as the unit of analysis, our theory speaks to the limits of legitimate parental authority over children. Taking the wider society, composed of many different families, as the relevant domain, it has things to say about the limits of legitimate parental partiality on behalf of children.

When we think about parents' rights to shape values, we mainly have in mind the need to protect and respect the separateness of their children. The problem is to work out what kinds of value-shaping activities, and interactions with their children, parents may claim as rights: something we try to do by looking at which activities and interactions need to be permitted in order for the family to realize its distinctive goods for its members. Those rights, as we have also argued, are themselves conditional on parents' fulfilling their duty of care to their children, which includes protecting *their* rights, including their right to develop the capacity for autonomy. Such issues are not entirely intrafamilial: third parties also have a stake in the doctrines that parents can raise their children to endorse, and, at least on some views of the proper demands of civic sense and civility, can set quite demanding constraints on what children must be brought up to believe. (Parents have no right, for example, deliberately to instill in their children the kind of racial prejudice that is likely to lead them to engage in racially motivated violence.)

But whereas, in the value-shaping case, there is at least the possibility of intrafamilial conflict—we are to some extent weighing the different interests of individual members of the same family—the conferral of advantage is entirely interfamilial. It concerns the right of parents to promote their children's interests in ways that create inequalities between them and others, so conflicts of interests between parents and children do not arise in the same way. The conflict is between the interests of particular families, parents and children taken together, and those of parents and children in *other* families. Parents may misjudge their children's interests, of course; things they take to be benefiting their children may in fact be doing them no good at all, or harming them. So there remains a question about who has the right to judge what is in children's interests, which takes us back toward the liberal challenge. But the right to confer advantage raises difficult and distinctive issues even in the standard scenario where parents are claiming the right to act in ways that will indeed be beneficial for their children.

Although a useful way of structuring our discussion, the distinction between conferring advantage and shaping values is rather artificial. One of the ways that parents try to benefit their children is by shaping their values. The benefit may be thought to derive simply from the holding of the values themselves: a devout parent who wants her child to share her beliefs does so partly because, for her, a life (or afterlife) in the true faith will be better than one outside it; the intellectual parent who wants to impart her love of learning may conceive the benefit very differently, but she too will probably be motivated partly by the simple idea that, other things equal, an educated reflective life is better than an ignorant thoughtless one. Here the benefits are conceived as intrinsic to the values, as it were. But of course parents may shape their children's values more instrumentally, with extrinsic advantages in mind. Given the role that educational qualifications play in allocating people to unequally rewarded positions in the occupational structure, for example, parents may seek to instill a love of learning in their children partly because that is a sensible strategy for preparing them to do well in the job market. Similarly, in some social milieus membership of the local church, synagogue, or mosque, and a reputation for piety, will be known to yield access to valuable networks, and may be encouraged partly for that reason. Whether the relation between value and benefit is conceived as intrinsic or extrinsic, parents' attempts to shape their children's values are nearly always also attempts to promote their interests. But in that case the egalitarian challenge arises here also: if raising a child in a particular faith, for example, is good for her, what gives a parent the right to bestow that benefit on her child rather than on another—perhaps one in greater need of that benefit?

The deep connection between the two issues, and the two challenges, is too rarely recognized. In particular, views about parents' rights to shape their children's values, arising in the context of the liberal challenge to the family, tend not to worry too much about the distributive issues that motivate the egalitarian challenge. We have separate chapters on the two topics partly because we want to engage with those views on their own terms. Many of our claims about the extent of parents' rights with respect to influencing children's values stand independently of any particular distributive concerns or commitments; they should be of interest to the (doubtless many) readers who will reject what we have to say about the limited extent of parents' rights to benefit their children. Still, we think it a merit of our theory that it provides an integrated way of approaching both topics.

Part 2 addressed the question of rights *to* family life: both children and adults have an interest in enjoying familial, parent-child, relationships that is important enough to imply duties for others, and thus allow us to think of those interests as grounding prima facie rights. Here, in part 3, we move on to consider what our theory implies about the rights *of* parents. Granted that children should indeed be raised in families, by parents, what rights do parents have with respect to the children they parent? That question too is best answered by an identification of the distinctive and extremely important goods that familial relationships contribute to human well-being, but, having identified them in part 2, we are now in a position to consider in more detail what it is that parents must be free to do to, with, or for their children, if those relationships are to make that contribution. Our relationship goods account helps us work out what room is necessary for the free and flourishing internal life appropriate to the family.[3] Parents have the right to engage in those activities and interactions with their children that facilitate the realization of the extremely valuable goods that justify the family in the first place. It is the interest in those relationship goods that grounds the rights. The result, as we will see, is a revisionist account of parents' rights.

It is revisionist in that it affords parents much less extensive rights over their children than they currently get as a matter of law; the rights are less extensive, too, than conventional views about the morally appropriate allocation of authority with respect to the raising of children. Even those who reject proprietarian accounts of the parent-child relationship tend still to think that parents should have far-reaching rights to control their children's lives. By offering a criterion for assessing precisely what kinds of things parents do indeed have a right to do to, with, or for their children, our theory of "family values" suggests that they are mistaken. What parents have a right to is a relationship of a certain kind: as we explained in part 2, children should be raised by parents because an intimate loving relationship, in which parents owe a fiduciary duty of care to those they are raising, makes a hugely important contribution to the well-being of both. Since parental rights protect the interest in having and maintaining a relationship of that kind, they are justified only insofar as they are required for protecting that relationship. From this perspective, many widely accepted parental rights look unwarranted. In particular, the relationship in question does not depend on parents' having a right to confer advantage on their children, nor to exert great influence over the content of their children's emerging beliefs. Unlike the interest in the familial relationship as we have described it, the interests that members of families have in being free to do *those* things are not weighty enough to ground duties in others.

But things are not that simple. The full extent of the complications, and the differences between the two cases, will become apparent in chapters 5 and 6. But some points that apply in both contexts—all of which render these rather extreme and general claims more precise—are worth making here, by way of clarification and orientation and, perhaps, to defuse skepticism.

First, when we say that parents do not have the rights in question, we mean specifically that they do not have a right that can properly be explained or described in that way. For example, parents may not defend decisions to bequeath their wealth to their children, or to send them to religious schools, by appealing to their rights to confer advantage on their children, or to influence their children's values. That's because, in our view, parents do not have the right to do the things so described. But that does not mean that they have no right to do things that will, as a matter of fact, confer advantage or influence their values. What they have a right to is a particular kind of relationship. The things that this does indeed give them a right to, the ways of interacting with their children that are part and parcel of the valuable intimate-but-authoritative relationship, may well have the effect of conferring advantage or influencing values. As far as values are concerned, such influence is inevitable; it is impossible to imagine an intimate relationship conducted in a way that involved no shaping of children's values. Chapter 5 will suggest that conferring advantage is different. Nonetheless, what parents have a right to are the activities internal to the valuable relationship; there is no right to bring about the external by-products of those activities, and that relationship, that might in fact arise in particular contexts.

Second, *some* deliberate conferring of advantage and shaping of values are themselves constitutive of that valuable relationship. One of the claims that we appealed to when justifying the family was that the parent-child relationship helps children's moral development. That idea makes no sense unless parents are involved in influencing their children's moral views; a parent who failed to teach her children right from wrong would be a failure as a parent. So there are some values that parents have not merely a right but a duty to instill in their children. Similarly, we cannot conceive of parents' having a duty of care to their children without regarding as it implying the right deliberately to confer advantage on them in at least some circumstances. This is true at the most general level—the basic reason why children should have parents is because children are better off for having parents, so in a world where some lack adequate parenting, successful parenting is itself a form of advantage-conferral. It would be incoherent to deny parents the right to bestow *any* advantages on their children. But it is also true with respect to more specific kinds of benefit: if the duty of care amounts to anything, it implies a duty to privilege one's own child over others with respect to life's necessities—subsistence, medical care—even where that will create distributive unfairness. When we deny that the interest in familial relationship goods generates a right to shape values or confer advantage, we mean specifically to reject the claim that it grounds any generalized or blanket rights of that kind.

Third, there is no way to respect parents' right to do the things with their children that they do indeed have the right to do without also affording them the opportunity to do things that they have no right to do. Healthy family life requires parents to enjoy a good deal of discretion over their children's lives, and to be experienced by their children as exercising authoritative judgments in many areas. This requires a substantial sphere of interaction unmonitored by other authorities. But parents cannot exercise that discretion and enjoy that unmonitored interaction without being allowed the space to make mistakes or, worse, deliberately to engage in activities that they have no right to engage in. Here readers may have in mind far worse ways in which parents may misuse their rights than by attempting to confer advantage on their children, or shape their values (though Richard Dawkins regards some forms of religious education as child abuse).[4] Again, it is important that we describe parents' rights carefully. Of course, parents have no right to abuse children—but they do have a right to the space within which abuse may occur. The same goes for conferring advantage and shaping values.

When we talk of parents' rights, we are talking very specifically about the rights that people have qua parents—the rights that attend, or perhaps even constitute, the role of parenting as we understand what that role is, or should be. This specificity raises some important and general issues. Recall our claim, emphasized in part 2, that the right *to* parent is grounded partly in the interests of adults. Recognizing adults' fundamental interest in parenting explains why it would be wrong to think that the sole criterion by which to assess child-rearing arrangements should be the well-being of children. Suppose that's right. That still leaves the question of whether the rights *of* parents—parents' rights—are grounded entirely in the interests of children.

The normative structure of those rights is complex. We identify parents' rights by thinking about children's interests: the rights that parents have over their children are rights that they have because it is in those children's interests that they be raised by people who have those rights. But, on our dual-interest account, the family is justified partly by appeal to adults' interest in parenting. Adults benefit greatly from exercising the rights (and discharging the duties) of parenthood; indeed, they benefit so much that the interest in parenting grounds a fundamental, nonfiduciary, right to parent. Children should be raised by adults who have a bundle of rights and duties with respect to them, and that bundle is identified entirely by consideration of children's interests. But adults have an interest in being, and a right to be, the people who get that bundle. It's good for children that their parents have certain rights over them, and certain duties toward them—it's good for children that it's their parents (rather than, say, state functionaries) who get to decide certain things about how they are raised, and are charged with the task of meeting some of their basic needs. So we work out what rights and duties parents have, qua parents, by thinking about what rights and duties it is in their children's interests that they have. But it's also good for adults that they get to do those things, good enough for us to think that adults have a right to exercise the rights and duties of parenthood.

Parents' rights and duties, then, are entirely fiduciary. Parents have just those rights and duties with respect to their children that it is in their children's interests for them to have. But there are two reasons why this does not make parents slaves to their children—two reasons why parents' every thought and action does not have to be aimed at promoting their children's interests.

The first is that, as explained in chapter 4, parents are not *only* parents (though it may seem like that sometimes!). They have the rights and duties that relate specifically to their relationship with their children, but they also have other rights and duties in virtue of other roles or statuses. Though not relating specifically to their relationship with their children, these too may nonetheless yield implications for the things they may properly do to, with, or for their children. When a parent takes his young child with him to visit a friend, or shopping, this need not be something that he does qua parent. He has the right to do it, let us assume, and his having the right makes a difference to what he may do with his child. But it need not be a parental right in the strict sense in which we are using the term. Parenting is a specific task or role.[5] (We can imagine the man breaking off the conversation with his friend to attend to his child's needs, saying, "Sorry, I have to stop for five minutes, time for a bit of parenting.") It is an unusually demanding and time-consuming role, and one the proper fulfillment of which has pervasive effects on the lives of those who fulfill it. But, even so, it is not all-consuming. It normally leaves space for those who are parents to live their lives with other purposes in view—including space to do things to and with their children that are not maximally in their children's interests.

So not all the rights that parents have, and that may properly influence what they do to, with, and for their children, are rights that they have qua parents. But the second reason why parents have rights to do things other than directly promote their children's interests *is* about parents' rights. It is about the rights that are needed by parents in order for them to play their fiduciary role. Here there is no avoiding a suggestion of paradox: it is in *children's* interests that their relationship with their parents is not one in which their parents always act with their children's best interests in mind. Parents have a fiduciary duty to do what they can to have a certain kind of relationship with their children, because it is in children's interests that their relationship with their parents is of that kind. But the kind of parent-child relationship that is in children's interests is not one in which parents are slaves, devoted exclusively to the promotion of their children's well-being. The relationship should be intimate, spontaneous, and emotionally honest; it should involve a genuine sharing of selves between parent and child, with the child experiencing its parent as a real person, with her own interests and enthusiasms, and the discretion to pursue them to some extent. Of course, there are crucial limits to this, limits that vary as the child develops. Sometimes playing the fiduciary role will indeed mean keeping children's interests clearly in mind; there are obviously limits on the kinds of sharing of selves, and ways of sharing selves, that are appropriate. But if we are clear that the child's interest is in a particular kind of intimate-but-authoritative relationship, and see the parent's fiduciary responsibility as that of developing one of *those* with her child, then it should be clear how parents' rights will include rights to do things to and with their children that do not directly aim at serving those children's interests.

CHAPTER 5

Conferring Advantage

Parents typically assume that they have the right to do things that benefit their children and not others. Indeed, they assume that showing favoritism toward their children—acting partially toward them—is morally required. That's what parents are *supposed* to do; it's part of the job. Our justification of the family invokes the value of parents' having a duty of care to their children, and that duty does indeed imply some putting of their children's interests ahead of other people's (including their own). Moreover, as we shall explain, wanting one's children's life to go well is part of what it means to love them. If I love my child and not yours, then I care more about my child's well-being than I care about yours. We accept that children benefit, in terms of familial relationship goods, from having parents who are able to express their love by favoring them over others. But that doesn't give parents a blank check, morally speaking. Our task here is to work out what ways of conferring advantage on their children parents do and do not have a right to engage in.

In our world, those with the resources can promote their children's interests by all manner of means. Wealthy parents send their children to elite private schools that may enhance their children's chances of entering good universities and getting good jobs, as well as providing educational experiences intrinsically superior to those provided by state-supported schools. Or they buy houses in neighborhoods that secure their children's admission to state schools believed to be superior to others. They take their children on fancy holidays and buy them expensive clothes and toys; invest in safer cars; buy life insurance to protect them against the parents' premature death; set up trust funds and bequeath them property; take them to museums; hire private tutors; send them to expensive summer camps; introduce them to well-connected adults; read them bedtime stories.

But it's not only advantaged parents who help their children. Although what parents *can* do may differ across the class structure, understood broadly in terms of both economic and cultural capital, the moral question needs addressing with respect to all parents. Those with above-average resources to devote to their children's well-being will doubtless constitute the majority of our readers, and there is indeed a sense in which our argument has particularly important implications for them. But the desire that one's children prosper is universal, and the sacrifice that parents are willing to undertake to that end is perhaps greatest among poor parents—think of economically and culturally disadvantaged immigrants desperate to give their children a decent start in life. Our theory must, and does, speak to their situation also.

Some Paradigm Cases

Our account of familial relationship goods yields a standard for assessing the kinds of things that parents can properly claim a right to do to, with, or for their children. There must be permission, and social support, for those activities and interactions between parents and children that facilitate the realization of the goods that justify the family, even where those may generate unfair inequalities between children born to different families. Certainly, these are prima facie rights; by the end of the chapter we will have discussed how they may be defeated by more important moral considerations. Still, the interest in a familial relationship of the kind we have described is weighty enough, and the implied duties not so burdensome, that we should regard as rights those conditions necessary for that relationship to make its crucial and distinctive contribution to human well-being.

We begin by contrasting some paradigm cases of activities that must be permitted, in order for familial relationships to flourish, with others that could normally be prohibited without jeopardizing the most valuable aspects of those relationships. The examples are highly simplified, and will be complicated over the course of the chapter, but they should serve to convey the core idea.

First, parents must be free to read bedtime stories to their children and should have considerable discretion over which books to read. Second, parents should be free to have their children accompany them to religious ceremonies and other valued activities and to enroll them in associations in which they will participate in the communities of value to which their parents belong (Hebrew school, the Ukrainian Youth League, cricket clubs, and so on). We shall discuss the latter in the next chapter. Here we consider the same kind of activity from a different perspective—its tendency, in some circumstances, to confer advantage in ways that disrupt fair equality of opportunity.

A parent reading a bedtime story is doing several things simultaneously. He is intimately sharing physical space with his child; sharing with her the content of a story selected by one of them; providing the background for future discussions; preparing her for her bedtime and, if she is young enough, calming her; reinforcing the mutual sense of identification one with another. He is giving her exclusive attention in a space designated for that exclusive attention at a particularly important time of her day. Having one's children accompany one to church is likewise a paradigm case because it involves similarly intimate interaction and produces similar mutual identification. Without substantial opportunity to share himself intimately with his child, in ways that reflect his own judgments about what is valuable, the parent is deprived of the ability to forge and maintain an intimate relationship, and the child is deprived of that relationship. The loss is to the core of what is valuable about the relationship. Imagine that parents are barred from engaging in these or relevantly similar activities, or, less drastically, that such activities are made very difficult: the opportunities for realizing the familial relationship goods that justify the family would be severely limited.

The contrast is with those things we do to, with, and for our children that are not essential for the realization of the relationship goods that we have identified. Again, there is a wide range. Think of a parent who invests all possible resources in securing competitive advantage for his child: perhaps, say, sending her to an expensive private school designed to optimize her chances in the competition for well-rewarded and interesting jobs, investing in a trust fund, and interacting with her on the basis of judgments about how best to develop her human capital. These activities are not protected by the considerations we have invoked concerning the value of the family. In normal circumstances at least, none of these is essential for the parent to carry out her special duty of care for the child—none is essential for the child's fundamental interests to be adequately met—and none is essential for the important goods distinctively made available by the familial relationship.

It would be convenient if the first kind of activity were less damaging to equal opportunity than the second. Some strands in the egalitarian tradition have tended to assume this, and that something close enough to fair equality of opportunity can be achieved through a combination of public education policies intended to marginalize the impact of expensive private schooling and tax-transfer policies designed to mitigate the effects of unequal parental wealth on life prospects. Things would be easier if the reason why inequality persisted across generations was that well-off parents bequeathed property to their children, or used their money to buy superior access to such advantage for their children. However, recent research in economics and sociology casts doubt on this assumption, suggesting that in fact parenting styles, culture, personality, and other factors that are, on our account, integral to valuable familial relationships, may have as much if not more impact on prospects for income and wealth than transfers from parents to children, or financial investment in their human capital.[1] Sociologists influenced by Pierre Bourdieu conjecture that as long as outcomes are substantially unequal, and the family remains in place, parents who win the competition for outcomes will, even if unintentionally, turn their winnings into opportunities for their children. Through the family children are acculturated into the expectations of life, including work life, of their parents and their parents' friends and acquaintances. Sometimes this is institutionalized: think of an apparently innocent phenomenon like "Take Our Daughters and Sons to Work Day," which encourages parents to introduce their children to the world of work, but does so by exposing them to their own position within the occupational structure. The family, even when kept within its genuinely valuable bounds, is more threatening to the prospects for equality of opportunity, even of the conventional kind, than many egalitarians might hope.

On our account of family values, it's important that parents and children really get to know each other; parents must be free to share their enthusiasms, to talk about the things that interest them, to conduct the common life of the family in ways that they are comfortable with, to take their children to visit the parents' friends, and so on. But these are some of the most important mechanisms that generate what sociologists call "cultural reproduction"—the tendency of norms, values, expectations, habits, perhaps personality types, to be transmitted, or "reproduced," between generations. So the mechanisms that yield familial relationship goods are also the mechanisms that tend to cause cultural reproduction within families. We might also think of them as the mechanisms that tend to "constitute" people as the people they are. Simplifying drastically, the day-to-day stuff of healthy familial relationships will tend to produce children who are somewhat like their parents.

As long as that day-to-day stuff does not conflict with children's right to autonomy, it seems hard to object to children's turning out somewhat like their parents. We all know families where children's mannerisms mirror those of their parents; an amused smile is the appropriate reaction. The problem is that these characteristics transmitted between generations within families cannot be conceived only in terms of "cultural reproduction." They are less innocent than that, for they are inextricably connected to the intergenerational reproduction of inequality, or what sociologists call "social" or "class" reproduction—the tendency of parents and children to occupy similar positions in the distribution of benefits and burdens. Consider the following observation from sociologist Annette Lareau, whose ethnography *Unequal Childhoods* identifies the ways in which middle-class parenting styles confer competitive advantage on their children:

> This kind of training developed in Alexander and other middle-class children a sense of entitlement. They felt they had a right to weigh in with an opinion, to make special requests, to pass judgment on others, and to offer advice to adults. They expected to receive attention and to be taken very seriously. It is important to recognize that these advantages and entitlements are historically specific. . . . They are highly effective strategies in the United States today precisely because our society places a premium on assertive, individualized actions executed by persons who command skills in reasoning and negotiation.[2]

Balancing family values and equality of opportunity is especially difficult because informal interactions within the family are so influential for children's prospects.[3]

Parents' Rights and Equality of Opportunity

So we have some paradigm cases of parent-child interactions that can, and cannot, be justified by appeal to the value of familial relationship goods. Those that can—bedtime stories, taking children to church and cricket—are the kind of thing that parents have a right to do with their children. Those that cannot—sending one's child to an elite private school, bequeathing her one's property—are not. Before going on to blur the boundaries between the two types of case, and complicating the story in several other ways, let's step back from the details and make four quite general points about the structure of the issue we are addressing.

The first emphasizes a particular implication of framing the distributive problem raised by parents' rights in terms of the conflict with fair equality of opportunity. We are focusing on the extent and nature of parents' rights to do things to, with, and for their children where doing those things confers on their children advantage of a particular kind: advantage, relative to otherwise similar children, in the competition for jobs and the rewards that go with them. Two aspects of this are worth distinguishing. One is that we are talking about the conferral of *advantage*, where that is understood in terms of a comparison with others (as in tennis). The issue is not what parents may do to benefit their children (i.e., to make them better off than they would otherwise be), but what they may do to confer advantage on them (i.e., to make them better off than others). On its own, that may seem trivial—a distinction of interest to philosophers but without any real moral or political significance. But add in the second aspect—that we are talking about the conferral of *competitive* advantage—and things become more interesting. The point about parents' rights to interact with their children in ways that confer *that* kind of advantage is, crucially, that if some children are getting it and others are not, then those who aren't are not just worse off than the others; they are worse off than they would have been if the others had not been getting it. (Again, think of tennis: the player who has "advantage" is not only better off than her opponent; she is better off in absolute terms—consider her chance of winning the game—than she was at "deuce.")

The issue at stake, when the conflict is with fair equality of opportunity, is not whether parents have the right to benefit their children. It's whether they have the right to benefit them in ways that confer competitive advantage on them. And that's an issue because whatever they do to confer competitive advantage is not neutral in its effects on other children—it does not leave untouched, but rather is detrimental to, those other children's prospects in the competition for jobs and associated rewards. Children who are not on the receiving end of competitive-advantage-conferring parental activities are worse off, at least in that respect, just because others are on the receiving end of them. Recalling the relation between rights and duties should bring out the structure of the moral issue. In thinking about what rights parents should have with respect to their children, we are necessarily thinking about the duties of others. Since permitting the conferral of advantage makes things worse for some children—those who don't get it—why exactly do we have a duty to let parents engage in these advantage-conferring activities, and, more specifically, what exactly do we have a duty to let them do?

Suppose that, because of its importance for familial relationship goods, a parent has a right to do something with her child that will in fact confer competitive advantage on the child. It doesn't follow that the parent has a right to confer that (or indeed any) advantage on the child. What is protected, on our account, is the parent-child interaction, not the advantage-conferral to which, in the imagined case, it gives rise. This is the second point: our account justifies a right to a particular kind of parent-child interaction because it realizes familial relationship goods, but it gives no reason for the state not to pursue other distributive goals, such as fair equality of opportunity, by taxing the benefit, or by breaking the connection between those goods and the other forms of advantage that might—and often do—otherwise accompany them. Suppose that the state did indeed break that connection, and did it so thoroughly that *none* of the familial interactions to which parents have rights any longer yielded *any* competitive advantage to their children. No parent could properly criticize the state for violating his right to confer that advantage on his child: he has no such right.

Whether, and to what extent, the practices that realize the goods of family life yield inequalities in the distribution of other goods depends on the design of social institutions. Take bedtime stories as our paradigm case of a protected parent-child interaction. Assume further that reading to one's children for fifteen minutes every evening has a demonstrable positive effect on both their expected lifetime income and their competitiveness for interesting and rewarding jobs. While, on our account, this tendency to upset fair equality of opportunity would not license attempts to prevent the reading of bedtime stories, that distributive goal could perfectly well be pursued by attempts to reduce the extent to which bedtime stories influence children's prospects for the goods governed by that principle. Governments might undertake measures designed to lessen the effect of such stories on lifetime expected income or on the other, less tangible, benefits attaching to occupations, such as how interesting they are, their status, and the self-fulfillment offered to those exercising the relevant responsibilities. This might involve a reduction in wage inequalities or the development of an occupational structure in which these other benefits were distributed more equally between occupations.[4] Even where the government may not—on pain of violating parents' rights—interfere with the intrafamilial processes that generate particular attributes in children, those rights do not protect the inequalities of opportunity that those processes currently tend to produce. The government may perfectly well seek to shape the social environment so as to diminish the extent of the influence of those attributes on children's prospects. It may, in other words, try to break the link between the kinds of parent-child interaction that make the family valuable, and which are protected by parents' rights, and the extrinsic goods that those interactions currently yield.

So we must be careful when specifying what is protected by parents' rights. Parents can have rights to do things to and with their children that generate certain attributes in those children, and, in certain circumstances, those attributes may give them competitive advantage over others. It is tempting to infer from this that they have the right to produce those attributes and confer that competitive advantage. In one, rather loose, sense, they do: preventing them from engaging in those activities, in the current circumstances where the competitive advantage results, would indeed violate their rights. But there is another sense in which they don't: parents do indeed have rights to interact with their children in particular ways, but they do not have rights to bring about the distributive outcomes that result from the way those attributes currently interact with, for example, the labor market or the tax and transfer system. There is plenty of room for governments to pursue egalitarian distributive goals while respecting parents' rights.

Parents, then, do not have rights to produce the inequalities of opportunity that in present circumstances result from those features of the parent-child relationship to which they can indeed claim rights. Nonetheless, and this is our third point, even if parents do not have rights to violate fair equality of opportunity, in the careful sense suggested, it could still be that, all things considered, governments would be justified in letting them do just that. Considerations concerning incentives and the efficiently productive use of resources may warrant permitting—and perhaps even encouraging—parents to do things for their children that exceed what they have a right to do for them. Even where conferring competitive advantage on their children is not something that parents can claim as a matter of right—because it is not susceptible to justification by appeal to children's interest in familial relationship goods—it may yet be justified for governments to adopt policies that allow them to do just that. That's because parents' rights and fair equality of opportunity do not exhaust the set of relevant normative considerations.

Toward the end of chapter 2 we emphasized the limits of fair equality of opportunity and discussed different ways in which equality of opportunity might be conceived. But we also mentioned the idea that, however conceived, *equality* might not be the most important distributive goal. Advocates of "prioritarianism," for example, think that what matters fundamentally is not that children should have equality of opportunity but that opportunities should be distributed in ways that reflect the weightier claims of the less advantaged. Suppose they are right: benefiting the less advantaged within a society is more important than providing its children with fair equality of opportunity.[5] In that case the government may be doing the right thing if it allows parents to favor their own children in ways that conflict with that kind of equality, even though parents lack the right to engage in that kind of favoring. For example, if disallowing a practice would reduce parents' tendency to deploy their productive assets to develop the human capital of others, in ways that would redound to the benefit of the less advantaged, the government might legitimately permit the practice. Even if parents have no right to bequeath property to their children, or to spend more money on their education than is available to other parents, how they would react to a policy denying them the freedom to do those things might warrant rejection of that policy.

We could think of this as a prioritarian harnessing of parents' motivation to benefit their children, analogous to the Pareto or "incentives" argument for permitting inequalities that will be familiar to readers of philosophical debates on distributive justice following Rawls's famous "difference principle." We are talking here about the equivalent argument, adapted to the parent-child, fair equality of opportunity, case. As far as that case is concerned, our view is that although a government may indeed be justified in harnessing parental motivations of this kind, in the relevant empirical circumstances, it remains the case that parents have no right to favor their children in these ways, unless they can be derived from our account of familial relationship goods.[6]

The previous points concerned the extent and specification of parents' rights to do things that would confer advantage on their children. By using fair equality of opportunity as the foil for our discussion, we have effectively been thinking of "conferring advantage" as equivalent to "giving children prospects greater than those they would have under fair equality of opportunity." So we, and doubtless our readers, have had in mind advantaged parents who do things to, with, or for their children that tend to give their children a better than fair chance, but whose familial interactions may be protected by the role they play in the production of familial relationship goods. But, as we said, a theory must address also the disadvantaged, who are just as likely to be motivated to promote their children's interests, even if they are less likely to possess the resources to do so effectively. For illiterate parents, for example, or for members of ethnic minorities whose children are known to suffer from various biases in education systems and labor markets, buying private tuition and, if they could afford it, elite private education, might have a rather different significance. When a parent living in a poor neighborhood with failing schools struggles to improve his daughter's prospects, he is, surely, trying to benefit her. But he may not be trying to confer advantage on her—not if "advantage" is understood in terms of a comparison with others. He may simply be acting to mitigate the disadvantage she would otherwise suffer—to provide her with more of the opportunities that she would have under a regime of fair equality of opportunity. So it's not obvious that we need to accord him any right to confer advantage on his daughter, and in that case the issue of parents' rights to confer advantage might not arise at all.

Alas, things are not that straightforward. The poverty-stricken parent may not be advantaging his daughter relative to children born to more prosperous families, but he will presumably be increasing her prospects relative to other children born into poverty. Indeed, although parents might indeed be aiming simply to give their own children the chances they would have under the principle of fair equality of opportunity, the effect of their actions may be to increase the deprivation of others as defined by that very principle. Other children, similarly talented and motivated, still have their prospects worsened; in that sense the parents' actions contravene, rather than being demanded by, fair equality of opportunity.[7] Does our account of the value of the family yield parents a right to seek that their own children achieve what they would have under fair equality of opportunity when they could be helping other people's children achieve it instead—perhaps, to combine it with the previous point, children with even worse prospects than their own?

As long as we are talking about prima facie rights, the answer is yes. This is where the parental duty of care is important. There is a distinct value to children that comes from their being raised by particular adults charged with the task of protecting their interests. Clearly there can be reasonable disagreement about the extent and kind of protection of children's interests that constitutes this fiduciary role, but in our view one has a prima facie duty, qua parent, to try not merely to avert outcomes that are bad for one's children in some absolute sense—such as malnutrition or a high risk of physical assault—but also to try to reduce the risk of those that would leave them unfairly disadvantaged relative to others. A parent-child relationship in which parents are not free to seek to promote their children's interests even to that limited extent does not take seriously enough the importance of the fiduciary role of parents—the benefit that comes to children from being raised by adults whose role is to try to ensure that they are not on the wrong end of unfair inequalities of opportunity. Parents' rights to confer advantage on their children, on our account, are much more limited than is commonly thought. Many kinds of favoritism or partiality that parents take for granted cannot in fact be justified by appeal to familial relationship goods. But we are talking specifically about conferring *advantage*. Parents' rights to counter their children's prospective disadvantage are different.

Wanting One's Loved One's Life to Go Better

With these general observations out of the way, we can get back to our paradigm cases and address a couple of the doubts and complications that may have led some readers to suspect us of sleight of hand. We have presented bedtime stories, and having one's children accompany one to church (or to cricket), as examples of the kinds of things that parents have a right to do with their children, and they have a right to do them even if that leads to unfair inequalities of opportunity. Spending one's money on elite private education, or bequeathing it to one's children, falls on the other side of the line; they are not the kind of parent-child interaction to which parents can claim rights. The difference, we have claimed, is that the former are needed for the familial relationship to make its distinctive contribution to children's flourishing, whereas the latter are not. There are two important objections to that claim. One is that loving parents will be motivated quite generally to promote their children's interests, and that anything that parents may do to that end should be regarded as realizing a kind of familial relationship good. The other is that there are situations in which activities like sending one's child to an elite private school or bequeathing her property do in fact contribute to the realization of familial relationship goods even on the account that we have given of what those goods are. The latter will be discussed in the next section. Here we consider the former.

Parents must be free to engage in activities such as reading bedtime stories and being accompanied to church because these actions contribute to the very valuable relationship goods that the family is distinctively able to provide to children. Parents' rights extend to those actions needed for the kind of relationship that will deliver those goods. But parents can be, and typically are, motivated by the more general desire to improve the quality of their children's lives. We care that all people's lives go well, but we care more, and in different ways, about the lives of those we love. And there is a distinctive value to having one's life go better because loved ones have acted to bring that about. It's good if nature or strangers bestow benefits on us, but it's good in a different and special way if those benefits come from those who love us, from those who have raised us and with whom we enjoy the distinctive parent-child relationship that lies at the heart of our account. The suggestion, then, is that the proposed approach to parents' rights, which derives them from children's interest in having a particular kind of relationship with those who raise them, can ground parents' rights to seek to benefit their children quite generally. Only if they are permitted to do that can the relationship yield these distinctive benefits to children.

Let's be clear how far this objection reaches. This chapter is about parents' rights to confer advantage on their children, not simply to benefit them. A loving parent may indeed want to promote her child's well-being, but it would be odd, perhaps even a little creepy, if the ultimate aim of her endeavors were that her child be better off than others. (Imagine a parent thinking: "I don't care how well her life goes. What matters is that it goes better than other people's." Imagine a child thinking: "I don't care whether my parents can make my life better. What matters is that they can make it go better than other people's.") So it's tempting to think that the objection is beside the point: we are interested in whether parents have rights to confer advantage on their children; but only creepy parents and children would be interested in doing and receiving that.

But that is too quick. When benefits are scarce, as they usually are, not everybody can get them. Parents who want their children to be among those who do get them will find themselves involved in the pursuit of competitive advantage; advantage over others is here valued instrumentally, as a means to the ultimate end of absolute benefit. So, given the way goods are allocated in societies such as ours, the sensible way to promote your child's well-being is indeed likely to be to improve her competitive position relative to others: that is, improving her relative advantage with respect to the various competitions—for schools, universities, jobs—by which those goods are distributed. That's why the objection cuts deep: if successful parent-child relationships require parents to be free to promote their children's interests in general, and putting them in a good position to succeed in the competitions that determine the allocation of goods is the way for them to do that, then by our own criterion for deciding the scope and content of parents' rights, they do indeed have the right to invest in their children's competitive advantage.

If the objection were valid, that would bring our view in line with the conventional wisdom. Parents are widely held to have the right to invest in their children's competitive advantage, and to bequeath them property, in order to promote their well-being. Indeed, parents are often thought to have a duty to do those things, where they can. To show why we persist in denying that parents have rights of that kind, we need to explain why the familial relationship goods that are invoked to support those rights are subordinate to the primary or core familial relationship goods that lie at the heart of our theory. For us, those goods are parasitic on those core goods, and they are secondary in the sense of being less important: children's interest in a relationship that permits *their* realization is not weighty enough to ground parents' having rights to act in ways that realize them.

Suppose parents were prevented from acting on their loving motivation generally to advance their children's well-being—by bestowing particular excellences or intrinsic goods on them, or by bestowing on them advantages in the competition to achieve positions from which they might secure those things for themselves in later life. Would they and their children be deprived of a good, and one that is distinctively made available by parent-child relationships? We think that they would. Consider this first from the parents' point of view: if people could pursue their own well-being, and could impartially act to promote the well-being of others, but were not allowed to pursue that of their loved ones in particular, they would indeed suffer a loss; forms of feeling for particular others, including the willingness to put the well-being of a loved one before one's own, would be denied a valuable mode of expression. And just as the goods realized in other kinds of intimate relationship are not, for many people, adequate substitutes for those achieved in parent-child relationships, so being free to further the interests of one's children allows expression of a distinctive kind of love: love for a person for whom one has acted as fiduciary, with whom one has enjoyed special and particular kinds of intimacy, and so on.

Since parents' rights are justified entirely by children's interests in being raised by parents who have those rights, the distinctive value to parents of the freedom to confer advantage on their children does not enter into their justification. We elaborate that value only to flesh out the sense in which the goods in question are distinctive. For analogous considerations apply from the child's perspective. Although we are talking now precisely of those kinds of advantage that could in one sense be received from anybody, there is a distinctive value to receiving those things *from one's parents*. Even where the purpose is the same— the general furthering of the recipient's interests rather than a more specifically "relationship" concern with intimacy, shared interests, or identification—the same bicycle, sports lessons, complete works of Shakespeare, or house will be valued differently depending on whether it comes from one's parents or from one's fellow citizens collectively, via the state, and rightly so. So children too have a distinct and specific interest in having their life made to go better by the loving acts of those with whom they have enjoyed the kind of intimate relationship that, on our account, gives the family its primary value. Refuse parents the freedom to promote their children's well-being in such ways and you deprive their children of a distinctively familial relationship good.

Why, then, don't parents have rights generally to benefit their children? Although distinctively familial relationship goods can indeed be realized when parents act in ways intended generally to help their children's lives go better than they otherwise would, *those* goods are simply not weighty enough to warrant the state's being under a duty to permit them to engage in those interactions or transmissions, where permitting them conflicts with other children's interest in fair equality of opportunity. The familial relationship goods that lie at the heart of our account make a hugely valuable contribution to human flourishing, sufficiently important to justify their protection by rights. But the good realized when parents act lovingly to promote their children's interests *in general* is nothing like as significant or substantial.

When we consider whether and why children should be raised by parents, rather than by state functionaries, the following answer has no appeal: "Yes, because there are distinctive and weighty contributions to well-being that can be realized only when parents and children enjoy an intimate, loving relationship *and when parents are permitted generally to promote the well-being of those whom they have raised.*" The goods made possible by the italicized condition are not only less important than those that precede it; they are parasitic on them. It is only because and where one has enjoyed a distinctive kind of relationship with a child that one can claim distinctive value for one's freedom generally to favor that child's interests. It is only because and where one has enjoyed that kind of relationship with a parent that one can claim distinctive value for the freedom to have one's interests promoted by that particular person. But these latter values are surely less important than the very relationship on which their value depends. As long as there is ample space available for parents to realize the more important familial relationship goods, those that yield our primary account of the family's value, parents can claim no right to the further freedoms that would be required for them to act on their loving motivation generally to further their children's interests.[8]

This analysis helps to explicate the sense of unease sometimes felt about parents who seem to care greatly that their children enjoy various material or cultural advantages but are less interested in actually spending time with them. That unease derives mainly from the view that such parents have misidentified what children really need from parents. Parents who, in order to earn the money required to send their children to expensive private schools, work such long hours that they hardly get to be with those children as they are growing up, or who send their young children away to schools believed likely to yield material and cultural benefits in due course, are, often, making a mistake about the ways in which parents can most effectively contribute to their children's well-being, all things considered (as well as missing out on a potential source of flourishing in their own lives). From this perspective, their failure should be conceived as an inefficiency; guided by a misunderstanding of what is important, parents are misallocating the resources (perhaps especially time) at their disposal.

But a nonprudential issue is also at stake in such cases. The interest in having one's well-being promoted by one's parents can be regarded as distinctively familial only where the interest is in having it promoted by someone with whom one has the particular kind of intimate, loving relationship that we have presented as justifying the institution of the family in the first place. Parents who seek generally to benefit their children *rather than* enjoying a relationship of that kind are not only (usually) misidentifying their children's (and their own) good, nor are they simply failing properly to balance their children's interests against those of other people's. They are engaging in the kind of favoritism that is simply not susceptible to justification by appeal to the value of the family. Of course, in practice, at least given contemporary views about parenting, things are unlikely to be quite so black-and-white. The father whose "love" for his children is expressed *entirely* by his paying for their nanny and school fees, and bequeathing them a share of his estate, is largely a thing of the past. Still, the analysis we have offered is helpful for understanding what was going wrong in such cases, and yields a framework for judging cases where the parent-child relationship has not gone quite as badly wrong as that.

The bottom line, then, is that parents do not have the right generally to benefit their children by conferring advantage on them in a way that undermines fair equality of opportunity. We do not dispute that distinctively familial relationship goods can be realized when they do so—there is indeed something special going on when parents act on their loving motivation to benefit their children. But parents' rights with respect to their children do not extend to all the actions that would produce all familial relationship goods. They have those rights required for the relationship to produce the core goods, which are indeed important enough to warrant holding others under the relevant duties. But children's interest in the secondary, parasitic relationship goods is simply not weighty enough to ground the corresponding rights. Denying parents the freedom generally to promote their children's interests indeed denies them the opportunity to express something valuable about familial love, and thereby to realize whatever value that expression has for their children (and for them). Still, it does not prevent them from realizing goods as valuable as the core familial relationship goods on which that value is parasitic.

Are Bequests and Bedtime Stories Really So Different?

The second objection to our attempt to distinguish between the paradigm cases of advantage-conferring activities to which parents have and don't have rights appeals not to a broader conception of familial relationship goods. Rather, it points out that there are situations in which activities like sending one's child to an elite private school or bequeathing her property do in fact contribute to the realization of the core familial relationship goods as we have defined them.

The challenge here runs as follows: It is one thing to provide an account of the properties that a particular parent-child interaction must have in order to ground a parental right to engage in that kind of interaction, another to determine whether a particular interaction, in a particular context, has those properties. What about circumstances where the success of the parent-child relationship itself depends on transfers and investments of the kind we have put on the wrong side of the line? A child might feel entitled to parental largesse, especially if she observes a cultural pattern of large-scale parent-child giving/ bequeathing within her milieu. She might similarly feel undervalued if she is consigned to the ordinarily resourced local school when she knows that her parents could readily pay for her to attend the outstandingly resourced private school some short distance away. A parent might feel that to do otherwise would be an expression of undervaluing her, and it might for that reason pollute the relationship.

One version of this phenomenon can readily be dealt with. The child who holds her parents hostage, as it were, by demanding that they provide various luxuries (sports car, ski trip) as the price of continuing the relationship, can be put to one side as a selfish brat. The relationship that she is demanding that price to continue is simply not the kind that yields its members the relationship goods we are talking about. It may indeed be that particular parents value particular kinds of interaction with their children enough to be willing to pay what those children demand for them, and we must of course acknowledge that familial relationships are complex, multifaceted, and likely to involve a mixture of healthy and unhealthy elements. Still, it is surely uncontroversial to claim that, the more a particular case tends toward the type described here, the more something has gone wrong—the relationship has become corrupted in ways that deprive it of the value central to our account.

More difficult are cases where no bargain is being struck, but where norms and conventions are such that even a nonmercenary child might experience a failure to bestow some forms of advantage as a failure of love. Here our response is somewhat conjectural. First, we doubt that such feelings would be prompted in a regime in which, for example, elite private schooling or large-scale gifting were effectively prohibited. If she is denied the opportunity to dispose of her resources in that way, a parent who does not use them to further her children's interests can hardly be doing anything that demonstrates her misevaluation of the child, and the child cannot reasonably believe that she is. Second, it is important to keep clearly in mind how much of the significance of particular kinds of parent-child interaction is conventional. As Samuel Scheffler points out,

> People's judgments about the circumstances in which, and the extent to which, they have reason to give special weight to the interests of their intimates and associates are highly sensitive to the norms they have internalized and to the character of the prevailing social practices and institu-

tions. Behaviour that is seen in one social setting as an admirable expression of parental concern, for example, may be seen in another setting as an intolerable form of favouritism or nepotism.[9]

We would argue that this conventional aspect extends to the significance that such norms have as expressions of parental love. Finally, even in a society where norms do firmly link loving to the conferral of various advantages, we conjecture that children who enjoy emotionally healthy relationships with their parents need not experience parental restraint as undervaluing. This is both because the parent has some influence over the emerging values of the child, as discussed in the next chapter, and because the parent has at her disposal many other ways to convey her love.

Quite apart from these general considerations about the expressive significance of acts of giving things to, or doing things for, one's children, there can also be more specific contexts in which instances of gifting and bequeathing, or of educational investment, are particularly valuable instantiations of the parent-child relationship. Consider the bequest of a house in which a family has lived, or a plot of land on which it has worked, for centuries. Perhaps, even though an egalitarian ethos and set of parental values could prevent children from feeling damaged by its unavailability, such a legacy, symbolizing the sense of continuity over time and between generations that is among our "family values," is an important good that would be lost in a regime of prohibition. Similarly, some parents wish their children to receive particular kinds of education neither because they want them to enjoy competitive advantage over others nor because they want them to partake of particular excellences that will make their lives go better, but because the parent-child relationship itself—or perhaps the child's sense of herself as a member of a particular familial tradition—depends on the child's knowing or understanding particular things (cricket, classical languages, music) not otherwise available, or, perhaps, on the child's attending the school that one of his parents and, maybe, one of his grandparents, attended. In such cases, familial relationship goods might indeed be invoked as grounds for permitting such bequests and educational choices.

Our response is simply to remind the reader of a point made earlier. Suppose that, in a particular context, sending one's child to a particular school, or kind of school, or bequeathing her a particular kind of property, would indeed realize such important familial relationship goods that parents may properly claim a right to engage in them. That implies no right to confer the incidental or contingent benefits that typically attend the receipt of the goods that have this distinctively familial significance. In our existing social and economic environment, inheriting a house early in adulthood, or having a secure prospect of that inheritance, constitutes a substantial financial benefit and changes hugely the ways in which beneficiaries can plan and live their lives. The beneficiary is freed from the necessity of rent or mortgage payments, or can rent the house out to offset his housing costs in another residence. Requiring that the beneficiary actually live in the house, taxing the financial benefit (including any eventual sale of the house) at 100 percent, so that only the sentimental benefit is realized, is entirely consistent with recognizing the relationship goods case for permitting the bequest. The fact, where it is one, that elite private schooling may be justified by appeal to family values in no way counts against governments' attempting to reconfigure the distribution of wages so that such schooling yields no earnings premium nor any of the other benefits that winners in the labor market tend currently to enjoy.

Alternatives, Discretion, and Spontaneity

A second response to the idea that familial relationship goods could justify bequests and educational choices is more complicated, raising issues far-reaching enough to warrant their own heading. It concerns the alternative means by which parents and children can realize familial relationship goods. Suppose a particular parent-child interaction is indeed, in the context, a vehicle for the realization of those goods. That is not enough to establish a right to that interaction, since there may be other means by which families can do as well, or well enough, in terms of "family values" but that are less disruptive of equality. Our reaction to a parent who appeals to the value of her familial relationship to ground a right to do something that confers substantial advantage on her child is to wonder whether she might not find other means of achieving her ends— means that are less detrimental to the interests of others.

We owe parents a set of means, or a range of options, by which to realize the goods that the family has to offer its members, but what means or options should go into that set is a complicated matter. Doubtless there are families for whom the bequest of property, or children's acquiring a particular accomplishment or attending a particular school, is indeed a means by which important familial relationship goods are realized. Were permitting such interactions the only way for families to realize those goods, that might indeed be sufficient to ground the corresponding right. Typically, however, there are, or can easily be, alternative mechanisms for their realization, mechanisms that conflict less with other valuable distributive goals, so the case for their protection is weak.

This observation raises a number of complexities. One concerns how we specify the interactions that require protection if familial relationship goods are to be realized. Our presenting bedtime stories as a paradigm case of a protected activity can now be seen to have begged a question about whether such stories are indeed "essential" or "necessary" for the familial relationship to yield its distinctive fruit. Are there no functional equivalents that might do as well in terms of family values while doing less to undermine fair equality of opportunity? What about lunchtime stories, or bedtime songs? Although, as our initial articulation of their paradigmatic status suggested, we suspect that there is indeed something special about a young child's bedtime, what our account actually identifies, at the fundamental level, is the case for protecting not any particular, tightly specified, kind of interaction but a harder-to-define set of options that between them afford families the space necessary for them to enjoy and realize the goods of family life. If it turned out that other activities could be substituted for bedtime stories, and that prohibition would result in no loss to the distinctive values that parents and children are able to derive from their relationship, then our account would have no grounds for objecting to their prevention.

But those are very big ifs. Any attempt to think seriously about the sphere of protected activity implied by our account has to bear in mind that different families will realize familial relationship goods through different kinds of interaction and shared activity, and, crucially, that healthy intimate relationships need to be spontaneous. While the family is not part of a "private sphere," a realm somehow beyond considerations of distributive justice and in principle immune to state action, the important kernel of truth in the privacy picture is that some degree of parental discretion is important, and that the monitoring and regulation of intimate relationships threaten to destroy the spontaneity on which much of their value depends. That is true whether the monitoring and regulation are carried out by the state or by the individuals themselves.

These points about parental discretion and spontaneity have to be treated carefully. Families are indeed different in ways that mean that successful parent-child relationships will tend to arise and be sustained through different kinds of interaction, or similar kinds of interaction focused on different particular activities. Still, their members can reasonably be expected to adapt, over time and within limits, some of which will be determined by other, not intrinsically familial, normative considerations (such as respect for parents' own views about what gives life value). Parents do not have a right to just that set of familial-relationship-good-realizing options that they would prefer, and some political actions aimed at shaping the mechanisms by which families realize the goods of family life may be legitimate. What parents have as a matter of right, however, at any particular time, is enough discretion over the detailed ways in which the parent-child relationship is conducted for it to be experienced as a spontaneous, loving, intimate sharing of lives. It's also important, for children's healthy moral and emotional development, that the parent should herself have some authority over what the child does, again within limits. The delivery, however conscientiously undertaken, of a sequence of state-prescribed bedtime stories is unlikely to fit the bill—or it will do that only if there are enough other arenas where children are subject to the loving authority of their parents and parents are free, both from external regulation and from continuous self-monitoring, to act on their natural, instinctive desire to share their lives and enthusiasms with their children.[10]

This claim about the value of spontaneity takes on extra significance in the light of our discussion in the previous section. We acknowledged there that a loving parent will be motivated quite generally to promote the well-being of her child, and that permitting her to act on that motivation would indeed realize goods distinctively made available by the familial relationship. But we argued that there was no right to act on that motivation *as long as there is ample space available for parents to realize the more important familial relationship goods, those that yield our primary account of the family's value.* Since successful intimate relationships require a good deal of relaxed spontaneity, and since a loving parent will be motivated spontaneously to promote her child's well-being, this italicized condition is important. A parent constantly monitoring herself to make sure that she does not act on her natural motivation to assist her children lest she do things—such as occasionally helping them with their homework— that may confer advantage on them is hardly going to be enjoying a relaxed relationship with them or making them feel special. To be sure, it is the *constancy* of the self-monitoring that is the problem, and there is a good deal more to be said about the kinds or degrees of self-monitoring that are and are not compatible with successful familial relationships. While we bracket that further discussion, it should at least be clear how our account gives parents a right to the spontaneous enjoyment of parent-child interactions—including those in which parents lovingly act to promote their children's well-being—even where such interactions will lead to the furthering of their child's interests in ways that would not be justified if parents were deliberately (i.e., nonspontaneously) aiming at them.

Unlike occasional helping with homework, however, the bequest of houses or other property, or the choice of elite private schools, is not the kind of child-favoring interaction the protection of which could be defended by appeal to the importance of spontaneous familial loving relationships.[11] As long as parents have an adequate set of means by which to realize those goods in other ways, they can hardly invoke the necessity of a space of unmonitored discretion to justify the inclusion of those particular, deliberate, choices within the set of familial interactions that they can claim as rights.

Beyond Fair Equality of Opportunity and Prima Facie Rights

In summary, then, parents have no right to confer advantage on their children but they do have the prima facie right to do things to, with, and for their children that may, in particular contexts, result in the conferral of competitive advantage. Children's interest in a familial relationship of the kind we have described is weighty enough for us to regard as prima facie rights the freedoms that parents need for that relationship to make its hugely important contribution to human well-being, which includes scope for discretion and spontaneity. Depending on the circumstances, particularly the way that the social environment is constructed, the exercise of those freedoms may result in some children's enjoying unfairly good, and others unfairly bad, prospects in the labor market—where "unfair" is defined relative to the principle of fair equality of opportunity. That principle gives us reason to reform the social environment—to decouple the interactions productive of our core familial relationship goods from the competitive advantage to which those interactions may give rise—but it would infringe parents' rights to attempt to promote that distributive ideal by denying them the freedom to engage in those interactions. Simply put, familial relationship goods are more important than fair equality of opportunity.

We must now acknowledge two kinds of incompleteness in the analysis. On the one hand, we have been talking only about prima facie rights. On the other hand, we have been discussing specifically the conflict between the family and fair equality of opportunity. As we explained in the introduction to part 2, prima facie rights may conflict with, and in particular circumstances be outweighed by, other prima facie rights. And, as we explained in chapter 2, fair equality of opportunity is a rather specific distributive principle. Suppose we are correct that children's interest in familial relationship goods is weighty enough to ground the prima facie parents' rights that we have derived from it; that interest is indeed sufficiently important to hold others under the corresponding prima facie duties. Suppose we are correct, also, in holding that the interest in those goods should win out in any conflict with the interest in fair equality of opportunity. What happens if *other* duties conflict with the duty to respect parents' rights, or if parents have duties to others that conflict with the prima facie rights that they have as parents? And what happens if family values can be realized only by the violation of distributive goals more urgent than fair equality of opportunity? Presenting our position on parents' rights as a claim about prima facie rights may have the advantage of corresponding to ordinary usage, but it leaves open the question of how they should be weighed against other moral considerations. And pitting the family against a conventional principle of fair equality of opportunity may yield a specific value conflict about which we can offer a relatively uncontroversial determinate judgment, but it is seriously misleading if understood as a description of the real-world situation and risks blinding us to the wider distributive questions.

When parents in affluent societies devote resources (time, energy, money) to their own children, they are not merely acting in ways that may deprive other children of fair equality of opportunity. They are acting in ways that leave others—adults as well as children, but let's just think of the children—in situations of dire need. That is true at the global level, where every day many are dying for lack of basic necessities, but not only at that level; even affluent societies like the United States and the United Kingdom allow some children to grow up in poverty. Suppose we have duties to assist those children, and suppose those duties are more urgent than at least some of the prima facie duties we owe our own children. In that case, many of the things that parents do to, with, or for their children, and which are indeed things to which they may claim a prima facie right, will simply be outweighed by the more pressing claims of others. Familial relationship goods are indeed extremely valuable, and we have emphasized how little, by way of advantage-conferral, can be justified by appeal to them. But it could still be that, given the extent of injustice in the world, or within our own societies, many of us would be overindulging in those goods even if we acted within the limits set down by our theory. Bedtime stories may indeed be crucial for familial relationship goods, but can parents really claim a right to read them in a world where their opportunity cost can be measured in the lives of others?

We cannot provide anything approaching a fully worked-out answer to these broader questions about our duties to others in an unjust world—not, alas, because we lack the space but because we do not have such an answer; judging the considerations at stake would require us to defend a general theory of global justice. But it is not our purpose, in this book, to persuade readers of any view of that kind. They will have their own opinions on these wider matters, and it would distract from our focus on the family if we sought to defend a particular position on, for example, the nature and weight of our duties to the global poor—or even to those living in poverty within our own societies. If correct, our theory of family values has radical implications even on rather modest or conventional understandings of the extent of our duties to others; it challenges much of what parents currently do to favor their children even at the level of prima facie rights and even when we are considering only the conflict with fair equality of opportunity. It challenges readers who think they have no duties to the global poor, for example, or who believe that their distributive duties to their fellow citizens can be discharged entirely by their supporting domestic policies that aim at fair equality of opportunity while respecting parents' rights. Placing our approach against the backdrop of more demanding distributive principles risks being a sidetrack or digression. Still, we cannot resist outlining a few ways in which our theory relates to that broader context, with implications for parents' rights all things considered (and not merely prima facie) to confer advantage on their children.

So far we have deliberately abstracted from the question of distributive justice among adults. We have been talking about the extent and nature of parents' rights to confer advantage on their children as if the only distributive issue raised by that conferral were the potential conflict with fair equality of opportunity. This can be thought of as focusing on the problem as entirely one of justice between children: what rights do parents have to act in ways that tilt the playing field for the next generation? But *that* is a good question even on the assumption that the resources available to parents are justly theirs. Whatever your preferred theory of distributive justice, imagine that all parents have exactly the resources—money, time, cultural capital—they should have. Perhaps all have the same, or perhaps there are inequalities but the inequalities are just because they have arisen in the right way in a context of just background conditions. (Perhaps, for example, they arose under conditions of fair equality of opportunity.) Even if parents have exactly what they can properly claim as their just entitlements, or just deserts (or however you want to think about the justice of the distribution of resources among parents), *still* there is an issue about what rights they have, qua parents, to use their justly held resources to confer advantage on their children. That, in fact, is what we have been discussing.

Readers who regard the current, actual, distribution of resources between parents as just will probably think that we have been focusing on the right—the relevant—issue. But some may suspect that, in the real world, many of those children who in fact enjoy unfairly superior prospects have parents who are themselves beneficiaries of an unjust distribution of resources. Perhaps their parents also had parents who were able to tilt the playing field in their favor, or perhaps the injustice came about by other means. In that case the question of their rights to confer advantage on their children looks rather different. Now we have to ask whether those parents have a duty to divest themselves of their unjust share of resources, and to direct them in ways that would most closely approximate their just distribution, before even thinking about their rights to use them to confer advantage on their children. Suppose that, in an otherwise just society, some large packet of resources that you knew to be stolen fell into your hands. Those resources aren't yours to devote to your children, or to devote to anything. They aren't yours at all. So it looks plausible that, whatever your prima facie rights qua parent, you have a more weighty duty to restore them to their rightful owners. (Of course, literally "restoring" the resources may not be appropriate or possible. Cultural capital, and, perhaps, time, cannot be returned in the same way that other more tangible and alienable forms of property can be. But the idea that one has a duty to compensate those who lack their just share of such resources still makes sense.)

Seeing parents' rights *stricto sensu*—that is, "all things considered" rather than prima facie—as depending on a broader account of one's distributive duties clearly opens up other questions. Philosophers working on distributive justice, for example, currently debate what members of rich countries owe to poor ones. Some think that the distributive duties that exist between members of states, or somewhat state-like schemes of cooperation, are different in kind from, and more extensive than, those that apply simply to people qua human beings. In their view, fellow citizens, or those cooperating within shared institutions, or those engaged in the shared project of collective self-rule, owe each other distinctively egalitarian forms of distributive justice. There is another big debate about the extent to which duties of distributive justice fall on individuals rather than being discharged primarily, and perhaps entirely, by collectives, via political institutions. Mere mention of these controversies may be enough to explain why we cannot provide a comprehensive treatment of how our theory of family values fits into a wider framework. Our best attempt at a general formulation of how it fits in is that our aim is to offer an account of the kind of parent-child interactions that are *susceptible to justification by appeal to the value of the family* and that must be permitted if people are to realize that value in their lives. We are happy to present our analysis in terms of prima facie rights, but offering any determinate judgments about what parents have the right to do, all things considered in the circumstances, to, with, and for their children would require us to bite more bullets than we have the appetite for, especially as we suspect that any biting that we might go in for would detract from the thrust of our argument.

Conclusion

We noted in chapter 2 that fair equality of opportunity is limited in various ways. One concerns the specification of the people between whom equality of opportunity is to pertain: it holds specifically that there should be equality of prospects between those of similar talents and willingness to use them. Another concerns what it is that those people should have equal opportunity for: the prospects are conceived in terms of positions in the occupational structure, and the kinds of rewards (money, opportunities for self-realization through work) that typically attach to them. But, as we also observed, it is perfectly coherent to endorse a distributive principle that applies much more broadly, to the opportunity for goods of a rather different kind. We might, for example, think about the distribution of opportunities for familial relationship goods themselves. So far this chapter has treated familial relationships as obstacles to the realization of egalitarian ideals. True, we have argued that the conflict between the family and equality is in fact much less stark than is commonly recognized; in our view, parents and children can enjoy healthy familial relationships, and parents can exercise all the rights needed for those relationships to make their distinctive contribution to well-being, without our having to tolerate anything like the kinds of inequalities of opportunity (for *anything*!) to which familial interactions currently give rise. But that argument, though important, still has family values on one side of the line and distributive considerations on the other. We conclude with the suggestion that the former be incorporated into the latter, as it were, by treating familial relationship goods as *distribuenda*: that is, as among the goods that people should have opportunities, perhaps equal opportunities, for.

Think of parents who attempt to raise their children in poverty in the United States. They cannot afford the more expensive housing that provides access to well-resourced schools in which their children can interact with a peer group with high aspirations, and most do not have the cultural capital that would enable them successfully to navigate the schools their children do attend. They may lack health insurance, and thus access to a primary care physician; their children are therefore more likely than others to miss school, or to be sick when at school. Their neighborhoods may be dangerous, or lack the concentration of social and cultural capital that contributes to children's and adults' ability to negotiate social institutions effectively.[12] To earn the income needed to compensate for these disadvantages, the parent may need to take two or more jobs, work long hours, perhaps with long travel times to and from work. Her attempt to serve her children's interests well thus militates against her ability to enjoy with them an intimate relationship of the kind that is often crucial to the children's emotional and moral development, quite apart from its value to the parent.

Our account of family values emphasizes adults' interest in acting as fiduciaries for children. But, of course, in the real world parenthood is for many a deep source of anxiety and frustration. There is great value in struggling with the challenges of parenthood, but family life contributes most to human flourishing only where those challenges can be met. Poverty and the multiple disadvantages that accompany it can easily create a microenvironment in which the task of parenting well is all but insuperable. Distributing opportunities for a more rewarding family life more equally requires the government to treat antipoverty measures as a matter of urgency.

Where the conventional framing pits parents' rights against equality, this alternative brings out a conflict between the (alleged) rights *of* parents and the right *to* parent, at least insofar as the latter is understood as a positive right to familial relationship goods. For those goods to be realized, it is not enough that adults have children to parent and that children get adults to parent them. Those are necessary conditions, but they are by no means sufficient. Also crucial is a social environment that allows the parent's relationship with her child to be about more than the struggle for life's necessities. Parents' rights, like "family values" generally, are often invoked against measures that mitigate inequality, such as estate or inheritance tax and the integration of schools.[13] On our analysis, it's not simply that that kind of rhetoric fails to withstand critical scrutiny. Worse, it fails to acknowledge the ways in which some parents' insistence on their supposed right to confer advantage on their children results in a failure to fulfill other parents'—and children's—genuine rights to familial relationship goods. Rather than conceiving them as obstacles to egalitarian goals, those who care about parents' rights and "family values" should be more specific about their content and worry more about those least able to enjoy them.

CHAPTER 6

Shaping Values

Where parents' right to confer advantage raises questions about distributions between families, their right to shape their children's values mainly raises issues concerning conflicts of interest within the family. Although third parties are also affected by the way that children are parented, and in ways that limit parents' rights to influence their children's beliefs and attitudes, the focus here will be on the need to protect children from excessive parental influence, while respecting the interest that both parents and children have in the right kind of parent-child relationship. The thrust of our argument will be to challenge widespread views about the extent of parents' rights to influence their children's emerging views of the world and what matters in it.

Many parents assume that they have the right to raise their children in ways that, while not perhaps guaranteeing that their children will become adults who subscribe to the parents' own beliefs and values, will more or less maximize the chances of their doing so. Some philosophers endorse that view. Recall, from chapter 1, Charles Fried's claim that the right to "form one's child's values, one's child's life plan" is grounded in the "basic right not to be interfered with in doing these things for oneself."[1] William Galston says that "the ability of parents to raise their children in a manner consistent with their deepest commitments is an essential element of expressive liberty."[2] As noted in the introduction to part 3, such views have already been subject to sustained critical attention, so both the topic addressed and the position argued for will be more familiar to those who have read the considerable academic literature on parents' rights with respect to their children's education. Still, in the wider culture it is widely held not only that parents may raise their children, at home, as members of particular faith or cultural communities but that they also have the right to have their children attend schools that will reinforce the message. Such claims are, indeed, written into key statements of international law: Article 26 of the UN

Universal Declaration of Human Rights subjugates the child's right to an education to parents' "prior right to choose the kind of education that shall be given to their children," while the International Covenant on Economic, Social and Cultural Rights asserts that parents have the liberty to "ensure the religious and moral education of their children in conformity with their own convictions."[3]

Our analysis of parents' right to shape children's values has the same basic structure as that of their right to confer advantage. In both cases, it is the core interest in a particular kind of relationship that yields the right to do some things—but not others—to, with, and for children. But while the parallels and structural similarities are important, so are the differences. Interactions leading to value shaping are more integral to family life, and, provided certain conditions are met, the implications of permitting such value shaping are less morally problematic. These two differences explain why our view on this topic is more conventional than that argued for in the previous chapter. Still, it is not entirely concessive. The "provided certain conditions are met" clause is important. Parents have a duty to do what they can to ensure not only that their children are properly equipped to function as citizens in a liberal democracy but also that they develop the capacity for autonomy. This part of the duty of care sets demanding limits on the way in which they may shape their children's values.

Shaping Values and Conferring Advantage

Rather than going back to square one and rehearsing the theoretical framework applied in the previous chapter, we shall just note the various ways in which the considerations discussed there arise when it comes to this second dimension of parents' rights. The basic idea is the same: parents have those rights over children that they need properly to discharge the parental role, on the understanding of that role which ties it to our conception of familial relationship goods. The rights they have to shape their children's values are derived from an account of the rights necessary for the kind of relationship we have described.

One way of seeing that we are covering the same terrain from a different angle is to recall the paradigm cases of parent-child interactions presented in the previous chapter as falling within the scope of parental rights: bedtime stories and having one's child accompany one to church (or a cricket match). Those were introduced as things that parents had the right to do with their children despite their tendency to confer advantage. But of course they are also mechanisms by which parents will tend to influence their children's values. Indeed, the second is a mechanism tending much more obviously and directly to that result than to the conferral of advantage. Moreover, our explanation of why parents had a right to have their children accompany them to church or cricket, despite possible conflict with fair equality of opportunity, appealed precisely to the claim that valuable familial relationships require parents to be free to engage with their children in ways that produce mutual identification and reflect the parents' judgments about what is valuable in life. It was the value-sharing aspect of such interactions that explained why parents had the right to engage in them. But there can be no value sharing without at least some degree of value shaping, so our argument in the previous chapter in effect appealed to the importance of value-shaping interactions to explain why parents had a right to them even where they tended to confer unfair advantage.

Before we get into the differences, it's worth recalling some of the similarities, identified in the introduction to part 3. One is that *some* shaping of values, like some conferring of advantage, is itself part of the parent's job. Not merely an inevitable by-product of, or accompaniment to, a successful familial relationship, it's what a parent's supposed to do, part of her role in overseeing her child's moral development. There will be other influences, of course, but instilling in children the virtue of honesty, or the ability to distinguish right from wrong, is a task primarily charged to parents and part of their fiduciary duty to their children (as well as being in the interests of third parties). But, for liberals, the kind of values that all children need to acquire as part of their moral development—the liberal virtues such as tolerance, respect for others, and what Rawls calls "a sense of justice"—are different from the kind that individuals may choose to endorse as a matter of private conscience, such as those attaching to full-blown religious systems or ethical doctrines.[4] We cannot here address difficult questions about the relations between the two. We note simply that the parental duty to oversee the moral development of her child is not the duty to instill a particular and comprehensive conception of how she should live her life; it is rather the duty to raise her as someone capable of moral judgment and, as we will see, judgment about how she should live her own life.

A second similarity is that, in both cases, we cannot respect parents' rights without giving parents the space to do what they have no right to. Just as parents given a good deal of discretion to conduct family life in their own way, itself required by our conception of familial relationship goods, may draw up and enact concerted advantage-conferral plans that far exceed what would be legitimate, so, of course, they may use that space and discretion to shape their children's values in ways that go beyond those that would be justified. The right to choose one's children's bedtime stories implies the opportunity to choose stories that will fill their heads with whatever parents want their heads to be filled with. In effect, then, there is a right to a sphere of discretionary authority within which the misuse of their rights may occur. Of course there are more or less subtle ways of monitoring, and the state can do some things to limit the opportunity for excessive value shaping while respecting the space and discretion that are needed for flourishing parent-child relationships.

Third, shaping one's children's values is, for most parents, itself a way of making their lives go better. Whether endorsing a particular belief system is held to be intrinsically valuable or the likely means to other forms of benefit, parents' attempts to influence their children's values are often motivated by the simple desire that their children's lives should go better than they otherwise would. This goes deeper than the observation that the same interactions could be seen under both aspects—as examples of interactions tending, as a matter of empirical fact, both to confer advantage and to shape values. What motivates parents when they aim to influence their children's values is, often, precisely a concern to benefit them.

This last point brings out clearly an unusual, and for some doubtless counterintuitive, feature of our theory. We emphasize the importance of those interactions between parent and child that allow that relationship to play its unique and very special role in people's lives. While acknowledging that there is a distinctive value to having one's life improved by a loving parent, rather than by a stranger or one's fellow citizens generally, we have insisted that that value is secondary and parasitic: secondary in being simply less important, and parasitic in that it arises only as a derivative good made possible by the loving parent-child relationship itself.[5] Value sharing, and hence value shaping, by contrast, lie close to the heart of that relationship. It is important that the parent shares herself with her child. That sharing should not be complete or entire; there are going to be *some* things about themselves that parents should try to withhold from their children. But a close, loving relationship will surely involve parents' honestly revealing their enthusiasms and aversions, their sense of what matters in life and what is trivial. So value-shaping interactions undertaken by parents in order to benefit their children may be indefensible under that description while being justified on the rather different grounds that they are contributing to a healthy, loving relationship between parent and child. This is somewhat paradoxical: if parents were doing only what they thought of themselves as doing—benefiting their children by increasing their chances of living a good life—then they might have no right to do it; but what they are also doing, and in our theory's terms what they are more importantly doing, is sharing themselves with their children, and *that* they do have a right to. The paradox is sharpened by our claim that parents' sharing themselves with their children is itself a way of benefiting those children, albeit specifically with respect to familial relationship goods.

This illustrates perhaps the main way that our theory implies a deep reevaluation of the point or purpose of familial relationships. Where parents often see their goal as promoting their children's well-being, by (almost) whatever means and with little or no regard to the interests of others, our conception of familial relationship goods puts the justificatory weight on the parent-child relationship itself. Parenting is about having a relationship of the right kind with one's child. Because people's values are central to who they are, because successful parenting requires parents to share themselves with their children, and because value sharing implies at least some degree of value shaping, value shaping is an inherent part of that kind of relationship. Of course, that kind of relationship also requires children to feel that their parents regard them as special, and care more about them than they do about other people's children. But, except for cases covered by the duty of care as discussed in the previous chapter, it does not, we claim, require parents to act on their natural and loving motivation generally to benefit their children where doing so will conflict with other children's interest in fair equality of opportunity.

Cases where the deliberate shaping of values is regarded by the parent as part of the duty of care are particularly difficult. Imagine a devout religious believer who thinks that her child will be condemned to eternal damnation if she is not raised in the true faith. The parent will take herself to be duty-bound to protect her child from that fate worse than death. Her duty of care, as she understands it, will require her to protect her child from any socializing influence that may reduce the chances of the child's coming to endorse the damnation-avoiding beliefs. Here we may hit bedrock disagreement between our, avowedly liberal, theory and the religious doctrine avowed by the parent. On our view, the parent is making a mistake about the content of her duty of care. She is misidentifying her child's true interests. She owes her child an upbringing that will equip him to judge for himself independently how to live his life—the child is a separate person, and is owed the opportunity to make his own judgments.

The Centrality of Value-Shaping Interactions to Familial Relationships

Putting that case to one side, we have now arrived at the first reason why our view on parents' rights to shape their children's values is more permissive than that on their rights to confer advantage. The kinds of interaction that lead to the shaping of children's values by parents are integral to family life, on our conception of it, because they are central to a successful parent-child relationship. We are not now talking about the shaping of the kind of value, such as a sense of justice, that is explicitly part of the parent's job description (on our understanding of what that is). The issue here rather concerns parents' engaging with their children in ways likely to influence their holding of particular, perhaps more controversial or comprehensive, views about what's good and bad. Familial relationship goods inevitably depend for their realization on interactions that will tend to have those effects too. This is so in various ways.

Some will arise as an unintended by-product simply of parents being themselves in their relationships with their children, and exercising in a more or less unreflective and personal way their sphere of discretion over the particular ways in which they interact with them. Of course there are limits: a parent who swears a lot in conversations with his friends may judge that some self-monitoring of his vocabulary is appropriate when around his children, even if only to save him or the child from embarrassment. (A friend once confessed that his son's third and fourth words, after "dog" and "duck," were "fucking buttons.") To be oneself is to respond at least somewhat spontaneously to situations and to express oneself through unthinking choices about how to spend time with one's children. People being themselves enthuse about things they value and denigrate things they detest. If a celebrity you think abhorrent comes on the TV news, a natural and spontaneous reaction may well reveal your abhorrence. Indeed, any decision about what to watch on TV in the first place, or whether to watch TV at all, or what to chat about over meals, or what books to read at bedtime, has some influence on children's views about what matters in the world. Or if, on a family trip, you pass an advertisement for a product that you judge absurdly frivolous, or that is selling it in an inappropriately sexual way, you must feel free to express your views. The idea that parents should constantly monitor themselves in their relations with their children in order to screen out anything that might have any influence on their children's emerging values is ludicrous. It would risk distancing them, creating artifice in the relationship, and depriving their children of the possibility of the warm, spontaneous, genuine relationship that they need. The spontaneous sharing with their children of at least some of who parents really are is crucial to healthy family life; that sharing is bound to result in some shaping of values.

Another, closely connected but analytically distinct, mechanism by which parents will tend to influence their children, and one to which our theory also implies they have a right, follows from our claim that loving parents will be motivated quite generally to promote their children's well-being. Our approach gives parents the right to a degree of unmonitored and spontaneous interaction with their children within which they might find themselves doing things, such as helping with homework, that they would not have a right to do if that were the result of a deliberate decision. Since, as we have said, much shaping of values is conceived by parents precisely as a way of benefiting their children—they think their children's lives will go better just because they have a proper understanding of what matters in life—that same consideration will grant parents some space spontaneously to shape their children's values. A loving parent who thinks that her child's life will benefit from a love of music, or of basketball, is bound to find herself nudging her in that direction simply because of her automatic and natural tendency to relate to her child in ways that she thinks will be good for her. The same applies to the natural tendency to denigrate, and unthinkingly steer her away from, bad influences.

Both previous cases put spontaneity center stage. The emphasis was on the children's interest in familial relationships in which parents can do things to, with, and for their children without undue reflection or deliberation. But our account also leaves some room for the deliberate shaping of values: that is, interactions undertaken with the aim of influencing the values that one's children will come to hold. When a Christian and cricket-loving parent takes his daughter to a cricket match, or to church, that is not usually an unthinking and automatic sharing of self between parent and child. It is more likely a deliberate decision to introduce the child to an activity, or a worldview, that the parent judges valuable. As long as that kind of deliberate shaping of values is needed for a close relationship between parent and child, and as long as it is done in a way that is consistent with the duty to develop the child's capacity for autonomy, then, on our account, parents have a right to engage in it. The shaping of values is deliberate, not an unintended by-product of spontaneity. But the shaping of values is itself, under this aspect, a means to a familial relationship of the kind that lies at the heart of our theory.

We are talking now about the right to seek deliberately to influence one's children in ways conducive to the enjoyment, and maintenance, of the familial relationship. In contrast to the case of conferring advantage, some deliberate shaping of values is justified precisely because it promotes or supports that kind of relationship. In order to have and sustain an intimate relationship with someone else, one must not only spend a good deal of time with the person; one must also have some interests and values in common with her. It is difficult to be precise about exactly how much needs to be shared, but it is easy to see why something must be shared. One can readily imagine intimacy despite people's having different religious beliefs, or different intellectual interests, or different aesthetic or sporting tastes, but without *some* overlap in interests and *some* overlap in values it is hard to for intimacy to have a basis. This applies both immediately, as it were, and in the longer term. Children have an interest in having a continued intimate relationship with their parents into adulthood. So that is a reason for a parent to increase the likelihood that he and his child will continue to have shared interests, and to value the same kind of thing, throughout the childhood and adulthood of the child.

This argument runs through the claim that parents have the right deliberately to act in ways likely to foster some degree of shared values. But it does *not* mean parents have the right that those values be the parents' own values. There is, to be sure, a crucial asymmetry between parent and child: in the earliest years, at least, it must be the parent who supplies the values. Moreover, since adults' values are less plastic than children's, the interest of both parent and child in a close relationship that extends into the child's adulthood is another ground for some degree of priority to the parent. The parent already has views about what she thinks matters in life, whereas the child is just learning to make such judgments. But these considerations enter at a secondary, derivative level, as opposed to the fundamental privileging of the parent's values that one finds in Fried's and Galston's claims about parents rights.[6]

This has implications for parents' rights in the relationship as the child develops and begins to become her own person. In later years the child will come to have her own interests and values, and any healthy intimate relationship involves give-and-take—some interests come from one, others from the other. Parents' values may be less plastic than children's, but they are by no means set in stone, and parents differ in their willingness to adapt to their children's emerging interests. A parent might have no interest at all in hip-hop music, but might succeed in fostering such an interest when his child becomes a hip-hop enthusiast or musician. He might be able to watch his child play soccer only under sufferance, but might endeavor really to learn about, and come to share, her interest in tortoises, or in high fashion. The parent's judgments have no deep priority, no fundamental claim to be the ones that are shared and, as shared, to be those shaping the relationship. In fact, we suspect that after the child has passed certain developmental landmarks—certainly by the age of ten or so—if the shared interests *all* originate from the parent, this is an indicator of something wrong, either because the child is too slavishly in thrall to the parent, or because the parent is too domineering within the relationship. Many parents, we would guess, will struggle to overcome their reluctance to develop new interests when doing so is part of maintaining a connection with their growing children, but, on our account, they have no justification for not trying—no right that the relationship be conducted on their terms.[7]

Of course, hip-hop, soccer, tortoises, and fashion may seem relatively trivial examples. Sometimes children will break with their parents' values in more serious ways: for example, by rejecting their cultural heritage or religion, or by adopting a religious worldview that is alien to their secular parents. Indeed, on our account of the duty of care, the parent is obliged to do what she can to ensure that her child has the capacity to do just that—to decide for herself how she is to live her life. We have two observations about that kind of case. One is simply that, in our view, a parent should be able to sustain a successful relationship without any *particular* shared interest or values. The parent who cuts off a child for marrying out, or for refraining from joining the military, or for entering a religious order, or for apostasy, or for becoming a corporate lawyer, fails as a parent. She has misunderstood her role, an important element of which was to attend to the development of her child's capacities to decide to do that kind of thing. Their familial lives together should not have been so focused on a single element, however important to the parent, that its rejection leaves nothing for parents and children to share, nothing to sustain the relationship in a different, perhaps inevitably more distant, but nonetheless still loving way.

The other observation is that the possibility of children's rejecting their parents' deepest value commitments is another reason why parents have the right deliberately to expose their children to those commitments. This may seem paradoxical, but as long as the autonomy duty is indeed discharged—and our analysis in this section assumes that condition is satisfied—it is better, in terms of familial relationship goods, for children to reject their parents' values from a position of experience and understanding of what those values are than to do so out of ignorance. It seems likely that, where the child *does* break from the parent's values, the parent-child relationship has a better chance of being sustained, and, when it is, sustained in a meaningful way, if child and parent are in a position at least to appreciate the other's point of view, to understand where the other is coming from. In the child's case, that can happen only if the parent has indeed made sure that the child has a real appreciation of how she lives her life and how she sees the world.

This raises questions about the role of the family in promoting a sense of continuity and shared identity across many generations. Chapters 3 and 4 discussed, and criticized, the view that genetic continuity is important, even to the particular, concrete relationship between parent and child, and we reject conceptions of the family that appeal to its role in facilitating multigenerational continuity of that kind. But cultural connectedness across generations is different. The family values argument for allowing parents some room to act on their hope that their children will come to share their view of the world, because familial relationships are likely to go better where parents are afforded that room, has implications for the multigenerational case. Many parents do not see the raising of their children in a particular religion or culture as simply a matter of sharing with their children something that is important to them. From their perspective, our analysis will seem doubly misguided. On the one hand, as already discussed, many would reject our emphasis on the *sharing* of a worldview between parents and children and see the weight we put on close familial relationships as mislocating the values at stake. *That's* not why they want to raise their children as Catholics, or Muslims, or atheists. On the other hand, many would deny also the importance we attach specifically to sharing *between parents and children*, which may seem a rather shortsighted perspective. What matters, for many, is the transmission of a way of life that has been endorsed and enacted by their family over many generations. To frame that in terms of the value of particular parent-child relationships is, again, to miss the point.

To respond properly to this charge of short-sightedness, we need to put some pressure on the question of what exactly is being claimed about the distinctively familial aspect of cultural continuity over time. Suppose it is valuable for human beings to feel connected to previous generations, and to future generations. Is it important that this sense of connection be realized *via* the vehicle of the family? Adults do not need to parent children in order to regard themselves as possessing crucial kinds of continuity with future generations. Similarly, children raised in state-run institutions could clearly be brought up to understand their own lives as critically connected to those of forefathers and descendants understood in a broader sense; much patriotic education involves precisely a widening of the sense of connection beyond children's own familial lines. Indeed, we could go further, and query the significance of particularity altogether. Is it important that the connection be felt with particular others, such as fellow nationals or coreligionists, rather than with, say, the entire human species? What would be lost if children were raised to think of themselves as intergenerationally connected, in both directions, to human beings as such?

To keep things manageable, let's put to one side the latter, more radical, suggestion and, granting the value of continuity with others more particular than the human species, focus on the value of those others' being members of one's family—in the extended sense of "family" that takes it beyond the immediate parent-child dyad that bears so much weight in our account. Granted that communes or monasteries or state institutions *could* raise children to have a strong sense of connectedness with past and future generations within particular ethnic, cultural, religious, or national communities, the question is whether anything valuable would be lost under such arrangements, compared with the world, like our own, in which, for many, parent-child relationships are an important medium of that sense. Is there a particular and distinctive value to being connected to previous and future generations through one's relationship with one's parent or child, and his relationship with his parent or child, and so on? If so, that would suggest that there is a familial relationship good realized when one is connected to the past and future *via one's family*, which would be at least the beginning of an argument for parents' having the right to raise their children in their familial culture.

We can think of two ways that argument might go. Both risk seeming reductive, since they insist on cashing out the value of the multigenerational connection in terms of concrete relationships between people who actually know each other. Neither concedes that there is a value to a sense of connection with one's great-great-grandparents, for example, that depends on the specific thought that one is part of the same multigenerational entity, or participants in the same multigenerational project. Nonetheless, both do give a genuine significance to the multigenerational aspect of familial relationships, even on our understanding of "familial," and acknowledge that there are distinctively familial relationship goods likely to be realized when parents are free to influence their children's values in ways that are at least somewhat continuous with the way the parents were influenced by *their* parents, and so on.

First, a relationship between parent and child is likely to be closer, deeper, and more enduring if it is developed and sustained through interactions that are informed by that parent's relationship with his parent. The same is true of his parent's relationship with his parent. And so on. Here the good, though realized by mechanisms that will certainly tend to the reproduction of values across many generations and may indeed lead to a sense of the family's having a continuing identity over those generations, is realized in the individual parent-child relationship. That relationship, we believe, takes on a distinctive character if it is informed by the parent's own upbringing, relationship with her parent's culture, and so on. When a child's father lulls her to sleep with the Gilbert and Sullivan songs, or hymns, or culturally laden fairy tales, with which his mother lulled him to sleep, that is a kind of deep or elemental sharing of parent with child that is likely to enrich their relationship. The child will grow up knowing his father not only for who he is now but for how he was as a child, and thus, in part, for how he got to be the way he is. The same applies when the father, replicating his own childhood experiences with his parents, takes his child to cricket, or to the mosque, or on country walks. The point is not that there is any particular value to doing the same kind of thing as one's never-known parents' parents' parents and their never-known parents and grandparents and so on— whether that be worshipping the same God, eating the same food, following the same sports, or reading the same books. The distinctively familial relationship good inheres entirely in the character of the actual, concrete relationship between individual parent and child. Still, there is indeed a distinctive interest in parents' being free to interact with their children in ways that will tend to shape their values not merely in ways informed by their own, but in ways informed by their own value-shaping interactions with their parents. Allowing parents that freedom will yield a tendency for families to share a sense of continuous identity across more than two generations.

But, second, we must also take into account the impact on relationships between members of the extended family. Our account gives a central role to the relationships between parents and children—indeed we have so far formulated all familial relationship goods in terms of the goods made possible specifically by that relationship—but we do not deny that relationships with grandparents, with uncles and aunts, and with cousins, and sometimes with great-grandparents, can also make a distinctively familial, albeit usually less weighty, contribution to people's well-being. By "distinctively familial," we mean analytically to isolate that aspect of the value of the relationship that derives specifically from the fact that such members of the extended family are connected to one another *via parent-child relationships*. Your aunt is your parent's parent's daughter.[8] Your first cousin is your parent's parent's child's child. Of course, your aunt or cousin may also be your best friend, and you may think of her primarily, perhaps entirely, as that. The value of relationships between members of extended families need not consist solely in the familial aspect; in some cases the familial dimension—the fact that the two people in question are connected via a web of parent-child relationships—is the least important thing about it. But the question now is whether factoring in extended familial relationships has any implications for the question of parents' interest in shaping, and hence potentially their right to shape, children's values in ways that reflect a shared family culture extending across many generations.

That it does is most easily seen in the case of relationships between children and grandparents. We are not talking now about those unusual cases where what are conventionally regarded as a child's grandparents in fact play the role of her parents; in such scenarios, the fact that the person parenting the child also parented her parent complicates matters. But in the standard, three-generational case of grandparent-parent-child, it seems obvious that, other things equal, the relationship between grandparent and child will be richer and deeper if the parent has raised his child in ways informed by the values and beliefs that in turn informed his own upbringing. The gain here is not to the parent-child relationship but to the grandparent-child relationship. And something similar, albeit often more attenuated, applies to other relationships with members of one's extended family. Cousins who have been brought up in ways that reflect their parents', and their grandparents', understandings of what matters in life, or perhaps simply of what is fun in life, will tend to understand each other better, will have the basis of a more substantial and affectionate relationship, than cousins whose parents have worked hard to shield their children from influence by a sense of the family's identity across generations. As before, this seems likely even in relationships between cousins some of whom have explicitly rejected the values and beliefs in which they were raised. The child raised as a practicing Jew who, as an adult, marries out and gives up all the traditions and rituals in which she was raised is in a better position to understand her observant cousins, and will have a deeper sense of who those cousins are, than the child whose parents raised her to be ignorant of her family's cultural and religious heritage. Whether the relationships with members of the extended family do in fact survive that kind of rejection is a further question. But at least there will be a continuing sense of something that was shared, if only in childhood, that has the potential to enrich those relationships if there is the will to continue them.

In these various ways, then, being connected to past and future generations via familial relationships does indeed seem to make possible distinctive goods in people's lives. The value, on our account, lies entirely in the impact on people's concrete relationships with actual other people. This is not the idea that there is value in families' existing as multigenerational entities, bequeathing and inheriting a distinctive set of values. What's good about parents' being free to shape their children's values is cashed out entirely in terms of goods accruing to particular individuals in their actual relationships with other individuals. This account of the value of intergenerational continuity within families will doubtless be too reductive for many readers. Still, it is sturdy enough to explain why parents can appeal to familial relationship goods to justify conducting their relationships with their children in ways informed by a sense of family history and, where appropriate, of the family's cultural or religious identity over time.

Cultural Reproduction and the Reproduction of Inequality

Early in the chapter we noted two reasons why our account of parents' rights to shape their children's values is more permissive than that of their rights to confer advantage on them. The previous section explained how the kinds of interaction that lead to value shaping are more worthy of protection. But the costs of such interactions are also less weighty. Compared to conferring advantage, and with two provisos in the form of the duty to facilitate the child's prospective autonomy and the relevant duties to third parties, there is simply less reason for parents *not* to shape their children's values. When parents act in ways that confer advantage on their children, they are undermining other children's claim to fair equality of opportunity. When they act in ways that shape their children's values, their actions need not have any adverse consequences for anybody.

Observing the way families currently operate, we can think of them as vehicles for two analytically distinct kinds of intergenerational transmission. On the one hand, children tend to end up in positions in the stratification system—in the distribution of benefits and burdens—similar to those of their parents. The association between the distributive position of parents and children is far from perfect, of course, since there is some social mobility, but it is substantial. Let's call the propensity of parent-child interactions to generate that kind of association their tendency to result in the intergenerational reproduction of *inequality*. On the other hand, children tend to end up endorsing values and beliefs somewhat similar to those of their parents. Again, the association between parent and child is far from perfect: children sometimes reject their parents' values outright, and they often adapt and adjust them somewhat. But it is considerable. Let's call the propensity of parent-child interactions to generate that kind of association their tendency to result in the intergenerational reproduction of *culture*. Nearly everybody thinks that the intergenerational reproduction of inequality raises a normative problem—even those who defend parents' rights to confer advantage on their children rarely deny that. But few people think the intergenerational reproduction of culture is similarly problematic. What's *bad* about the fact that there's an association between parents' and children's place in the distribution of values or beliefs?

Some mechanisms by which that association is generated may, of course, have bad aspects. If parents transmitted their values to their children by making them take value-determining pills, bypassing all capacity for autonomous judgment, that would be bad. (It would be bad even if they didn't make them take such pills, but merely offered them!) If they achieved that outcome by denying their children access to alternatives (e.g., perhaps, through some kinds of homeschooling), or by taking advantage of their hugely privileged position with respect to the child's emotional needs (e.g., using the sanction of withheld intimacy and affection), that would be bad too. The autonomy proviso, to be discussed shortly, addresses such concerns. There might also be things that are bad about the segregation of a society into overly distinct, familially transmitted, cultures. A concern for civic integration and a common culture may yield reason to mitigate the intergenerational transmission of familial pluralism. And, of course, some of the content of the values and beliefs that are being transmitted intergenerationally may be bad. There are reasons to deny parents the freedom to raise their children in a family culture of thievery, or of corruption or manipulation of democratic political processes. But these are not objections to intergenerational association as such. Such cases aside, it may be hard to see what is troubling about parents' deliberately shaping their children's values.

The intrafamilial intergenerational transmission of culture is in this respect very different from the intrafamilial intergenerational transmission of advantage. Recall, from the previous chapter, our claim that, where a parent-child interaction to which parents could claim a right by appeal to the interest in familial relationship goods resulted in the conferral of advantage (to which, on our analysis, they have no right), it would be justified for the state to tax that advantage. It may not, in practice, be possible for the benefit to be taxed, but, as a matter of principle, the disruption to equality could properly be neutralized. There is nothing analogous to this in the current case—no adverse consequences for others follow simply from the fact of parents' raising their children in ways that tend to result in those children's sharing their view of the world. Provided that the considerations discussed in the previous paragraph are not in play—a very hefty proviso—the state should not normally seek to reduce parents' influence over their children's values. After all, children's values are going to be shaped willy-nilly, by some complex set of agents with whom they interact, directly or indirectly (e.g., through the media). It's not as if the default is *no* shaping of children's values. As long as they are simultaneously discharging their duties to their children and third parties, we see no harm in their playing an important role in that process. Indeed, we have explained why there is considerable value in their playing precisely such a role.

Still, deliberately shaping other people's values is always potentially problematic—whether they are children or adults—and it is especially so when one stands in such an influential position as parents do with respect to their children. This remains the case even when the autonomy condition, and duties to third parties, are satisfied. The autonomy condition does not require that children should have an entirely "open future";[9] even where that condition is met, children will be more likely to lead some lives than others. So there are questions both about why it can be legitimate for anybody intentionally to shape their values and, if that can be answered, why it should be their parents in particular who get to play such an important role in the process.[10] Our account of its significance for familial relationship goods is supposed to answer those questions.

The Duty to Facilitate Autonomy

We have claimed that parents have only those rights that it is in their children's interests for them to have. We have also claimed that children have an interest in the development of their capacities for considered and reflective judgment. They are different, separate, people from their parents, and they should become able to make independent judgments about which values are to guide them, and should, within limits, be able to act on those judgments. They have an interest, in other words, in becoming autonomous. Here we explain what autonomy is, and why developing it is so valuable. Our aim is not to offer an original or distinctive account, but to show that some of the features found in most accounts are important enough that its development should be an important goal of a child's upbringing.[11]

Immanuel Kant contrasts autonomy with heteronomy. A person acts autonomously when she acts on laws or rules that she has given to herself; when she acts under compulsion, whether from another person, or driven by her physical desires, she acts heteronomously. (Kant's account of autonomy is accompanied by a controversial metaphysical theory, but the usefulness of the contrast does not depend on one's endorsing that.) There is no particular value in being able to make and act on judgments different from those of one's community or one's parents, if those judgments are determined either by somebody else again, or by desires over which one has no control. The value is in being able to make independent and critical judgments about what one values, and how to act on those judgments in the world. This requires knowledge of what different values one might hold, and how one might reason concerning them, as well as some degree of strategic knowledge of how different actions might work out in specific circumstances, and the ability to understand connections between those actions, their consequences, and the value judgments that have informed them.

On most conceptions of autonomy at least the following kinds of belief and preference formation are potentially problematic: preferences and beliefs formed where someone deliberately manipulates an agent by providing false information about the options available or costs and benefits attached to the options; preferences or beliefs unconsciously adapted to apparently unchangeable circumstances (as in the fabled case of the fox who, finding the delicious-looking grapes out of reach, declares them sour); preferences deliberately accommodating unjust background conditions (as in the case of the slave who, believing himself unable to alter his condition, fosters a stoical attitude).[12] Some of these processes are somewhat present in each of our lives. However, teachable skills, combined with the right emotional traits and dispositions, can enable us to avoid or overcome many instances of them. Broadly speaking, the capacities involved in critical reflection help us to live autonomously. We can learn methods for evaluating the truth and falsehood, or relative probability, of various claims about the world. We can be taught, for example, the difference between anecdotal and statistical evidence, and the differences in their reliability. We can avoid manipulation, to some extent, by ensuring that we have the developed ability to investigate truth claims with somewhat reliable tools, on our own. We can learn that adaptive and accommodating preference formations happen, and that one can sometimes avoid them by stepping back from one's commitments and reflecting on how they were formed.

Processes of preference and belief formation are *potentially* problematic. But many of our commitments must be formed nonautonomously. Many of our most deeply held beliefs were selected not through careful and rational weighing of reasons, but by internalizing impressions, by trusting the testimony of others, or our intuitions or hunches, or through participating in a community of belief and practice and (often unconsciously) internalizing shared commitments. A theory of autonomy that impugned all such beliefs or commitments would make autonomy a rare and hard-to-attain condition. What makes these processes *actually* problematic is agents' inability to reflect on and revise them using their capacity for independent judgment; it is not the genesis of one's beliefs and commitments that tells us whether they are autonomous, but their relationship with one's current judgment. Commitments generated by nonautonomous processes become autonomous when the agent reflects on them with an appropriate degree of careful critical attention: when she is able, for example, to detect inconsistencies among her beliefs, and is able to compare her own commitments with those of others, critically reflecting on the reasons for and against revising them.

This makes it sound like a purely cognitive matter, a question of exercising rationality in solving puzzles. But autonomy requires certain emotional traits as well. Being able to subject one's commitments to scrutiny in a way that might lead to reasonable revision and subsequent action requires some self-confidence, but not so much that one is overconfident about one's prior judgments. One also needs a certain amount of courage, the ability and willingness to scrutinize one's first "gut" reactions as well as the judgments and habits of those one is close to, especially those who have exerted a great deal of influence in shaping one's commitments and habits. One must be able to listen to, and hear, criticism, but not be overwhelmed by it. Aligning one's actions with one's judgments can require the capacity to conquer some of one's emotional reactions. One might, for example, judge that homosexuality is morally innocent, and therefore that one should be open to friendship with someone one knows to be gay, but still be repulsed by thoughts of homosexual practices or inhibited by the knowledge that one's community abhors them. It is not rationality, or any cognitive trait, but a certain kind of emotional strength that enables one either to eliminate such revulsion or inhibitions or to accept or offer friendship while they remain. Finally, one needs some level of sensitivity to when reflection is important, when it is valuable, when it is unimportant, and when it is futile. Someone who is constantly engaged in reflection, or in whom reflection is too easily triggered, is inhibited from acting on her judgments: the autonomous person understands that rational reflection does not resolve everything and has quite limited power with respect to some commitments (whom to love, for example).[13]

Why is autonomy important? The case is overdetermined, but it's worth being clear that our arguments do not imply that it is necessary for someone to be autonomous in order for her to have a successful life. There have been and still are societies that discourage autonomy with respect to certain kinds of commitment, and it is implausible that nobody in those societies has enjoyed a flourishing life, or even that the only people who have were those lucky enough to have developed the relevant skills and traits despite society's influence. Some people, even in complex modern societies, are lucky enough to be raised in communities of practice in which they can live lives that they can endorse without alienation, and flourish despite not having reflected much about their deep commitments.

As we noted in chapter 3, the arguments break down into two main kinds. Some emphasize autonomy's value for the well-being of the autonomous agent, while others stress the importance of people's being authors of their own lives independently of its effects on their well-being.

We can distinguish two plausible reasons why autonomy tends to be important for well-being. The first appeals to the complexity of the kinds of societies we live in, the rapidity of change, and the dangers to the person of being inflexible in response to those changes. We need to be able to reflect in response to changes in our environment, in order to be able to make the kinds of judgments and choices that will be better rather than worse for us. As Joseph Raz puts it:

> fast changing technologies and free movement of labour . . . call for an ability to cope with changing technological, economic and social conditions, for an ability to adjust, to acquire new skills, to move from one subculture to another, to come to terms with new scientific and moral views.[14]

This flexibility in the face of complexity and change requires both the cognitive skills and the dispositions we have described. Autonomy is not, for all people, a necessary condition of their well-being, but it improves the chances that one's life will go well.

The second focuses on the fact that people vary considerably in their basic constitutions and personalities. Conceptions of the good that can be endorsed and followed without alienation by some people may clash with the needs of others. Different ways of life elevate different virtues, and some children are ill constituted to develop the particular virtues endorsed by their parents. Some persons' constitutions will not allow them to live some ways of life "from the inside."[15] To give a stark example, some people experience their sexuality as fixed. A homosexual who experiences his homosexuality as unchangeable simply cannot live, from the inside, a way of life that requires heterosexual marriage. He will be alienated: it may be a very good way of life, but it is not one that *he* can endorse, and is therefore not one that *he* can live well. Similarly, some religious ways of life that impose on women the duties of modesty and fidelity in marriage conflict with the natures of some women who are raised in those religions. Again, autonomy is not a necessary condition of being able to find a way of life that fits with one's constitution, but it is extremely important for those not lucky enough to be raised within a way of life that fits them well.[16]

The second kind of argument for valuing autonomy claims that there is independent value to being an author of one's own life, making one's own choices and judgments independently, which is not reducible to its contribution to one's well-being. This is the thought that there is an interest in dignity, which played a role in our earlier discussions of rights and of agency. Suppose a parent has a pill that will, if administered to his daughter, guarantee that she will not only follow his religion but also be so constituted as to flourish doing so—and flourish as much as anybody who adopted the religion autonomously. Is it permissible for him to administer the pill? If not, that must be because there is a value to a person's living a life as a result of evaluating the reasons in favor of living that kind of life, knowing at least some alternatives. Is it, truly, her own life, if she does not?

There are risks, as well as benefits, to becoming autonomous. One may end up having a sense of responsibility for one's life that, if it goes badly, makes it feel worse. Some argue, too, that autonomy can endanger involvement in very closely tied communities of practice. Both may be true. Our conjecture is that this risk is one worth taking because it makes it much more likely that one's life will go well, and makes that life one's own.

We have argued that autonomy is important enough to hold parents under a duty that is a condition on their having the right to parent. But what, exactly, does that duty consist in? One thought would be that parents have the duty to ensure that the child becomes autonomous. But no parent can *guarantee* the child's prospective autonomy. Social institutions other than the family cooperate with or frustrate parental efforts to serve a child's interests, and the interest in autonomy is no different from others in this respect. A public culture that emphasizes instant gratification, and in which large sums are spent promoting materialism and shaping teens' and young adults' perspectives on sex, places considerable demands on parents. Given the difficulty of the task, parents should *try to ensure* that their children become autonomous. This formulation implies that the pursuit of the child's prospective autonomy must be quite self-conscious, but allows that a parent may fulfill her duty even though, owing to factors outside her control, her child does not in fact become autonomous. It also leaves open just how much the parent should try to ensure autonomy: we cannot be precise about this because how much the parent should try depends on how much the child's other interests are threatened.

The social environment within which a parent raises a child can make it impossible to meet all the child's interests. In such circumstances the responsible parent will do a triage among the child's interests, and may well judge that she should neglect the interest in autonomy. To give a stylized example, suppose that a parent in a poor area in an inner city has the choice between sending her child to a local religious school, the walk to which is short and safe, or a multicultural school that is more distant and the walk to which involves passing through an area in which gunfire is frequently heard. The parent may consider the child's physical safety to be at a premium, and compromise an opportunity to expand her child's horizons for that reason. This is quite different from a case in which the parent is predisposed against the child's prospective autonomy, even if the end result is the same.

Religious and Secular Upbringings

Parents have the rights over children that it is in their children's interests for them to have. *Some* shaping of the child's values is an inevitable result of a healthy intimate relationship and the proper exercise of those parental rights. But the child's interest in autonomy means that parents do not have the right to shape values in ways that prevent the child from becoming autonomous.

What does this mean for religious parents? May they raise their children as members of their religion? Matthew Clayton argues that they may not, drawing a parallel between the situation of parents vis-à-vis their children, and the situation of the state vis-à-vis its citizens. The state is, he thinks, subject to Rawls's requirement of liberal legitimacy:

> Our exercise of political power is fully proper only when it is exercised in accordance with a constitution the essentials of which all citizens as free and equal persons may reasonably be expected to endorse in the light of principles and ideals acceptable to their common human reason.[17]

This requirement is justified because the political relationship is nonvoluntary in the sense that we neither enter nor leave it voluntarily; it is coercive because the use of power is backed up by the use of sanctions; and the basic structure has profound effects on the lives of individuals. But the situation of children with respect to their parents, as Clayton observes, is analogous: they are in a situation that has profound effects on their lives, and is coercive and nonvoluntary.

> If the parallels between the political and parental case are sound, the conclusion can be drawn that parental conduct, as well as political conduct, should be in accordance with the ideal of liberal legitimacy. That is, parents should exercise their authority in accordance with public reason, in a way that is capable of acceptance by free and equal persons.[18]

They therefore have an obligation to exercise that power legitimately. In the case of the state Clayton thinks, following Rawls, that the principle of legitimacy yields a requirement that coercion be used in accordance with constitutional essentials that can be justified only by appeal to public reason.

> Parental conduct should be guided by ideals and principles that do not rest on the validity of any particular reasonable comprehensive doctrine. The ideals that guide parents must not, for example, be secular or religious ideals, which are disputed by reasonable persons. Clearly, this is a significant restraint that prohibits what many parents believe to be routinely acceptable forms of appeal to ideals and values which animate their lives.[19]

This, he thinks, supports the idea that the state may not attempt to enroll citizens who are not autonomous into a comprehensive conception of the good. Similarly, parents must not enroll their children (who are not yet autonomous) into a comprehensive conception of the good. To do so would be to exercise illegitimately the coercive power they (rightly) have over children. They must wait until their children's autonomy is secure before attempting to influence the child to adopt their conception of the good. For Clayton, children's autonomy should be regarded as a "precondition" of any such attempt.

We disagree. The three conditions he identifies do, indeed, hold, in the parent-child relationship. But it would be too costly, in terms of familial relationship goods, for most parents to refrain from acting on their own judgments about how to live their lives in their dealings with their children, because those are so intertwined in healthy parent-child relationships. A relationship in which both parent and child are enjoying the relationship goods that drive our account of parents' rights is one in which a great deal is shared between parent and child, and in which the parent exhibits a limited but considerable amount of spontaneity. Most of us cannot simultaneously shield our children from those values and commitments that are central to our identities and share ourselves with them in the way that the healthy parent-child relationship demands. Clayton is of course right that if one raises a child in one's religion, one will be using coercive power to shape her values without her consent. This, though, is consistent with proper attention to her autonomy on our understanding of its significance—as a capacity, an "end state," to be achieved.

It does not follow from this that there is a right to raise a child in one's religion. In fact, we think there is not a general answer to that question. Whether a parent may do so depends on two things. One is whether the religious upbringing she is offering is consistent with autonomy. Shelley Burtt argues that most religions, even in most of their deeply traditionalist versions, contain reflective and interpretative components that require the use of critical thinking, such that being raised in the religion will usually suffice to develop the relevant skills and traits:

> Questions such as "Who am I? What goods ought to compel my allegiance? What weight do I give to the different components that make up my identity?" all encourage reflection on what counts as the good life for me without requiring extensive familiarity with how very different sorts of people from very different circumstances choose to live their lives. In fact, resources for this sort of education exist within the cultural scripts of most comprehensive religions or cultural identities.[20]

Bringing children up within *some* religions certainly seems to be consistent with autonomy—take, for example, the Anglican churchgoer who believes in

God but does not take that belief to be a precondition of, or even much of an aid to, salvation; such a believer can raise her child within the practices of her religious community, can teach him her faith, and can also expose him to a wide range of influences some of which may lead him to break with that faith. She can even encourage him to follow some of those influences. Other faiths, especially those for which belief and practice are preconditions of salvation, are less consistent with an upbringing that encourages autonomy. Paula McAvoy discusses the situation of an interviewee, Emily, who was raised Old Order Mennonite:

> Deciding to leave a fundamentalist community also requires one to accept a future in hell. When Emily left her parents' house at age 19 she believed she would "spend eternity in a napalm environment." At first she hoped to live at home and simply live her own life, but after three days she packed her bags and went to live with her aunt. As she explained:
>
>> My mother cried constantly. My brother yelled at me—he had left and come back twice—and he felt I was making a very bad mistake and he wanted to keep me from making the same one. My sister was confused. I still feel *awful* for, I mean I cut my family out of my life basically for a few months, because I did not have the capacity, or the level of judgment necessary to deal with their pain and stay the course that I had chosen.
>
> At the time she told herself that she would be back one day, but six months later she married a person "of the world" and knew she had left forever. As she describes it, it took years to come to believe she had not, in fact, chosen hell. During those years her anxiety about the afterlife woke her up at night.[21]

Given Emily's testimony it is hard to believe that her prospective autonomy was adequately protected (even though she ultimately defected and seems capable of extremely thoughtful reflection on her decisions). In Emily's case the religious aspect of the upbringing seems to be implicated, because it is clear that Emily's mother is a sincere believer and also appears to love her child unconditionally. But it is often hard to tell whether it is indeed the religious character of an upbringing that inhibits autonomy. Parents who terrorize children with fear of eternal damnation are sometimes simply exercising their own overbearing desire for control, rather than following the requirements of their religion.

Whether a particular religious upbringing is consistent with autonomy depends on how it interacts with the surrounding culture. Think of the difference between a child being reared Amish in an Amish village with very little contact with the surrounding "English" world, and a child being reared in a home with very similar religious beliefs and practices but in a neighborhood in which there is a lot of contact with children and adults living very different lives. Being raised in a diverse environment is more likely to support the development of autonomy than being raised in an enclave, even when the home values and the home culture are not, themselves, any different.

Some readers may find it easy to see how children raised in a religion can autonomously become secular, but harder to envisage how those raised outside any faith can autonomously become religious. But, if religious lives are effectively shut off from children raised in secular homes, how can we think of *those* children as having their prospective autonomy safeguarded? To be autonomous, it might be argued, children need the deep familiarity with religious commitment that can be attained only if one is raised within a religion.

People do, indeed, convert to faiths as adults, after having secular upbringings, and we see no reason to think that all of these conversions are either insincere or the result of psychological imbalance. Many, we think, occur in well-balanced autonomous persons. But, just as a religious upbringing in which one is psychologically abused with excessive fear of hell makes it extremely difficult for people to exit autonomously from a religious way of life, so a secular upbringing in which one imbibes contempt and hatred, or even just disdain, for religion makes autonomous conversion problematic. Shelley Burtt is right to observe that the prescription that children should get "educations which challenge rather than affirm their parents' values and ways of life" is "rarely applied with vigor to enthusiasts of the mainstream secular, consumer culture": for children with secular upbringings to become autonomous they must, indeed, have their received values challenged, and need intimate contact with real people for whom a spiritual faith is woven into the fabric of their daily lives.[22] There are other serious threats to autonomy than parents attempting to inculcate their own commitments: parents who neglect their children's autonomy sometimes put it at risk as much as—sometimes more than—parents who consciously seek to block its development, certainly in a social environment that is materialistic and commercialized. This is one reason that the ideal of the common school has some force: children raised in nonreligious households are more likely to befriend children from religious households, and thus to have the meaningful contact with a religious life that is, for many, a precondition of autonomous conversion.

For parents to raise their children successfully they must establish themselves as loving authorities. But if they succeed in that, their children will be

inclined to follow their lead in many things, including in their most fundamental commitments. And in order to have the ability to shape values in the
ways that are legitimate, and indeed the ability to fulfill children's other interests, parents need a great deal of power and latitude over their children.
They have to be able to share their space, and their lives, with them. This gives
them plenty of emotional power to inhibit their children's recourse to critical
reflection. If a child knows that her parents think some ways are good and
some bad, perhaps very bad, then she will be under considerable emotional
pressure to go along with that, even if they attempt not to pressure her, let
alone if they are more forceful. The emotional cost of breaking from the views
in which she was raised and will have been raised to treat as gospel, and the
analytically distinct emotional cost of breaking from what she knows to be
her parents' views, and the emotional rupture likely to be involved in that,
mean that it is very hard to do. People who do it do so by resisting pressures
that may not be formally or legally coercive but are experienced by many as
emotionally coercive. Parents can affect the emotional costs borne by their
children should they decide to reject the parents' views. It would be extremely
difficult for parents completely to remove the emotional costs to the child of
revising her received commitments, and we suspect that doing so would often
require seeming to be indifferent to what the child decides in a way that will be
inauthentic and may seem uncaring, thus affecting the relationship negatively
in other ways. But a parent, whether religious or secular, who ensures scrupu-
lously that his child has the cognitive skills and information needed for autonomy but then deliberately raises the emotional costs of revision has surely
not met his obligation. We have acknowledged that a child's prospective autonomy depends on more than the will and action of the parent, but the duty
that parents are under is complex and burdensome. It includes restraining
themselves from exerting the emotional pressure that they may be tempted
deliberately to impose on the child to refrain from revising her received
commitments.

Parents' rights to shape their children's values are limited by the condition
that they must adequately attend to their children's interests, which include the
interest in becoming autonomous. Clayton's "precondition" approach, we believe, is counterproductive in that the kind of withholding from the child that
the parent will have to engage in will hamper the development of an emotionally healthy relationship, which might itself be regarded as needed for the development of autonomy. So raising one's child within one's religion is morally
permissible—as long as that is done in a way consistent with the development
of her autonomy.

Conclusion

The basic point is simple. Children are separate people, with their own lives to lead, and the right to make, and act on, their own judgments about how they are to live those lives. They are not the property of their parents. As Kahlil Gibran says, in the poem that serves as our book's epigraph: "Your children are not your children. . . . though they are with you yet they belong not to you." And because they are not property, and yet parents are—rightly—accorded such power over them, it is wrong for parents to treat them as vehicles for their own self-expression, or as means to the realization of their own views on controversial questions about how to live. The desire to extend oneself into the future, and to influence the shape that future takes, can be satisfied in other ways, without a parent's relying on that authority over her children that, for us, is justified on other grounds.

Gibran continues: "You may give them your love but not your thoughts, / For they have their own thoughts." Whether they have their own thoughts, or how much of their thinking is indeed their own, depends a good deal on how they are raised. We agree that they should have their own thoughts, or at least be able to have them. But the giving of thoughts and the giving of love cannot be so readily separated. The loving parent will care for her child's moral development. More, some spontaneous expression of self, and demonstration of one's desire to promote one's children's well-being, are healthy elements in a loving familial relationship, and both are likely to lead to some giving of thoughts. Further, because of the role that shared values and mutual understanding play in loving relationships, some deliberate introduction of children to parents' views about what matters in life can itself be justified as conducive to the relationship goods at the heart of our theory. Still, the very fact that value-shaping interactions of this kind are inevitable aspects of such relationships makes it all the more important that parents not exceed the limits implied by the duty to enable their children to become autonomous adults.

Conclusion

Rather than concluding with a summary rehearsal of our arguments, we end by pointing out some of their limitations. We might think of these, more positively, as an agenda for future research.

We have shied away from concerns about what children owe their parents. Our analysis has been limited to "the family" conceived narrowly in terms of the parent-child relationship, but even within that we have concentrated on parents' rights over, and duties to, their children. Questions of filial obligation raise different problems, and the issue of what adult children owe their elderly parents in particular is clearly very important.[1] For policymakers in aging societies, the problem is how to divide responsibility between family and state. For individuals, the issues raised are often emotionally complex, to say the least. Might it be productive to frame at least some of these matters in terms of "familial relationship goods"? Perhaps some such goods are realized when adult children care for their own parents. Perhaps they are realized—albeit to a lesser extent—when adult children provide the resources needed for that care to be provided by others. In one sense, of course, adults' looking after dependent parents are experiencing an inversion of the familial relationship that we have focused on. But, from a broader perspective, it might rather be conceived as a continuation or completion of that relationship.

A rather different way forward would be to move beyond the family altogether, applying the concept of "relationship goods" to other kinds of relationship. Those who argue that we have special responsibilities to our fellow nationals, or to our fellow citizens, often appeal to an analogy with the family, the general idea being that particular modes of association or relationship, and perhaps certain kinds of shared identity, permit, or even demand, particular forms of partiality toward particular others. Our approach to the question of legitimate parental partiality focuses attention on the specific contribution to well-being that is made by familial relationships, and we suspect that approach can usefully be applied to these, supposedly analogous, cases. To what extent do current arguments in this area invoke claims that might helpfully be framed in terms of relationship goods?[2] Is it true that the relationship of shared nationality, for example, contributes particular goods to people's lives? If so, what forms of interaction—and what forms of partiality—must be permitted for the relationship to make that contribution? Similar questions can be asked about the civic relationship—about the goods made possible by citizens' sharing membership of a state.[3] It may be, further, that thinking in terms of relationship goods and the conditions of their realization can illuminate other areas, such as the obligations and permissions of friendship.[4] If one is willing to countenance the idea that one has a relationship with oneself—and we do sometimes think in terms of people's being alienated from themselves—it might even help us think about the nature and limits of partiality toward self.

But another research agenda suggested by our theory concerns its policy implications. It's unlikely, of course, but suppose you agreed with everything so far: we are right about why there should be families, about what kinds of families are valuable, and about what rights parents should (and shouldn't) have over their children. What you would be agreeing with are some rather abstract, philosophical claims, but it's far from clear what they mean for policymakers—or for us as citizens, democratically deciding the framework of rules and regulations we are to live under. Some critics of political philosophy object to its tendency to operate at a level so removed from the world of real politics and practical decision making. They think that more should be done to explain how its grand theories might translate into prescriptions for action, what those theories mean for government policy here and now.

We share this concern, and would be delighted to conclude with a comprehensive and detailed set of concrete proposals that follow from our theory of family values.[5] But philosophy, even political philosophy, has only a modest and specific part to play when it comes to policy prescriptions. Much of what is at stake in policy debates concerns disputes on which philosophers have no particular expertise, disputes that turn on complex empirical considerations. The main way for philosophers to contribute to those debates is to make their arguments available to nonspecialists in an accessible form, which is what we've tried to do in this book.

That said, we trust that the reader interested in its political implications will keep in mind the key big-picture aspects of our approach to family values. Though we cannot ourselves pursue them to their conclusions, it should be clear that, if accepted, that approach would have radical consequences across a wide range of policy domains. Three take-home messages stand out. The first is that children come first. True, unlike the proponents of some purely child-centered approaches, we have argued for a dual-interest view, insisting that adults' interest in parenting (and not only children's interest in being parented) helps us to understand the moral basis of the family. But our claim that the adult interest is in acting as a child's fiduciary, and that the weighty adult interest in a parent-child relationship is an interest in the kind of relationship that serves children's interests, substantially reduces the practical significance of that aspect. Our theory yields a much more constrained account of parents' rights over their children than is widely accepted. Compared to the status quo, with its more-than-residual elements of the idea that children belong to their parents in a way that licenses their being treated as means to their parents' ends, a concern for the family as a source of familial relationship goods will give parents considerably less discretion over their children's upbringing than they currently enjoy.

Second, respect for the family is much less of an obstacle to egalitarian goals than is often claimed. Family values are often regarded as grounds for resisting redistributive measures (such as inheritance taxes), and policy generally defers to widely held claims that parents must have extensive freedom to promote their children's interests (for example, by investing in their education). Focusing carefully on the distinct contribution that familial relationships can make to people's flourishing suggests that many such invocations of the family cannot be sustained. We insist, moreover, that familial relationship goods matter for everyone, not just for those who invoke the family to defend their advantages. By conceiving those goods as distribuenda, and noticing the way in which public policy and the social environment massively affect their distribution, family values not only lose much of their force as grounds for resisting egalitarian policies; they provide a strong basis for endorsing them.

Third, our account of the family's value gives no fundamental significance to biological connection between parent and child. We reject, in particular, the conventional claim that adults have a right to parent a child who shares their genetic material. Since we accept that it will generally be in children's interests to be raised by their biological parents, and that there are practical limits on the state's (or anybody's) capacity to identify exceptions, this does not immediately imply extremely radical conclusions at the level of policy. One area where it will have bite, however, concerns state support for adoption. Many would-be parents do not even consider the possibility of adopting until attempts to produce biologically connected children have failed. It can be very hard, and very costly, for parents to adopt; there looks to be a strong case for the state's subsidizing and in other ways promoting adoption, partly by tackling widespread norms and taken-for-granted assumptions about what constitutes a proper family. Such measures could be seen as helping us to discharge our collective duty to provide parents for those children who lack them.[6] There will also, of course, be implications for policy concerning assisted reproduction.

At a more fundamental level, our skepticism about the significance of biological connection will have implications for what might call "procreation policy"—an area we think likely to become very salient in the next few decades as the implications of global population growth become impossible to ignore. The alleged "right to procreate" derives much of its appeal from an implicit claim about the value of getting to parent the child one has procreatively produced. Calling that into question suggests a substantial reframing of the normative issues around political attempts to control population growth.[7]

Some may object to any attempt to infer policy implications from our theory. An influential view in political philosophy holds that the state acts illegitimately if its policies are justified by appeal to controversial philosophical doctrines, including controversial conceptions of human well-being. The state is, at root, a coercive apparatus—an instrument for preventing people from doing some things, and making them do others. In liberal democracies, citizens are rightly regarded as free and equal, and the state as belonging to them jointly. Those thoughts are taken by some to imply that the state should act only as an impartial umpire, providing a level playing field: a neutral framework in which individuals are left free to pursue their own goods in their own way. Since there is reasonable disagreement about what constitutes human flourishing, it is wrong for government to enact policies that rely on any particular conception—even if the decisions are made democratically. Doing that involves using the coercive power of the state in support of a particular sectarian doctrine. The proper role of the state is to prevent harm and ensure just background conditions against which people can make their own choices about how to live. It is not to promote well-being.[8]

It should be clear how this line of argument might challenge any attempt to derive policy implications from our theory. From this perspective, a policy premised on the value of familial relationship goods looks objectionably "perfectionist," for it involves harnessing the coercive power of the state to promote a controversial understanding of what makes people's lives go well. True, such policies might be only *mildly* perfectionist. The state would not be endorsing a single, monistic, vision of how people should live their lives as a whole, and there need be no suggestion that it would be willing directly to coerce people into realizing the particular goods to which its policies did indeed appeal. Still, it does look as if a government that took our argument to heart and attempted to put it into practice would have to acknowledge being not entirely neutral between citizens' views about the value and significance of the family.

Those who demand that the state should refrain from grounding its policies in a controversial view about well-being need not deny the validity of that view. It is entirely coherent for someone to accept our account of family values—to think we are right about the way in which familial relationships contribute to human flourishing and what it implies for parents' discretion over their children's upbringing—while denying that it would be legitimate for the state to implement policies based on that account. She could, for example, regard our theory as providing valid guidance for her own attempts to parent her children. But all-things-considered assessments of political action must weigh not only the outcomes they can be expected to promote but also the means by which they are to be promoted. The antiperfectionist derives, from respect for the value of citizens' freedom and equality, a procedural concern that the state acts illegitimately when it endorses a particular controversial doctrine—even when that doctrine is correct and its political enactment would indeed promote flourishing. For the antiperfectionist, those "political" values weigh more heavily than even the "comprehensive" values connected to a correct account of human flourishing.[9]

We cannot here evaluate the cases for and against mild state perfectionism. We can, however, explain why some measures that governments might take in attempting to put our theory into practice need not be as perfectionist as they might seem. The centrality of our account of children's interests is the key here; *those* interests should be regarded as a legitimate basis for state action even by those committed to state neutrality. One might plausibly deny that government policy may properly promote adults' interest in parenting—by, for example, subsidizing the use of artificial reproductive technology, or encouraging people to become parents by subsidizing the costs of child rearing. After all, one might think, individual adults can and should make their own judgments about how to spend their resources; rather than endorsing a contentious view about how familial relationship goods contribute to adult flourishing, the proper role of the state is to provide adults with their just share of resources and leave it to them to decide whether they want to spend them on raising children. But it is much less plausible to object to children's interest in being well parented, and to our interests as third parties in their being so, as legitimately guiding policy. And, we would suggest, our account of those interests is considerably less controversial. Indeed, we think they could not reasonably be rejected.

It is important, then, that many policies that would serve the adult interest in parenting can be justified by a less controversial appeal to the interests of children (and, to some extent, of third parties). Poverty is a major barrier to adults' capacity to participate in the relationships we have described. The conscientious parent, living in poverty, doing her best to provide her child with a decent start in life, may find herself working longer hours, or trying to hold down two or more jobs, in a way that makes it very difficult for her to enjoy an intimate relationship with that child. Even many affluent parents in wealthy societies face significant barriers to enjoying relationships of the kind we have described. Professional and nonprofessional jobs, especially in the United States, frequently lack the kind of employment protection that enables parents to negotiate their hours of work to fit with the demands of parenting, and jobs are often structured in such a way that wholehearted involvement in them is strongly in tension with wholehearted involvement in family life and parenting. Policies to combat poverty, to socialize the costs of children's education and health care, and to help even affluent parents achieve better work-life balance do serve the interests of parents, but of course they serve children's interests too. Children's interests in growing up well (and other people's interest in their growing up that way) may be quite sufficient justifications of many of the policies that would be advocated by a state deliberately promoting adult well-being through encouraging parenting. Policy aimed at tackling those aspects of poverty most damaging to a flourishing parent-child relationship, or at enabling even affluent parents to achieve a better work-life balance, help parents in large part by helping them do what parents should be able to do *for their children*. If it is good for the parent to be home from work in time to read bedtime stories to her children, that is in large part (though not entirely) because it is good for children to have bedtime stories read to them by the parent. We contribute to parents' flourishing indirectly, as it were, by policies justified primarily on child-centered, and less controversial, grounds.

It remains possible, of course, that children's interests will not justify all the policies that a perfectionist state promoting adults' interest in parenting would endorse. This leads us to our second point. Insofar as policy prescriptions did appeal to claims about parents' interests, they might be conceived and presented as correcting or compensating for biases that make it unduly difficult, given current incentive structures, for adults to experience the kind of relationships that we claim to be distinctively valuable. Institutional arrangements and social norms influence not only the distribution of resources, and the costs and benefits attaching to particular choices about how to deploy those resources; they also influence people's preferences and inclinations. Of course it is a complicated question how we should conceive the baseline against which to assess any claim about bias, and one would need to do a good deal of work to show that, say, existing arrangements were tilted against parenting in a way that would justify pro-family policies as consistent with an egalitarian or neutralist conception of distributive justice.[10] Those mindful of the interests of future generations might well regard those arrangements as far too *generous* to parents, since those who become parents by procreation are not required to bear the costs that their choices will impose on others via, for example, effects on the environment. Those attentive to the influence of social norms might think them biased in *favor* of the decision to become a parent; childless women, especially, are often expected to explain the absence of children, or at least that absence is the subject of others' speculation, in a way that mothers are not expected to explain their presence. Still, especially where fertility rates are falling, it is important to keep in mind the possibility that some of us live in societies that have tilted the balance against parenthood. Most analyses in affluent societies think about falling fertility rates as an economic problem. Our approach suggests a different kind of worry. People whose lives would go better were they to become parents may be missing out. Insofar as their decision to remain childless reflected our having made the costs of parenting unduly high, efforts to correct the imbalance could be justified without any appeal to perfectionist considerations.

We should note, finally, the rhetorical appeal of family values, an appeal that can be acknowledged even by those who, philosophically speaking, would object to state action motivated exclusively by such considerations. For the antiperfectionist, the ideal is to secure a just distribution of resources, and then leave it to individuals to make their own judgments about what to spend them on, without good-specific subsidy. In our societies that distribution is, in fact, unjust; many people cannot make the choices (and, sometimes, do not make the judgments) that they would make in just circumstances. In the absence of a just distribution, invoking family values may be a good way to motivate support for policies that would be justified on other grounds.

NOTES

Preface

1. Plato advocated such arrangements only for prospective philosopher kings; *The Republic*, ed. G.R.F. Ferrari (Cambridge: Cambridge University Press, 2000).

2. Martin Johnson, "A Biomedical Perspective on Parenthood," in *What Is a Parent?*, ed. Andrew Bainham et al. (Oxford: Hart Publishing, 1999), pp. 47–71.

3. Brenda Almond, a trenchant critic of "the new ideology of the family," would doubtless include us among those she accuses of adopting "the Humpty Dumpty view that words can mean whatever we want them to mean." *The Fragmenting Family* (Oxford: Oxford University Press, 2006), p. 9.

4. Colin Macleod defines a family as "a social institution composed of one or more adults and children linked together through close and distinctive affective ties and in which the adults have special responsibilities and a measure of authority in supervising the rearing of children." "Conceptions of Parental Autonomy," *Politics & Society* 25, no. 1 (1997): 117–140, p. 137.

5. See, for example, the *Report of the Commission on the Measurement of Economic Performance and Social Progress*, set up by the French president Nicolas Sarkozy, published in 2009 and available at www.stiglitz-sen-fitoussi.fr.

6. Richard Layard, *Happiness: Lessons from a New Science* (Harmondsworth: Penguin, 2011).

7. See Elizabeth Burney and Loraine Gelsthorpe, "Do We Need a 'Naughty Step'? Rethinking the Parenting Order after Ten Years," *Howard Journal of Criminal Justice* 47 (2008): 470–485. For the United States, see Paul Tough, *Whatever It Takes* (New York: Houghton Mifflin, 2009).

8. The seminal contribution is Susan Moller Okin, *Justice, Gender, and the Family* (New York: Basic Books, 1989). See also Mary Lyndon Shanley, "'No More Relevance than One's Eye-Color,'" in *Toward a Humane Justice*, ed. Debra Satz and Rob Reich (Oxford: Oxford University Press, 2009), pp. 113–128; Will Kymlicka, "Rethinking the Family," *Philosophy & Public Affairs* 20, no. 1 (1991): 77–97; Anca Gheaus, "Gender Justice," *Journal of Ethics & Social Philosophy* 6, no. 2 (2012): 1–24.

9. See, for example, Harry Brighouse and Erik Olin Wright, "Strong Gender Egalitarianism," *Politics & Society* 36, no. 3 (2008): 360–372; Anca Gheaus and Ingrid Robeyns, "Equality-Promoting Parental Leave," *Journal of Social Philosophy* 42, no. 2 (2011): 173–191.

10. The seminal contribution here is Carol Gilligan, *In a Different Voice: Psychological Theory and Women's Development* (Cambridge, MA: Harvard University Press, 1982). Important subsequent contributions in moral and political philosophy include Joan Tronto, *Moral Boundaries: A Political Argument for an Ethic of Care* (London:

Routledge, 1993); Diemut Bubeck, *Care, Gender and Justice* (Oxford: Oxford University Press, 1995); Nel Noddings, *Caring: A Feminine Approach to Ethics and Moral Education* (Berkeley: University of California Press, 2003); Virginia Held, *The Ethics of Care: Personal, Political and Global* (New York: Oxford University Press, 2006); Daniel Engster, *The Heart of Justice: Care Ethics and Political Theory* (Oxford: Oxford University Press, 2007).

11. D. W. Winnicott, *The Family and Individual Development* (London: Tavistock Publications, 1965); Bruno Bettelheim, *A Good Enough Parent* (London: Thames and Hudson, 1987); John Bowlby, *Secure Base: Parent-Child Attachment and Healthy Human Development* (London: Routledge, 1988).

12. Shelley Day Sclater and Candida Yates, "The Psycho-Politics of Post-Divorce Parenting," in *What Is a Parent?*, ed. Andrew Bainham et al. (Oxford: Hart Publishing, 1999), pp. 271–293.

Introduction to Part One

1. See, for example, Samuel Bowles and Herbert Gintis, "The Inheritance of Economic Status: Education, Class and Genetics," in *International Encyclopedia of the Social and Behavioral Sciences: Genetics, Behavior and Society*, ed. Marcus Feldman and Paul Baltes (New York: Oxford University Press and Elsevier, 2001), pp. 4132–4141; Samuel Bowles, Herbert Gintis, and Melissa Osborne-Groves, eds., *Unequal Chances: Family Background and Economic Success* (Princeton, NJ: Princeton University Press, 2005); John Ermisch, Markus Jantti, and Timothy Smeeding, *From Parents to Children: The Intergenerational Transmission of Advantage* (New York: Russell Sage Foundation, 2012).

2. UN General Assembly, Universal Declaration of Human Rights, 10 December 1948, 217 A (III), Article 16.3, available at http://www.refworld.org/docid/3ae6b3712c .html; Council of Europe, European Convention for the Protection of Human Rights and Fundamental Freedoms, as amended by Protocols Nos. 11 and 14, 4 November 1950, ETS 5, Articles 8 and 12, available at: http://www.refworld.org/docid/3ae6b3b04 .html.

3. The most important moves in the direction of appropriate specification have been made by Francis Schrag, "Justice and the Family," *Inquiry* 19, nos. 1–4 (1976): 193–208; Ferdinand Schoeman, "Rights of Children, Rights of Parents, and the Moral Basis of the Family," *Ethics* 91, no. 1 (1980): 6–19; Jeffrey Blustein, *Parents and Children: The Ethics of the Family* (New York: Oxford University Press, 1982); Samantha Brennan and Robert Noggle, "The Moral Status of Children: Children's Rights, Parents' Rights, and Family Justice," *Social Theory and Practice* 23, no. 1 (1997): 1–26; Veronique Munoz-Darde, "Is the Family to Be Abolished, Then?" *Proceedings of the Aristotelian Society* 99, no. 1 (1999): 37–56; Shelley Burtt, "What Children Really Need: Toward a Critical Theory of Family Structure," in *The Moral and Political Status of Children*, ed. David Archard and Colin M. Macleod (Oxford: Oxford University Press, 2002), pp. 231–252; Colin Macleod, "Conceptions of Parental Autonomy," *Politics & Society* 25, no. 1 (1997): 117–140, and "Liberal Equality and the Affective Family," in *The Moral and Political Status of Children*, ed. David Archard and Colin M. Macleod (Oxford: Oxford University Press, 2002), pp. 212–230; David Archard, *Children, Family and the State* (Aldershot: Ashgate, 2003), and *The Family: A Liberal Defence* (Basingstoke: Palgrave Macmillan, 2011); Matthew Clayton, *Justice and Legitimacy in Upbringing* (Oxford: Oxford University Press,

2006); Michael W. Austin, *Conceptions of Parenthood: Ethics and the Family* (Aldershot: Ashgate, 2007); Norvin Richards, *The Ethics of Parenthood* (New York: Oxford University Press, 2010).

CHAPTER 1

Liberalism and the Family

1. http://communitariannetwork.org/communitarian-vision/marriage-and-family/.

2. Ibid.

3. William Galston, Mary Ann Glendon, Jean Bethke Elshtain, Enola Aird, Amitai Etzioni, Martha Minow, and Alice Rossi, "A Communitarian Position Paper on the Family," http://www.gwu.edu/~ccps/pop_fam.html (original emphasis).

4. David Popenoe, "Family Values: A Communitarian Position," in *Macro Socio-Economics: From Theory to Activism*, ed. David Sciulli (Armonk, NY: M. E. Sharpe, 1996), 165–183, p. 169, cited in Eva Feder Kittay, "A Feminist Public Ethic of Care Meets Family Policy," *Ethics* 111, no. 3 (2001): 523–547.

5. Nor would we seek to conceal the *lack* of overlap. For critiques of communitarian thinking about the family with which we largely concur, see Kittay, "A Feminist Public Ethic of Care"; Burtt, "What Children Really Need," pp. 231–52; Elizabeth Frazer, "Unpicking Political Communitarianism: A Critique of 'The Communitarian Family,'" in *Changing Family Values*, ed. Gill Jagger (London: Routledge, 1999), pp. 150–164.

6. For a detailed account of the relationship between liberalism and communitarianism at the philosophical level, see Stephen Mulhall and Adam Swift, *Liberals and Communitarians*, 2nd ed. (Oxford: Blackwell, 1996); for a more accessible summary from a more political perspective, see Adam Swift, *Political Philosophy: A Beginners' Guide for Students and Politicians*, 3rd ed. (Cambridge, MA: Polity, 2013), chap. 4.

7. See works cited in n. 10 of the preface, but also John Hardwig, "Should Women Think in Terms of Rights?" *Ethics* 94, no. 3 (1984): 441–455. For a subtle discussion that transcends this crude framing and addresses both adults and children within the family, see Martha Minow, *Making All the Difference: Inclusion, Exclusion, and American Law* (Ithaca, NY: Cornell University Press, 1990).

8. Aristotle, *The Politics*, trans. Carnes Lord (Chicago: University of Chicago Press, 1985).

9. Will Kymlicka, "Rethinking the Family," *Philosophy & Public Affairs* 20, no. 1 (1991): 77–97.

10. David Archard, *Children, Family and the State* (Aldershot, UK: Ashgate, 2003), pp. 123–124.

11. See Carole Pateman, "Feminist Critiques of the Public/Private Dichotomy," in her *The Disorder of Women: Democracy, Feminism, and Political Theory* (Stanford, CA: Stanford University Press, 1989), pp. 118–140; Ruth Gavison, "Feminism and the Public/Private Distinction," *Stanford Law Review* 45, no. 1 (1992): 1–45; Sandra Berns, "Liberalism and the Privatized Family: The Legacy of Rousseau," *Res Publica* 11, no. 2 (2005): 125–155. For a view closer to our own, see Corey Brettshchneider, "The Politics of the Personal: A Liberal Approach," *American Political Science Review* 101, no. 1 (2007): 19–31.

12. Bruce W. Frier and Thomas A. J. McGinn, *A Casebook on Roman Family Law*, American Philological Association Classical Resources Series (New York: Oxford University Press, 2004); John Locke, *Two Treatises of Government*, ed. Peter Laslett (Cambridge: Cambridge University Press, 1988).

13. Robert Nozick, *The Examined Life: Philosophical Meditations* (New York: Simon and Schuster, 1989), p. 28.

14. Charles Fried, *Right and Wrong* (Cambridge, MA: Harvard University Press, 1976), p. 152.

15. William Galston, *Liberal Pluralism: The Implications of Value Pluralism for Political Theory and Practice* (Cambridge: Cambridge University Press, 2002), p. 102.

16. Eamonn Callan, *Creating Citizens* (Oxford: Oxford University Press, 1997), p. 143.

17. Barbara Arneil, "Becoming versus Being: A Critical Analysis of the Child in Liberal Theory," in *The Moral and Political Status of Children*, ed. David Archard and Colin M. Macleod (Oxford: Oxford University Press, 2002), pp. 70–94.

18. Shelley Burtt, "The Proper Scope of Parental Authority: Why We Don't Owe Children an 'Open Future,'" in *Nomos XLIV: Child, Family, and State*, ed. Stephen Macedo and Iris Marion Young (New York: New York University Press, 2003), pp. 243–270, p. 253.

19. Arneil, "Becoming versus Being," p. 81.

20. Burtt, "The Proper Scope of Parental Authority," p. 253.

21. Ibid., p. 258.

22. Ibid., p. 259.

23. John Eekelaar, "The Emergence of Children's Rights," *Oxford Journal of Legal Studies* 16, no. 2 (1986): 161–182, at 169.

24. Arneil, "Becoming versus Being," p. 82

25. Immanuel Kant, *The Metaphysics of Morals*, trans. Mary Gregor (Cambridge: Cambridge University Press, 1996), p. 161, cited in S. Matthew Liao, "The Right of Children to Be Loved," *Journal of Political Philosophy* 14, no. 4 (2006): 420–440.

26. Joseph Raz, *The Morality of Freedom* (Oxford: Oxford University Press, 1986), p. 56.

27. Jeremy Waldron, "When Justice Replaces Affection: The Need for Rights," in his *Liberal Rights* (Cambridge: Cambridge University Press, 1991). Waldron is discussing the need for rights held by adult members of failing or dissolving love relationships, but the analysis applies just as well to parent-child relationships.

28. For relevant debate, see S. Matthew Liao, "The Idea of a Duty to Love," *Journal of Value Inquiry* 40, no. 1 (2006): 1–22, and "The Right of Children to Be Loved," pp. 420–440; Mhairi Cowden, "What's Love Got to Do with It? Why a Child Does Not Have a Right to Be Loved," *Critical Review of International Social and Political Philosophy* 15, no. 3 (2012): 325–345, and the subsequent exchange in the same journal.

29. Lisa Cassidy, "That Many of Us Should Not Parent," *Hypatia* 21, no. 1 (2006): 40–57.

30. Cf. David Archard, *The Family: A Liberal Defence* (Basingstoke: Palgrave Macmillan, 2011).

CHAPTER 2
Equality and the Family

1. For the suggestion that parenting involves a loss of autonomy and that society owes parents something in return for that loss, see Anne Alstott, *No Exit: What Parents Owe Their Children and What Society Owes Parents* (Oxford: Oxford University Press, 2005).

2. Laurence Thomas, *The Family and the Political Self* (Cambridge: Cambridge University Press, 2005), p. 80. Gary Becker's influential *A Treatise on the Family* (Cambridge, MA: Harvard University Press, 1991) similarly conceives concern for family members as "altruistic."

3. For the idea of concentric circles, see David Miller, *On Nationality* (Oxford: Oxford University Press, 1995).

4. Thomas, *The Family and the Political Self*, p. 77.

5. Alexandra Kollontai, *Selected Writings of Alexandra Kollontai*, trans. Alix Holt (London: Allison and Busby, 1977), p. 259.

6. As Robert Nozick puts it: "We should note in passing the ambivalent position of radicals toward the family. Its loving relationships are seen as a model to be emulated and extended across the whole of society, at the same time that it is denounced as a suffocating institution to be broken and condemned as a focus of parochial concerns that interfere with achieving radical goals." *Anarchy, State, and Utopia* (New York: Basic Books, 1974), p. 167.

7. Samuel Scheffler, *Boundaries and Allegiances: Problems of Justice and Responsibility in Liberal Thought* (Oxford: Oxford University Press, 2003), p. 85.

8. For variations on this theme, see Elizabeth Anderson, "What Is the Point of Equality?" *Ethics* 109, no. 2 (1999): 287–337; Samuel Scheffler, "What Is Egalitarianism?" *Philosophy & Public Affairs* 31, no. 1 (2003): 5–39; and Jonathan Wolff, "Fairness, Respect, and the Egalitarian Ethos," *Philosophy & Public Affairs* 27, no. 2 (1998): 97–122.

9. Paul Adams et al., *Children's Rights: Toward the Liberation of the Child* (New York: Praeger Publishers, 1971); Howard Cohen, *Equal Rights for Children* (Totowa, NJ: Rowman and Littlefield, 1980).

10. E.g., Francis Schrag, "Children and Democracy: Theory and Policy," *Politics, Philosophy & Economics* 3, no. 3 (2004): 365–379; Andrew Rehfeld, "The Child as Democratic Citizen," *Annals of the American Academy of Political and Social Science* 633, no. 1 (2011): 141–166.

11. For the idea of failure of justification as a failure of relationship (or, as he mainly puts it, "community"), see G. A. Cohen, *Rescuing Justice and Equality*: (Cambridge, MA: Harvard University Press, 2008), chap. 1, especially pp. 41–46.

12. On different conceptions of equality of opportunity, see Adam Swift, *Political Philosophy: A Beginners' Guide for Students and Politicians*, 3rd ed. (Cambridge: Polity, 2013), and Richard Arneson's entry "Equality of Opportunity," in *The Stanford Encyclopedia of Philosophy* (Fall 2008 edition), ed. Edward N. Zalta, http://plato.stanford .edu/archives/fall2008/entries/equal-opportunity/.

13. See Devah Pager, *Race, Crime and Finding Work in an Era of Mass Incarceration* (Chicago: University of Chicago Press, 2007), who finds that, in the labor market she

studied, being black counts against men in labor market competition as much as having a criminal record does.

14. John Rawls, *Justice as Fairness: A Restatement* (Cambridge, MA: Harvard University Press, 2001), pp. 43–44.

15. John Schaar, "Equality of Opportunity, and Beyond," in *Nomos IX: Equality*, ed. Roland J. Pennock and John Chapman (New York: Atherton Press, 1967), pp. 228–249; reprinted in *Equality: Selected Readings*, ed. Louis P. Pojman and Robert Westmoreland (New York: Oxford University Press, 1997), pp. 137–147.

16. Adam Swift and Gordon Marshall, "Meritocratic Equality of Opportunity: Economic Efficiency, Social Justice, or Both?" *Policy Studies* 18, no. 1 (1997): 35–48.

17. The classic exposition of this kind of argument is Nozick's Wilt Chamberlain example in his *Anarchy, State, and Utopia*, pp. 161–163.

18. See Samuel Bowles, Herbert Gintis, and Melissa Osborne-Groves, eds., *Unequal Chances: Family Background and Economic Success* (Princeton, NJ: Princeton University Press, 2005); see also Bowles and Gintis, "The Inheritance of Inequality," *Journal of Economic Perspectives* 16, no. 3 (2002): 3–30.

19. Charles Dickens, *Bleak House* (Oxford: Oxford University Press, 2008).

20. In Rawls's formulation: "supposing that there is a distribution of *native endowments*, those who have the same level of talent and ability and the same willingness to use these gifts should have the same prospects of success regardless of their social class of origin" (our italics). Rawls, *Justice as Fairness*, p. 44.

21. What children are like at the moment of birth is itself a function of their social context. Mothers' nutrition, levels of anxiety, and various other characteristics clearly attributable to "social" phenomena—and highly correlated with socioeconomic position—are known to affect the child in utero. And how the genetic characteristics of newborns develop and materialize over time likewise depends on the environments in which they are raised. See Joseph Fishkin, *Bottlenecks: A New Theory of Equal Opportunity* (Oxford: Oxford University Press, 2014).

22. John Rawls, *A Theory of Justice*, rev. ed. (Cambridge, MA: Harvard University Press, 1999), p. 265.

23. See David Miller, *Principles of Social Justice* (Cambridge, MA: Harvard University Press, 2001), especially chaps. 7–10, for a sophisticated defense of this "conventional" conception of desert. See also George Sher, *Desert* (Princeton, NJ: Princeton University Press, 1989).

24. All conceptions of equality of opportunity share the same structure: X is (or should be) equal to Y with respect to the opportunity for Z. They differ in how they specify X, Y, and Z. Whereas the previous point concerned who counts as X and Y—that is, between whom should opportunities be equal?—this one is about Z—that is, opportunities for what? See Peter Westen, "The Concept of Equal Opportunity," *Ethics* 95, no. 4 (1985): 837–850; Adam Swift, "Class Analysis from a Normative Perspective," *British Journal of Sociology* 51, no. 4 (2000): 663–679; and Hugh Lazenby, "The Concept of Equality of Educational Opportunity" (unpublished paper given at Children, Education and Philosophy Group, University of Warwick, 6 September 2013).

25. Cf. Paul Gomberg, *How to Make Opportunity Equal: Race and Contributive Justice* (Oxford: Blackwell, 2007).

26. For discussions of global justice, see Gillian Brock, *Global Justice: A Cosmopolitan Account* (Oxford: Oxford University Press, 2009); Simon Caney, *Justice beyond Borders* (Oxford: Oxford University Press, 2006); Richard W. Miller, *Globalizing Justice* (Oxford: Oxford University Press, 2010); Thomas Nagel, "The Problem of Global Justice," *Philosophy & Public Affairs* 33, no. 2 (2005): 113–147; and A. J. Julius, "Nagel's Atlas," *Philosophy & Public Affairs* 34, no. 2 (2006): 176–192.

27. T. M. Scanlon, *The Difficulty of Tolerance* (Cambridge: Cambridge University Press, 2003), chap. 11.

28. Notice that Rawls himself, who gives fair equality of opportunity lexical priority over the (prioritarian) difference principle, seems also (and apparently somewhat inconsistently) to nod in this direction when he allows that "an inequality of opportunity must enhance the opportunities of those with the lesser opportunity" (Rawls, *A Theory of Justice*, rev. ed., p. 266).

29. The locus classicus is Derek Parfit, "Equality or Priority?" in *The Idea of Equality*, ed. Matthew Clayton and Andrew Williams (Houndmills, Basingstoke: Palgrave Macmillan, 2002), pp. 81–125. For objections specifically to fair equality of opportunity along these lines, see Richard Arneson, "Against Rawlsian Equality of Opportunity," *Philosophical Studies* 93, no. 1 (1999): 77–112; Matthew Clayton, "Rawls and Natural Aristocracy," *Croatian Journal of Philosophy* 1, no. 3 (2001): 239–259. For its application to issues of educational justice in particular, see our "The Place of Educational Equality in Educational Justice," in *Education, Justice and the Human Good*, ed. Kirsten Meyer (London: Routledge, 2014), pp. 14–33.

30. Brighouse and Swift, "Equality, Priority and Positional Goods," *Ethics* 116, no. 3 (2006): 471–497.

31. Ronald Dworkin, *Justice for Hedgehogs* (Cambridge MA: Harvard University Press, 2011). For an accessible version of his methodological position, see "Do Equality and Liberty Conflict?" in *Living as Equals*, ed. Paul Barker (Oxford: Oxford University Press, 1999), pp. 39–58.

Introduction to Part Two

1. Jennifer Roback Morse, "No Families, No Freedom: Human Flourishing in a Free Society," *Social Philosophy and Policy* 16, no. 1 (1999): 290–314.

2. For useful discussions of well-being, see James Griffin, *Well-Being* (Oxford: Oxford University Press, 1989); L. W. Sumner, *Welfare, Happiness and Ethics* (Oxford: Oxford University Press, 1999); Thomas Hurka, *Perfectionism* (New York: Oxford University Press, 1996); Richard Kraut, *What Is Good and Why: The Ethics of Well-Being* (Cambridge, MA: Harvard University Press, 2009); Martha Nussbaum, *Women and Human Development: The Capabilities Approach* (Cambridge: Cambridge University Press, 2000); Martha Nussbaum and Amartya Sen, eds., *The Quality of Life* (Oxford: Oxford University Press, 1993).

3. See Joseph Raz, *The Morality of Freedom* (Oxford: Oxford University Press, 1986), chaps. 7 and 8.

4. Neil MacCormick, "Rights in Legislation," in *Law, Morality and Society: Essays in Honour of H.L.A. Hart*, ed. Peter Hacker and Joseph Raz (Oxford: Oxford University Press, 1977), pp. 189–209.

5. On "compossibility," see Hillel Steiner, *An Essay on Rights* (Oxford: Blackwell, 1994), and on "specificationism," see Christopher Heath Wellman, "On Conflicts between Rights," *Law and Philosophy* 14, nos. 3–4 (1995): 271–295; John Oberdiek, "Specifying Rights Out of Necessity," *Oxford Journal of Legal Studies* 28, no. 1 (2008): 127–146.

CHAPTER 3

Children

1. In ordinary language, this is thought of as a metaphorical application of the second sense, though philosophers are more likely to offer stipulative definitions along these lines, defining "child" and "adult" (or, sometimes, "person") in terms of the nonpossession and possession of certain characteristics. See, for example, Tamar Schapiro, "What Is a Child?" *Ethics* 109, no. 4 (1999): 715–718.

2. See Eva Feder Kittay, *Love's Labour: Essays on Women, Equality and Dependency* (London: Routledge, 1998). See especially chaps. 1, 2, and 6 for helpful and careful discussions of rearing children with cognitive disabilities.

3. T. Berry Brazelton and Stanley I. Greenspan, *The Irreducible Needs of Children: What Every Child Must Have to Grow, Learn, and Flourish* (Cambridge, MA: Da Capo Press, 2000).

4. On the kind of intensive attention needed in the early stages, see Sue Gerhardt, *Why Love Matters: How Affection Shapes a Baby's Brain* (London: Routledge, 2004).

5. Child development takes place within a social environment. Some variant of this brief account taken from Brazelton and Greenspan, *The Irreducible Needs of Children*, would be accepted by most child development researchers writing by and for inhabitants of modern Western countries, and arrived at using modern scientific techniques observing large numbers of children growing up in the modern Western cultures. Not only is there variance in the ages at which milestones are achieved within those cultures, but it may be that in other cultures children simply do not reach those milestones, or have reached them at significantly different ages, or reach other milestones that are not measured. We are not claiming that the developmental course outlined here is universal. However, as we argue later in the chapter, observing that childhood is socially constructed is consistent with thinking that there are better and worse ways of developing, and in our view a society that inhibited the emotional development of children along the lines described by Brazelton and Greenspan is, *in that respect*, worse (and its children worse off) than one that facilitates that development.

6. Martha Nussbaum, *Women and Human Development: The Capabilities Approach* (Cambridge: Cambridge University Press, 2000), pp. 78–80.

7. See Ronald Dworkin, *Sovereign Virtue* (Cambridge, MA: Harvard University Press, 2000); Will Kymlicka, *Liberalism, Community and Culture* (Oxford: Oxford University Press, 1989), chap. 8.

8. See James Griffin, *Well-Being* (Oxford: Oxford University Press, 1989); Joseph Raz, *The Morality of Freedom* (Oxford: Oxford University Press, 1986).

9. Gerhardt, *Why Love Matters*, pp. 5–6.

10. See Samantha Brennan, "The Goods of Childhood and Children's Rights" in *Family-Making: Contemporary Ethical Challenges*, ed. Françoise Baylis and Carolyn McLeod (Oxford: Oxford University Press, 2014), pp. 29–45. See also Colin Macleod, "Primary Goods, Capabilities, and Children," in *Measuring Justice*, ed. Ingrid Robeyns and Harry Brighouse (Cambridge: Cambridge University Press, 2010); David Archard, *Children: Rights and Childhood*, 2nd ed. (London: Routledge, 2004).

11. See Brennan, "The Goods of Childhood," and Anca Gheaus, "The 'Intrinsic Goods of Childhood' and the Just Society," in *The Well-Being of Children in Theory and Practice*, ed. Alexander Bagattini and Colin M. Macleod (Dordrecht: Springer, forthcoming). Gheaus suggests that adults could, in fact, experience some of these "special goods" more often than they currently do, and that it would be good if they did.

12. UN Convention on the Rights of the Child, 20 November 1989, available at http://www.ohchr.org/EN/ProfessionalInterest/Pages/CRC.aspx.

13. Laura Purdy, *In Their Best Interests: The Case against Equal Rights for Children* (Ithaca, NY: Cornell University Press, 1992); Onora O'Neill, "Children's Rights and Children's Lives," *Ethics* 98, no. 3 (1988): 445–463.

14. Raz, *The Morality of Freedom*, chaps. 7 and 8.

15. For our purposes the term "paternalism" is doubly unfortunate, carrying with it not only familial but also gendered baggage. When the state is said to treat its citizens "paternalistically," it is being likened to a parent, specifically to a father, as if the father-child relationship were the paradigm for the phenomenon. But we are considering the question of whether children should have parents in the first place (more precisely, at this point, whether they have a *right* to a parent), and the argument in favor of paternalism is only part of that. One could accept that children should be treated paternalistically without agreeing that there should be such things as parents who are to treat them that way. And of course one can endorse the idea that much of children's paternalistic treatment should indeed come from a parent, as we will argue that it should, without committing oneself to anything about the parent's gender. In the absence of a suitable alternative, and despite these inappropriate resonances, we will continue to use "paternalism" in the sense specified above.

16. The loci classici here are Mary Wollestonecraft, *A Vindication of the Rights of Woman*, ed. Sylvana Tomaselli (Cambridge: Cambridge University Press, 1995); John Stuart Mill, *On the Subjection of Women*, in *"On Liberty" and Other Writings*, ed. Stefan Collini (Cambridge: Cambridge University Press, 1989).

17. Priscilla Alderson, *Children's Consent to Surgery* (Milton Keynes: Open University Press, 1993), p. 154. Alderson concludes that "competence is more influenced by the social context and the child's experience than by innate ability," and that we should not "think in sharp dichotomies of wise adult/immature child, infallible doctor/ignorant patient, but . . . see wisdom and uncertainty shared among people of varying ages and experience" (p. 158).

18. E.g., Allison James, "Understanding Childhood from an Interdisciplinary Perspective," in *Rethinking Childhood*, ed. Peter Puffall and Richard Unsworth (New Brunswick, NJ: Rutgers University Press, 2004), pp. 25–37.

19. Michael Freeman, "Why It Remains Important to Take Children's Rights Seriously," *International Journal of Children's Rights* 15 (2007): 5–23, p. 13.

20. Hillary Clinton, *It Takes a Village: And Other Lessons Children Teach Us* (New York: Simon and Schuster, 1996).

21. The special significance of the parent-child bond, and of parents' authority over their children, does not imply that parents should have complete control over whether other adults can interact with their children, or in what ways. It is plausible that parents owe children a duty to facilitate their getting to know adults beyond the immediate, or extended, family. See Claudia Card, "Against Marriage and Motherhood," *Hypatia* 11, no. 3 (1996): 1–23; Anca Gheaus, "Arguments for Nonparental Care for Children," *Social Theory and Practice* 37, no. 3 (2011): 483–509.

22. Shelley Burtt, "What Children Really Need: Toward a Critical Theory of Family Structure," in *The Moral and Political Status of Children*, ed. David Archard and Colin M. Macleod (Oxford: Oxford University Press, 2002), pp. 231–252; see pp. 244–247.

23. Gerhardt, *Why Love Matters*.

24. E.g., Miri Scharf, "A 'Natural Experiment' in Childrearing Ecologies and Adolescents' Attachment and Separation Representations," *Child Development* 72, no. 1 (2001): 236–251; Rachel Levy-Schiff, "Adaptation and Competence in Early Childhood: Communally Raised Kibbutz Children versus Family Raised Children in the City," *Child Development* 54, no. 6 (1983): 1606–1614.

25. Sara McLanahan and Gary Sandefur, *Growing Up with a Single Parent: What Hurts, What Helps* (Cambridge, MA: Harvard University Press, 1994).

26. Burtt, "What Children Really Need."

27. http://www.fathers-4-justice.org/.

28. Charlotte J. Patterson, "Lesbian and Gay Parents and Their Children: Summary of Research Findings," in *Lesbian and Gay Parenting: A Resource for Psychologists*, 2nd ed. (Washington, DC: American Psychological Association, 2005). (But see Loren Marks, "Same-Sex Parenting and Children's Outcomes: A Closer Examination of the American Psychological Association's Brief on Lesbian and Gay Parenting," *Social Science Research* 41, no. 4 [2012]: 735–751, for a skeptical analysis.) For more recent and specific studies, see Rachel H. Farr, Stephen L. Forssell, and Charlotte J. Patterson, "Parenting and Child Development in Adoptive Families: Does Parental Sexual Orientation Matter?" *Applied Developmental Science* 14, no. 3 (2010): 164–178; Daniel Potter, "Same-Sex Parent Families and Children's Academic Achievement," *Journal of Marriage and Family* 74, no. 3 (2012): 556–571. For a more general summary of research in this area, see Abbie E. Goldberg, *Lesbian and Gay Parents and Their Children: Research on the Family Life Cycle* (Washington, DC: American Psychological Association, 2010).

Note that even if children did have a right not to be parented by same-sex parents, or would generally be better raised by opposite-sex parents, allowing same-sex parents to parent them might nonetheless be the best available policy. If children in institutional care are failing to get anything like what they need, even would-be parents who can offer less-than-optimal parenting should surely be allowed to take on the task. See Morris B. Kaplan, "Legal Fictions and Family Romances: Contrasting Paradigms of Child Placement," in *NOMOS XLIV: Child, Family and State*, ed. Stephen Macedo and Iris Marion Young (New York: New York University Press, 2003), pp. 170–210.

29. J. David Velleman, "Family History," *Philosophical Papers* 34, no. 3 (2005): 357–378, p. 357.

30. Ibid., p. 361. Similarly, Velleman, pp. 361–362, regards as "important" the right stated in the United Nations Convention on the Rights of the Child, Article 7, paragraph 1, that "the child . . . shall have . . . as far as possible, the right to know *and be cared for by* his or her [biological] parents" (our emphasis).

31. Velleman, "Family History," p. 368.

32. David Howe and Julia Feast, "The Long-Term Outcome of Reunions between Adult Adopted People and Their Birth Mothers," *British Journal of Social Work* 31, no. 3 (2001): 351–368, pp. 364–365; cited in Sally Haslanger, *Resisting Reality: Social Construction and Social Critique* (Oxford: Oxford University Press, 2012), p. 172.

33. Haslanger, *Resisting Reality*, p. 172.

34. Caroline Whitbeck, "The Maternal Instinct," in *Mothering: Essays in Feminist Theory*, ed. Joyce Trebilcot (Totowa, NJ: Rowman and Allanheld, 1984), pp. 185–191, cited in Anca Gheaus, "The Right to Parent One's Biological Baby," *Journal of Political Philosophy* 20, no. 4 (2012): 432–455.

35. Gheaus, "The Right to Parent One's Biological Baby," p. 451.

36. On the duty to have children, see Anca Gheaus, "Could There Ever Be a Duty to Have Children?" in *Permissible Progeny?*, ed. Sarah Hannan, Samantha Brennan, and Richard Vernon (Oxford: Oxford University Press, forthcoming).

37. It is natural to think that biological parents are the primary duty-bearers, at least in cases where they can properly be held responsible for the child's existence. Even in those cases, however, it is arguable that the duties are owed not to the child directly. Perhaps we owe it to other adults that they not be saddled with duties as a result of our procreative activity, and that is why it is procreators who have the duty to ensure that the child is parented (which is different from having the duty to parent it oneself).

CHAPTER 4

Adults

1. Frederick Schoeman puts the interest in intimacy central but fails to recognize the distinctive features of the intimacy specific to parent-child relationships. See his "Rights of Children, Rights of Parents, and the Moral Basis of the Family," *Ethics* 91, no. 1 (1980): 6–19. An account that shares some of the features of ours can be found in Colin Macleod's "Liberal Equality and the Affective Family," in *The Moral and Political Status of Children*, ed. David Archard and Colin M. Macleod (Oxford: Oxford University Press, 2002), pp. 212–230.

2. Locke says that "parents were, by the Law of Nature, under an obligation to preserve, nourish, and educate the Children they had begotten; [though] not as their own Workmanship, but as the Workmanship of their own Maker, the Almighty to whom they were to be accountable for them." John Locke, *The Second Treatise of Government*, in *Two Treatises of Government*, ed. Peter Laslett (Cambridge: Cambridge University Press, 1988), paragraph 56. Contemporary theorists who emphasize the fiduciary interest, despite giving otherwise different accounts of the relationships, include Rob Reich, *Bridging Liberalism and Multiculturalism in American Education* (Chicago: University of Chicago Press, 2002), pp. 148–151; William Galston, *Liberal Pluralism: The Implications of Value Pluralism for Political Theory and Practice* (Cambridge: Cambridge University

Press, 2002), pp. 101–106; Eamonn Callan, *Creating Citizens* (Oxford: Oxford University Press, 1997), chap. 6; James G. Dwyer, *Religious Schools v. Children's Rights* (Ithaca, NY: Cornell University Press, 1999); Samantha Brennan and Robert Noggle, "The Moral Status of Children: Childrens' Rights, Parents' Rights, and Family Justice," *Social Theory and Practice* 23, no.1 (1997): 1–25; David Archard, *Children: Rights and Childhood*, 2nd ed. (London: Routledge, 2004).

3. Nannies sometimes experience a variant of the full package—effectively doing most of the parenting. In our view, one of the tragedies in that relationship is that its security is vulnerable to the arbitrary power of the child's official "parents."

4. Hugh LaFollette, "Licensing Parents Revisited," *Journal of Applied Philosophy* 27, no. 4 (2010): 327–343; Jurgen De Wispelaere and Daniel Weinstock, "Licensing Parents to Protect Our Children?" *Ethics and Social Welfare* 6, no. 2 (2012): 192–205; Michael McFall, *Licensing Parents: Family, State, and Child Maltreatment* (Lanham, MD: Rowman and Littlefield, 2009).

5. Liam Shields, "How Bad Can a Good Enough Parent Be?" (unpublished). Available at http://www.academia.edu/1528782/How_Bad_Can_a_Good_Enough_Parent_Be.

6. Callan, *Creating Citizens*, p. 142.

7. Lisa Cassidy, "That Many of Us Should Not Parent," *Hypatia* 21, no. 4 (2006): 40–57.

8. For a book-length treatment of the reasons for (and against) having children, see Christine Overall, *Why Have Children? The Ethical Debate* (Cambridge, MA: MIT Press, 2012). Overall's focus is on procreation, rather than parenting, though of course, in the standard case, people's reasons for wanting to do the former are so that they can get to do the latter.

9. Colin M. Macleod, "Parental Responsibilities in an Unjust World," in *Procreation and Parenthood*, ed. David Archard and David Benatar (Oxford: Oxford University Press, 2010), pp. 128–150, p. 142.

10. Edgar Page, "Parental Rights," *Journal of Applied Philosophy* 1, no. 2 (1984): 187–203, p. 200.

11. Ibid., p. 196 (our emphasis).

12. Cf. Michael W. Austin, "The Failure of Biological Accounts of Parenthood," *Journal of Value Inquiry* 38, no. 4 (2004): 499–510, pp. 507–509.

13. See Yonathan Reshef, "Rethinking the Value of Families," *Critical Review of International Social and Political Philosophy* 16, no. 1 (2013): 130–150, for an account of the parent-centered value of the family that appeals to the importance of shared identity—"a strong sense of interconnectedness and continuity between the parent's and child's identities that is established during childhood by a process of reproducing some of the parent's characteristics in the child." Reshef's paper appeared too recently for us adequately to respond to it here.

14. Mary Warnock, *Making Babies: Is There a Right to Have Children?* (Oxford: Oxford University Press, 2002), p. 4.

15. John Robertson, "The Question of Human Cloning," in *The Human Cloning Debate*, ed. Glenn McGee (Berkeley, CA: Berkeley Hills Books, 2002), pp. 42–57, p. 46. Robertson infers from this a positive right to technological assistance: "Infertile couples have the same interests in reproducing as coitally fertile couples, and the same abilities to rear children. That they are coitally infertile should no more bar them from repro-

ducing with technical assistance than visual blindness should bar a person from reading with Braille or the aid of a reader."

16. Carson Strong, "Cloning and Infertility," originally published in *Cambridge Quarterly of Healthcare Ethics* 7, no. 3 (1998); reprinted in *The Human Cloning Debate*, ed. Glenn McGee (Berkeley, CA: Berkeley Hills Books, 2002), pp. 184–211. See pp. 202–204.

17. Page, "Parental Rights," pp. 199–200.

18. Ibid., p. 201.

19. Anca Gheaus, "The Right to Parent One's Biological Baby," *Journal of Political Philosophy* 20, no. 4 (2012): 432–455, pp. 436, 450.

20. Judith Jarvis Thomson, "A Defense of Abortion," *Philosophy & Public Affairs* 1, no. 1 (1971): 47–66.

21. Gheaus, "The Right to Parent One's Biological Baby," pp. 453, 455, 436.

Introduction to Part Three

1. Amy Gutmann, *Democratic Education*, rev. ed. (Princeton, NJ: Princeton University Press, 1999); Eamonn Callan, *Creating Citizens* (Oxford: Oxford University Press, 1997); Meira Levinson, *The Demands of Liberal Education* (Oxford: Oxford University Press, 2002); James G. Dwyer, *Religious Schools v. Children's Rights* (Ithaca, NY: Cornell University Press, 2001); Rob Reich, *Bridging Liberalism and Multiculturalism in American Education* (Chicago: University of Chicago Press, 2002).

2. That, at least, is what she says in *The Positively True Adventures of the Alleged Texas Cheerleader-Murdering Mom* (dir. Michael Ritchie, Frederick S. Pierce Company, 1993). See also Anne McDonald Maier, *Mother Love, Deadly Love*. (New York: St. Martin's Paperbacks, 1994).

3. For Rawls, we need to distinguish between "the point of view of people as citizens and their point of view as members of families and of other associations. As citizens we have reasons to impose the constraints specified by the political principles of justice on association; while as members of associations we have reasons for limiting those constraints so that they leave room for a free and flourishing internal life appropriate to the association in question." *Justice as Fairness: A Restatement* (Cambridge, MA: Harvard University Press, 2001), p. 165.

4. "The phrase 'child abuse' is no exaggeration when used to describe what teachers and priests are doing to children whom they encourage to believe in something like the punishment of unshriven mortal sins in an eternal hell." Richard Dawkins, *The God Delusion* (Wilmington, MA: Mariner Books, 2008), p. 358.

5. For an account that has influenced our thinking, see Sarah Hannan and Richard Vernon, "Parental Rights: A Role-Based Approach," *Theory and Research in Education* 6, no. 2 (2008): 173–189.

CHAPTER 5

Conferring Advantage

1. See Kenneth Arrow, Samuel Bowles, and Steven Durlauf, eds., *Meritocracy and Economic Inequality* (Princeton, NJ: Princeton University Press, 2000); Samuel Bowles, Herbert Gintis, and Melissa Osborne-Groves, eds., *Unequal Chances: Family Background and Economic Success* (Princeton, NJ: Princeton University Press, 2005); Greg

Duncan and Dick Murnane, eds., *Whither Opportunity?* (New York: Russell Sage Foundation; Chicago: Spencer Foundation, 2011); Lee Rainwater and Timothy Smeeding, *Poor Kids in a Rich Country* (New York: Russell Sage Foundation, 2005); John Ermisch, Markus Jantti, and Timothy Smeeding, eds., *From Parents to Children: The Intergenerational Transmission of Advantage* (New York: Russell Sage Foundation, 2012); and, for a qualitative account, Annette Lareau, *Unequal Childhoods*, 2nd ed. (Berkeley: University of California Press, 2011). For a careful account of how this plays out specifically with respect to the uptake of education in American schools, see Richard Rothstein, *Class and Schools: Using Social, Economic, and Educational Reform to Close the Black-White Achievement Gap* (Washington, DC: Economic Policy Institute and Teachers College, 2004).

2. Lareau, *Unequal Childhoods*, p. 133.

3. See also Samuel Bowles and Herbert Gintis, "The Inheritance of Inequality," *Journal of Economic Perspectives* 16, no. 3 (2002): 3–30.

4. For a sustained argument for a radical reform of the occupational structure, see Paul Gomberg, *How to Make Opportunity Equal: Race and Contributive Justice* (Oxford: Blackwell, 2007).

5. On prioritarianism, see the works cited in chap. 2, n. 28.

6. John Rawls, *A Theory of Justice* (Cambridge MA: Harvard University Press, 1971); G. A. Cohen, *Rescuing Justice and Equality* (Cambridge, MA: Harvard University Press, 2008).

7. For this objection to a less nuanced version of the current argument, see Matthew Clayton and David Stevens, "School Choice and the Burdens of Injustice," *Theory and Research in Education* 2, no. 2 (2004): 111–126.

8. See Paul Bou-Habib for the alternative view that it is not in parents' interests to favor their children in ways that exceed the morally permissible: "The Moralized View of Parental Partiality," *Journal of Political Philosophy* 22, no. 1 (2014): 66–83.

9. Samuel Scheffler, *Boundaries and Allegiances: Problems of Justice and Responsibility in Liberal Thought* (New York: Oxford University Press, 2001), p. 123. Scheffler continues: "Social institutions can vary considerably in their character while still leaving ample room for people to behave in ways that give expression to the value they attach to their interpersonal relationships. Within a fairly broad range, people can modify the behaviour that serves this function to fit the institutional and normative context in which they find themselves. In particular, they can adapt their behaviour to more or less egalitarian institutions and policies. People who live in societies with relatively more extensive social welfare programmes, or more extensive policies of redistributive taxation, are not thereby prohibited from giving meaningful expression to the value they place on their most treasured relationships. To be sure, this kind of flexibility is not unlimited, and it is an interesting question where the limits lie. However, it is not necessary to fix those limits with any precision to see that a general practice of honouring special responsibilities need not preclude the implementation of significantly egalitarian policies, or deprive a professed commitment to equality of all practical implications." We are offering an answer to the interesting question of where the limits lie.

10. Discretion and spontaneity have important implications for state attempts to promote good parenting. Richard Rothstein expresses rare skepticism that reading to children will produce cognitive benefit if the parent is unenthusiastic (see *Class and Schools*, chap. 2); but, even if parents could promote their children's cognitive development when they would rather be doing something else, there would still be a loss in terms of other aspects of the relationship. Reading to one's child will be less expressive of, and hence less likely to foster, an intimate loving relationship if one is not independently invested in it. With regard to that goal, it may well be counterproductive.

11. With respect to private schooling, we here disagree with Colin Macleod, "The Puzzle of Parental Partiality," *Theory and Research in Education* 2, no. 3 (2004): 309–321.

12. See Stephen Macedo, "School Reform and Equal Opportunity in America's Geography of Inequality," *Perspectives on Politics* 1, no. 4 (2003): 743–755; Annette Lareau, *Home Advantage* (Berkeley: University of California Press, 2000).

13. In the U.S. case, see, for example, Michael J. Graetz and Ian Shapiro, *Death by a Thousand Cuts: The Fight over Taxing Inherited Wealth* (Princeton, NJ: Princeton University Press, 2006); Nathan Glazer, "Separate and Unequal," *New York Times Book Review*, 25 September 2005, pp. 12–13.

CHAPTER 6

Shaping Values

1. Charles Fried, *Right and Wrong* (Cambridge, MA: Harvard University Press, 1976), p. 152.

2. William Galston, *Liberal Pluralism: The Implications of Value Pluralism for Political Theory and Practice* (Cambridge: Cambridge University Press, 2002), p. 102.

3. UN General Assembly, Universal Declaration of Human Rights, 10 December 1948, 217 A (III), Article 7, available at http://www.refworld.org/docid/3ae6b3712c .html; International Covenant on Economic, Social and Cultural Rights, 16 December 1966, United Nations, Treaty Series, vol. 993, p. 3, available at http://www.refworld.org /docid/3ae6b36c0.html.

4. John Rawls, *A Theory of Justice*, rev. ed. (Cambridge, MA: Harvard University Press, 1999), pp. 41, 414–419, and "The Sense of Justice," in *Collected Papers*, ed. Samuel Freeman (Cambridge, MA: Harvard University Press, 1999), chap. 5, pp. 96–116. (Originally published in *Philosophical Review* 72, no. 3 [1963]: 281–305.)

5. There is also distinctive value to a parent's having her life improved by a loving child. We cannot here explore how our theory might be extended to consider children's rights and duties to benefit their parents (legitimate *filial* partiality), for example when parents are elderly and in need of care, but we hope that we or others will address that agenda in due course. For an attempt to invoke relationship goods to explain filial duties, see Jonathan Seglow, *Defending Associative Duties* (London: Routledge, 2013, chap. 4.

6. See Colin M. Macleod, "Conceptions of Parental Autonomy," *Politics & Society* 25, no. 1 (1997): 117–141, for the idea that parents should be free provisionally to privilege their own beliefs in their relations with their children.

7. See Michael Sandel, *The Case against Perfection* (Cambridge, MA: Harvard University Press, 2009), pp. 52–62, for a nice discussion of the phenomenon he calls "hyperpar-

enting." See also Leon Kass, "The Wisdom of Repugnance," *New Republic*, 2 June 1997, pp. 17–26.

8. Of course, your aunt is also your parent's sibling. We cannot here explore the implications of our theory for the analysis of the value of sibling relationships. The thought, from which such an analysis would begin, is that the special—distinctively familial—aspect of sibling relationships derives from the fact that siblings are raised by the same parent(s).

9. See Joel Feinberg, "The Child's Right to an Open Future," in *Freedom and Fulfillment: Philosophical Essays* (Princeton, NJ: Princeton University Press, 1994), pp. 76–97; Claudia Mills, "The Child's Right to an Open Future," *Journal of Social Philosophy* 34, no. 4 (2003): 499–509.

10. The first question is posed most thoroughly by Matthew Clayton, *Justice and Legitimacy in Upbringing* (New York: Oxford University Press, 2006), and "The Case against the Comprehensive Enrolment of Children," *Journal of Political Philosophy* 20, no. 3 (2011): 353–364. We discuss Clayton's position further below. For critical discussion of Clayton's view, see Tim Fowler, "The Problems of Liberal Neutrality in Upbringing," *Res Publica* 16, no. 4 (2010): 367–381; Christina Cameron, "Clayton on Comprehensive Enrolment," *Journal of Political Philosophy* 20, no. 3 (2011): 341–352.

11. On different views of autonomy and its value, see, for example, Harry Frankfurt, "Freedom of the Will and the Concept of a Person," in *The Importance of What We Care About* (Cambridge: Cambridge University Press, 1987), chap. 2, pp. 11–25; Gary Watson, "Free Agency," *Journal of Philosophy* 72, no. 8 (1975): 205–220; Joseph Raz, *The Morality of Freedom* (Oxford: Oxford University Press, 1986), chaps. 14 and 15; Gerald Dworkin, *The Theory and Practice of Autonomy* (New York: Cambridge University Press, 1988); Thomas Hurka, "Why Value Autonomy?" *Social Theory and Practice* 13, no. 3 (1987): 361–382; Marilyn Friedman, "Autonomy and the Split-Level Self," *Southern Journal of Philosophy* 24, no. 1 (1986): 19–35; Christine Korsgaard, *Creating the Kingdom of Ends* (Cambridge: Cambridge University Press, 1996), chap. 13; Barbara Herman, *The Practice of Moral Judgment* (Cambridge, MA: Harvard University Press, 1993), especially chaps. 1, 4, 7, and 9.

12. See Jon Elster, *Ulysses and the Sirens* (Cambridge: Cambridge University Press, 1982), for a nice discussion of such departures from autonomy.

13. For valuable correctives to overintellectualized ways of thinking about autonomy, see Shelley Burtt, "Comprehensive Educations and the Liberal Understanding of Autonomy," in *Citizenship and Education in Liberal Democratic Societies: Teaching for Cosmopolitan Values and Collective Identities*, ed. Walter Feinberg and Kevin McDonough (Oxford: Oxford University Press, 2003), pp. 179–207; Eamonn Callan, "Autonomy, Childrearing and Good Lives," in *The Moral and Political Status of Children*, ed. David Archard and Colin M. Macleod (Oxford: Oxford University Press, 2002), pp. 118–141.

14. Raz, *The Morality of Freedom*, pp. 369–370.

15. See Will Kymlicka, *Liberalism, Community and Culture* (Oxford: Oxford University Press, 1989), chapters 8 and 9, for an extensive discussion of the interest in living a life from the inside and its significance for cultural reproduction.

16. Harry Brighouse, "Liberal Legitimacy and Civic Education," *Ethics* 108, no. 4 (1998): 719–745.

17. John Rawls, *Political Liberalism* (New York: Columbia University Press, 1993), p. 137.

18. Clayton, *Justice and Legitimacy in Upbringing*, p. 94.

19. Ibid., p. 95.

20. Burtt, "Comprehensive Educations and the Liberal Understanding of Autonomy," p. 202.

21. Paula McAvoy, "There Are No Housewives on *Star Trek*: A Reexamination of Exit Rights for the Children of Insular Fundamentalist Parents," *Educational Theory* 62, no. 5 (2012): 535–552.

22. Burtt, "Comprehensive Educations and the Liberal Understanding of Autonomy," p. 201.

Conclusion

1. See Christina Sommers, "Filial Morality," *Journal of Philosophy* 83, no. 8 (1986): 439–456; Norman Daniels, *Am I My Parents' Keeper? An Essay on Justice between the Young and the Old* (New York: Oxford University Press, 1990); Simon Keller, "Four Theories of Filial Duty," *Philosophical Quarterly* 56, no. 223 (2006): 254–274; Claudia Mills, "Duties to Ageing Parents," in *Care of the Aged*, ed. James M. Hurber and Robert F. Almeder (Totowa, NJ: Human Press, 2003), pp. 147–166; Anders Schinkel, "Filial Obligations: A Contextual, Pluralist Model," *Journal of Ethics* 16, no. 4 (2012): 395–420.

2. For a sustained investigation along these lines, see Jonathan Seglow, *Defending Associative Duties* (London: Routledge, 2013).

3. For some very preliminary thoughts, see Harry Brighouse and Adam Swift, "Legitimate Partiality, Parents and Patriots," in *Arguing for Justice: Essays for Philippe Van Parijs*, ed. Axel Gosseries and Yannick Vanderborght (Louvain-la-Neuve: Presses Universitaires de Louvain, 2011), pp. 115–124. For relevant discussion, see Anna Stilz, *Liberal Loyalty: Freedom, Obligation, and the State* (Princeton, NJ: Princeton University Press, 2008); Seth Lazar, "The Justification of Associative Duties," *Journal of Moral Philosophy* (forthcoming).

4. See Simon Keller, *Partiality* (Princeton, NJ: Princeton University Press, 2013).

5. For some attempts in this direction, and discussion of the complications involved in those attempts, see our "The End of the Tory War on Single Parents?" *Public Policy Research* 14, no. 3 (2007): 186–192; "Social Justice and the Family," in *Social Justice and Public Policy*, ed. Tania Burchardt, Gary Craig, and David Gordon (Bristol: The Policy Press, 2008), pp. 139–156; "Family Values and School Policy: Shaping Values and Conferring Advantage," in *Education, Justice, and Democracy*, ed. Danielle Allen and Rob Reich (Chicago: University of Chicago Press, 2013), pp. 199–220.

6. See Françoise Baylis and Carolyn Macleod, eds., *Family Making* (Oxford: Oxford University Press, 2014).

7. See Sarah Hannan, Samantha Brennan, and Richard Vernon, eds., *Permissible Progeny?* (New York: Oxford University Press, forthcoming).

8. John Rawls, *Political Liberalism* (New York: Columbia University Press, 1993). For a brief account of the issues raised by this position, intended to be accessible to the nonspecialist, see Adam Swift, *Political Philosophy: A Beginners' Guide for Students and Politicians*, 3rd ed. (Cambridge, MA: Polity Press, 2013), pp.167–170. For thorough defenses of the position, see Jonathan Quong, *Liberalism without Perfection* (Oxford:

Oxford University Press, 2011); and Steven Lecce, *Against Perfectionism: Defending Liberal Neutrality* (Toronto: University of Toronto Press, 2008). The seminal defense of perfectionist liberalism is Joseph Raz, *The Morality of Freedom* (Oxford: Oxford University Press, 1986).

9. For an approach to the issue of bequest and inheritance that contrasts nicely with ours in chapter 5, see Matthew Clayton, "Equal Inheritance: An Anti-Perfectionist View," in *Inherited Wealth, Justice and Equality*, ed. Guido Erreygers and John Cunliffe (London: Routledge, 2013), pp. 98–118.

10. For philosophical work on this topic, see Paula Casal and Andrew Williams, "Equality of Resources and Procreative Justice," in *Dworkin and His Critics*, ed. Justine Burley (Oxford: Blackwell, 2004), pp. 150–169; Matthew Clayton, *Justice and Legitimacy in Upbringing* (Oxford: Oxford University Press, 2006), pp. 61–75; Serena Olsaretti, "Choice, Circumstance and the Cost of Children," in *Hillel Steiner and the Anatomy of Justice*, ed. Stephen de Wijze, Matthew H. Kramer, and Ian Carter (London: Routledge, 2009), pp. 70–84, and "Children as Public Goods," *Philosophy & Public Affairs* 41, no. 3 (2013): 226–258; Patrick Tomlin "Should Kids Pay Their Own Way?," *Political Studies* (forthcoming 2014). Because these contributions operate at an abstract level, their claims would need to be combined with complex empirical assessments to yield concrete policy implications here and now.

BIBLIOGRAPHY

Adams, Paul, et al. *Children's Rights: Toward the Liberation of the Child.* New York: Praeger Publishers, 1971.

Alderson, Priscilla. *Children's Consent to Surgery.* Milton Keynes: Open University Press, 1993.

Almond, Brenda. *The Fragmenting Family.* Oxford: Oxford University Press, 2006.

Alstott, Anne. *No Exit: What Parents Owe Their Children and What Society Owes Parents.* Oxford: Oxford University Press, 2005.

Anderson, Elizabeth. "What Is the Point of Equality?" *Ethics* 109, no. 2 (1999): 287–337.

Archard, David. *Children: Rights and Childhood.* 2nd ed. London: Routledge, 2004.

———. *Children, Family and the State.* Aldershot, UK: Ashgate, 2003.

———. *The Family: A Liberal Defence.* Basingstoke: Palgrave Macmillan, 2011.

Archard, David, and David Benatar, eds. *Procreation and Parenthood.* Oxford: Oxford University Press, 2010.

Archard, David, and Colin M. Macleod, eds. *The Moral and Political Status of Children.* Oxford: Oxford University Press, 2002.

Aristotle. *The Politics.* Translated by Carnes Lord. Chicago: University of Chicago Press, 1985.

Arneil, Barbara. "Becoming versus Being: A Critical Analysis of the Child in Liberal Theory." In *The Moral and Political Status of Children,* edited by David Archard and Colin M. Macleod, 70–94. Oxford: Oxford University Press, 2002.

Arneson, Richard. "Against Rawlsian Equality of Opportunity." *Philosophical Studies* 93, no. 1 (1999): 77–112.

———. "Equality of Opportunity." In *The Stanford Encyclopedia of Philosophy* (Fall 2008 edition), edited by Edward N. Zalta. http://plato.stanford.edu/archives/fall2008/entries/equal-opportunity/.

Arrow, Kenneth, Samuel Bowles, and Steven Durlauf, eds. *Meritocracy and Economic Inequality.* Princeton, NJ: Princeton University Press, 2000.

Austin, Michael W. *Conceptions of Parenthood: Ethics and the Family.* Aldershot: Ashgate, 2007.

———. "The Failure of Biological Accounts of Parenthood." *Journal of Value Inquiry* 38, no. 4 (2004): 499–510.

Bagattini, Alexander, and Colin M. Macleod, eds. *The Well-Being of Children in Theory and Practice.* Dordrecht: Springer (forthcoming).

Baylis, Françoise, and Carolyn Macleod, eds. *Family-Making: Contemporary Ethical Challenges.* Oxford: Oxford University Press, 2014.

Becker, Gary. *A Treatise on the Family.* Cambridge, MA: Harvard University Press, 1991.

Berns, Sandra. "Liberalism and the Privatized Family: The Legacy of Rousseau." *Res Publica* 11, no. 2 (2005): 125–155.

Bettelheim, Bruno. *A Good Enough Parent*. London: Thames and Hudson, 1987.

Blustein, Jeffrey. *Parents and Children: The Ethics of the Family*. New York: Oxford University Press, 1982.

Bou-Habib, Paul. "The Moralized View of Parental Partiality." *Journal of Political Philosophy* 22, no. 1 (2014): 66–83.

Bowlby, John. *Secure Base: Parent-Child Attachment and Healthy Human Development*. London: Routledge, 1988.

Bowles, Samuel, and Herbert Gintis. "The Inheritance of Economic Status: Education, Class and Genetics." In *International Encyclopedia of the Social and Behavioral Sciences: Genetics, Behavior and Society*, edited by Marcus Feldman and Paul Baltes, 4132–4141. New York: Oxford University Press and Elsevier, 2001.

———. "The Inheritance of Inequality." *Journal of Economic Perspectives* 16, no. 3 (2002): 3–30.

Bowles, Samuel, Herbert Gintis, and Melissa Osborne-Groves, eds. *Unequal Chances: Family Background and Economic Success*. Princeton, NJ: Princeton University Press, 2005.

Brazelton, T. Berry, and Stanley I. Greenspan. *The Irreducible Needs of Children: What Every Child Must Have to Grow, Learn, and Flourish*. Cambridge, MA: Da Capo Press, 2000.

Brennan, Samantha. "The Goods of Childhood and Children's Rights." In *Family-Making: Contemporary Ethical Challenges*, edited by Françoise Baylis and Carolyn McLeod, 29–45. Oxford: Oxford University Press, 2014.

Brennan, Samantha, and Robert Noggle. "The Moral Status of Children: Children's Rights, Parents' Rights, and Family Justice." *Social Theory and Practice* 23, no. 1 (1997): 1–25.

Brettshchneider, Corey. "The Politics of the Personal: A Liberal Approach." *American Political Science Review* 101, no. 1 (2007): 19–31.

Brighouse, Harry. "Liberal Legitimacy and Civic Education." *Ethics* 108, no. 4 (1998): 719–745.

Brighouse, Harry, and Adam Swift. "The End of the Tory War on Single Parents?" *Public Policy Research* 14, no. 3 (2007): 186–192.

———. "Equality, Priority and Positional Goods." *Ethics* 116, no. 3 (2006): 471–497.

———. "Family Values and School Policy: Shaping Values and Conferring Advantage." In *Education, Justice, and Democracy*, edited by Danielle Allen and Rob Reich, 199–220. Chicago: University of Chicago Press, 2013.

———. "The Goods of Parenting." In *Family-Making: Contemporary Ethical Challenges*, edited by Françoise Baylis and Carolyn McLeod, 11–28. Oxford: Oxford University Press, 2014.

———. "Legitimate Parental Partiality." *Philosophy and Public Affairs* 37, no. 1 (2009): 43–80.

———. "Legitimate Partiality, Parents and Patriots." In *Arguing for Justice: Essays for Philippe Van Parijs*, edited by Axel Gosseries and Yannick Vanderborght, 115–124. Louvain-la-Neuve: Presses Universitaires de Louvain, 2011.

———. "Parents' Rights and the Value of the Family." *Ethics* 117, no. 1 (2006): 80–108.

———. "The Place of Educational Equality in Educational Justice." In *Education, Justice and the Human Good*, edited by Kirsten Meyer, 14–33. London: Routledge, 2014.

———. "Social Justice and the Family." In *Social Justice and Public Policy*, edited by Tania Burchardt, Gary Craig, and David Gordon, 139–156. Bristol: The Policy Press, 2008.

Brighouse, Harry, and Erik Olin Wright. "Strong Gender Egalitarianism." *Politics & Society* 36, no. 3 (2008): 360–372.

Brock, Gillian. *Global Justice: A Cosmopolitan Account*. Oxford: Oxford University Press, 2009.

Bubeck, Diemut. *Care, Gender and Justice*. Oxford: Oxford University Press, 1995.

Burney, Elizabeth, and Loraine Gelsthorpe. "Do We Need a 'Naughty Step'? Rethinking the Parenting Order after Ten Years." *Howard Journal of Criminal Justice* 47 (2008): 470–485.

Burtt, Shelley. "Comprehensive Educations and the Liberal Understanding of Autonomy." In *Citizenship and Education in Liberal Democratic Societies: Teaching for Cosmopolitan Values and Collective Identities*, edited by Walter Feinberg and Kevin McDonough, 179–207. Oxford: Oxford University Press, 2003.

———. "The Proper Scope of Parental Authority: Why We Don't Owe Children an 'Open Future.' " In *Nomos XLIV: Child, Family, and State*, edited by Stephen Macedo and Iris Marion Young, 243–270. New York: New York University Press, 2003.

———. "What Children Really Need: Toward a Critical Theory of Family Structure." In *The Moral and Political Status of Children*, edited by David Archard and Colin M. Macleod, 231–52. Oxford: Oxford University Press, 2002.

Callan, Eamonn. "Autonomy, Childrearing and Good Lives." In *The Moral and Political Status of Children*, edited by David Archard and Colin M. Macleod, 118–141. Oxford: Oxford University Press, 2002.

———. *Creating Citizens*. Oxford: Oxford University Press, 1997.

Cameron, Christina. "Clayton on Comprehensive Enrolment." *Journal of Political Philosophy* 20, no. 3 (2011): 341–352.

Caney, Simon. *Justice beyond Borders*. Oxford: Oxford University Press, 2006.

Card, Claudia. "Against Marriage and Motherhood." *Hypatia* 11, no. 3 (1996): 1–23.

Casal, Paula, and Andrew Williams. "Equality of Resources and Procreative Justice." In *Dworkin and His Critics*, edited by Justine Burley, 150–169. Oxford: Blackwell, 2004.

Cassidy, Lisa. "That Many of Us Should Not Parent." *Hypatia* 21, no. 1 (2006): 40–57.

Clayton, Matthew. "The Case against the Comprehensive Enrolment of Children." *Journal of Political Philosophy* 20, no. 3 (2011): 353–364.

———. "Equal Inheritance: An Anti-Perfectionist View." In *Inherited Wealth, Justice and Equality*, edited by Guido Erreygers and John Cunliffe, pp. 98–118. London: Routledge, 2013.

———. *Justice and Legitimacy in Upbringing*. Oxford: Oxford University Press, 2006.

———. "Rawls and Natural Aristocracy." *Croatian Journal of Philosophy* 1, no. 3 (2001): 239–259.

Clayton, Matthew, and David Stevens. "School Choice and the Burdens of Injustice." *Theory and Research in Education* 2, no. 2 (2004): 111–126.

Clinton, Hillary. *It Takes a Village: And Other Lessons Children Teach Us*. New York: Simon and Schuster, 1996.

Cohen, G. A. *Rescuing Justice and Equality*. Cambridge, MA: Harvard University Press, 2008.

Cohen, Howard. *Equal Rights for Children*. Totowa, NJ: Rowman and Littlefield, 1980.

Communitarian Network. http://communitariannetwork.org/communitarian-vision/.

Council of Europe. European Convention for the Protection of Human Rights and Fundamental Freedoms, as amended by Protocols Nos. 11 and 14. 4 November 1950. ETS 5, Articles 8 and 12. http://www.refworld.org/docid/3ae6b3b04.html.

Cowden, Mhairi. "What's Love Got to Do with It? Why a Child Does Not Have a Right to Be Loved." Critical Review of International Social and Political Philosophy 15, no. 3 (2012): 325–345.

Craig, Gary, and David Gordon, eds. Social Justice and Public Policy. Bristol: The Policy Press, 2008.

Daniels, Norman. Am I My Parents' Keeper? An Essay on Justice between the Young and the Old. New York: Oxford University Press, 1990.

Dawkins, Richard. The God Delusion. Wilmington, MA: Mariner Books, 2008.

De Wispelaere, Jurgen, and Daniel Weinstock. "Licensing Parents to Protect Our Children?" Ethics and Social Welfare 6, no. 2 (2012): 192–205.

Dickens, Charles. Bleak House. Oxford: Oxford University Press, 2008.

Duncan, Greg, and Dick Murnane, eds. Whither Opportunity? New York: Russell Sage Foundation; Chicago: Spencer Foundation, 2011.

Dworkin, Gerald. The Theory and Practice of Autonomy. New York: Cambridge University Press, 1988.

Dworkin, Ronald. "Do Equality and Liberty Conflict?" In Living as Equals, edited by Paul Barker, 39–58. Oxford: Oxford University Press, 1999.

———. Justice for Hedgehogs. Cambridge MA: Harvard University Press, 2011.

———. Sovereign Virtue. Cambridge, MA: Harvard University Press, 2000.

Dwyer, James G. Religious Schools v. Children's Rights. Ithaca, NY: Cornell University Press, 1999.

Eekelar, John. "The Emergence of Children's Rights." Oxford Journal of Legal Studies 16, no. 2 (1986): 161–182.

Elster, Jon. Ulysses and the Sirens. Cambridge: Cambridge University Press, 1982.

Engster, Daniel. The Heart of Justice: Care Ethics and Political Theory. Oxford: Oxford University Press, 2007.

Ermisch, John, Markus Jantti, and Timothy Smeeding, eds. From Parents to Children: The Intergenerational Transmission of Advantage. New York: Russell Sage Foundation, 2012.

Farr, Rachel H., Stephen L. Forssell, and Charlotte J. Patterson. "Parenting and Child Development in Adoptive Families: Does Parental Sexual Orientation Matter?" Applied Developmental Science 14, no. 3 (2010): 164–178.

Feinberg, Joel. "The Child's Right to an Open Future." In Freedom and Fulfillment: Philosophical Essays, 76–97. Princeton, NJ: Princeton University Press, 1994.

Fishkin, Joseph. Bottlenecks: A New Theory of Equal Opportunity. Oxford: Oxford University Press, 2014.

Fowler, Tim. "The Problems of Liberal Neutrality in Upbringing." Res Publica 16, no. 4 (2010): 367–381.

Frankfurt, Harry. "Freedom of the Will and the Concept of a Person." In The Importance of What We Care About, 11–25. Cambridge: Cambridge University Press, 1987.

Frazer, Elizabeth. "Unpicking Political Communitarianism: A Critique of 'The Communitarian Family.'" In Changing Family Values, edited by Gill Jagger, 150–164. London: Routledge, 1999.

Freeman, Michael. "Why It Remains Important to Take Children's Rights Seriously." *International Journal of Children's Rights* 15 (2007): 5–23.

Fried, Charles. *Right and Wrong.* Cambridge, MA: Harvard University Press, 1976.

Friedman, Marilyn. "Autonomy and the Split-Level Self." *Southern Journal of Philosophy* 24, no. 1 (1986): 19–35.

Frier, Bruce W., and Thomas A. J. McGinn. *A Casebook on Roman Family Law.* American Philological Association Classical Resources Series. New York: Oxford University Press, 2004.

Galston, William. *Liberal Pluralism: The Implications of Value Pluralism for Political Theory and Practice.* Cambridge: Cambridge University Press, 2002.

Galston, William, Mary Ann Glendon, Jean Bethke Elshtain, Enola Aird, Amitai Etzioni, Martha Minow, and Alice Rossi. "A Communitarian Position Paper on the Family." http://www.gwu.edu/~ccps/pop_fam.html.

Gavison, Ruth. "Feminism and the Public/Private Distinction." *Stanford Law Review* 45, no. 1 (1992): 1–45.

Gerhardt, Sue. *Why Love Matters: How Affection Shapes a Baby's Brain.* London: Routledge, 2004.

Gheaus, Anca. "Arguments for Nonparental Care for Children." *Social Theory and Practice* 37, no. 3 (2011): 483–509.

———. "Could There Ever Be a Duty to Have Children?" In *Permissible Progeny?* Edited by Sarah Hannan, Samantha Brennan, and Richard Vernon. Oxford: Oxford University Press (forthcoming).

———. "Gender Justice." *Journal of Ethics & Social Philosophy* 6, no. 2 (2012): 1–24.

———. "The 'Intrinsic Goods of Childhood' and the Just Society." In *The Well-Being of Children in Theory and Practice,* edited by Alexander Bagattini and Colin M. Macleod. Dordrecht: Springer (forthcoming).

———. "The Right to Parent One's Biological Baby." *Journal of Political Philosophy* 20, no. 4 (2012): 432–455.

Gheaus, Anca, and Ingrid Robeyns. "Equality-Promoting Parental Leave." *Journal of Social Philosophy* 42, no. 2 (2011): 173–191.

Gilligan, Carol. *In a Different Voice: Psychological Theory and Women's Development.* Cambridge, MA: Harvard University Press, 1982.

Glazer, Nathan. "Separate and Unequal." *New York Times Book Review,* 25 September 2005, 12–13.

Goldberg, Abbie E. *Lesbian and Gay Parents and Their Children: Research on the Family Life Cycle.* Washington, DC: American Psychological Association, 2010.

Gomberg, Paul. *How to Make Opportunity Equal: Race and Contributive Justice.* Oxford: Blackwell, 2007.

Graetz, Michael J., and Ian Shapiro. *Death by a Thousand Cuts: The Fight over Taxing Inherited Wealth.* Princeton, NJ: Princeton University Press, 2006.

Griffin, James. *Well-Being.* Oxford: Oxford University Press, 1989.

Gutmann, Amy. *Democratic Education.* Rev. ed. Princeton, NJ: Princeton University Press, 1999.

Hannan, Sarah, Samantha Brennan, and Richard Vernon, eds. *Permissible Progeny?* New York: Oxford University Press (forthcoming).

Hannan, Sarah, and Richard Vernon, "Parental Rights: A Role-Based Approach." *Theory and Research in Education* 6, no. 2 (2008): 173–189.

Hardwig, John. "Should Women Think in Terms of Rights?" *Ethics* 94, no. 3 (1984): 441–455.

Haslanger, Sally. *Resisting Reality: Social Construction and Social Critique.* Oxford: Oxford University Press, 2012.

Held, Virginia. *The Ethics of Care: Personal, Political and Global.* New York: Oxford University Press, 2006.

Herman, Barbara. *The Practice of Moral Judgment.* Cambridge, MA: Harvard University Press, 1993.

Howe, David, and Julia Feast. "The Long-Term Outcome of Reunions between Adult Adopted People and Their Birth Mothers." *British Journal of Social Work* 31, no. 3 (2001): 351–368.

Hurka, Thomas. *Perfectionism.* New York: Oxford University Press, 1996.

———. "Why Value Autonomy?" *Social Theory and Practice* 13, no. 3 (1987): 361–382.

James, Allison. "Understanding Childhood from an Interdisciplinary Perspective." In *Rethinking Childhood,* edited by Peter Puffall and Richard Unsworth, 25–37. New Brunswick, NJ: Rutgers University Press, 2004.

Johnson, Martin. "A Biomedical Perspective on Parenthood." In *What Is a Parent?,* edited by Andrew Bainham et al., 47–71. Oxford: Hart Publishing, 1999.

Julius, A. J. "Nagel's Atlas." *Philosophy & Public Affairs* 34, no. 2 (2006): 176–192.

Kant, Immanuel. *The Metaphysics of Morals.* Translated by Mary Gregor. Cambridge: Cambridge University Press, 1996.

Kaplan, Morris B. "Legal Fictions and Family Romances: Contrasting Paradigms of Child Placement." In *NOMOS XLIV: Child, Family and State,* edited by Stephen Macedo and Iris Marion Young, 170–210. New York: New York University Press, 2003.

Kass, Leon. "The Wisdom of Repugnance." *New Republic,* 2 June 1997, 17–26.

Keller, Simon. "Four Theories of Filial Duty." *Philosophical Quarterly* 56, no. 223 (2006): 254–274.

———. *Partiality.* Princeton, NJ: Princeton University Press, 2013.

Kittay, Eva Feder. "A Feminist Public Ethic of Care Meets Family Policy." *Ethics* 111, no. 3 (2001): 523–547.

———. *Love's Labour: Essays on Women, Equality and Dependency.* London: Routledge, 1998.

Kollontai, Alexandra. *Selected Writings of Alexandra Kollontai.* Translated by Alix Holt. London: Allison and Busby, 1977.

Korsgaard, Christine. *Creating the Kingdom of Ends.* Cambridge: Cambridge University Press, 1996.

Kraut, Richard. *What Is Good and Why: The Ethics of Well-Being.* Cambridge, MA: Harvard University Press, 2009.

Kymlicka, Will. *Liberalism, Community and Culture.* Oxford: Oxford University Press, 1989.

———. "Rethinking the Family." *Philosophy & Public Affairs* 20, no. 1 (1991): 77–97.

LaFollette, Hugh. "Licensing Parents Revisited." *Journal of Applied Philosophy* 27, no. 4 (2010): 327–343.

Lareau, Annette. *Home Advantage.* Berkeley: University of California Press, 2000.

———. *Unequal Childhoods.* 2nd ed. Berkeley: University of California Press. 2011.

Layard, Richard. *Happiness: Lessons from a New Science.* Harmondsworth: Penguin, 2011.

Lazar, Seth. "The Justification of Associative Duties." *Journal of Moral Philosophy*, (forthcoming).

Lazenby, Hugh. "The Concept of Equality of Educational Opportunity." Unpublished paper given at Children, Education and Philosophy Group, University of Warwick, 6 September 2013.

Lecce, Steven. *Against Perfectionism: Defending Liberal Neutrality.* Toronto: University of Toronto Press, 2008.

Levinson, Meira. *The Demands of Liberal Education.* Oxford: Oxford University Press, 2002.

Levy-Schiff, Rachel. "Adaptation and Competence in Early Childhood: Communally Raised Kibbutz Children versus Family Raised Children in the City." *Child Development* 54, no. 6 (1983): 1606–1614.

Liao, S. Matthew. "The Idea of a Duty to Love." *Journal of Value Inquiry* 40, no. 1 (2006): 1–22.

———. "The Right of Children to Be Loved." *Journal of Political Philosophy* 14, no. 4 (2006): 420–440.

Locke, John. *Two Treatises of Government.* Edited by Peter Laslett. Cambridge: Cambridge University Press, 1988.

MacCormick, Neil. "Rights in Legislation." In *Law, Morality and Society: Essays in Honour of H.L.A. Hart,* edited by Peter Hacker and Joseph Raz, 189–209. Oxford: Oxford University Press, 1977.

Macedo, Stephen. "School Reform and Equal Opportunity in America's Geography of Inequality." *Perspectives on Politics* 1, no. 4 (2003): 743–755.

Macleod, Colin M. "Conceptions of Parental Autonomy." *Politics & Society* 25, no. 1 (1997): 117–141.

———. "Liberal Equality and the Affective Family." In *The Moral and Political Status of Children,* edited by David Archard and Colin M. Macleod, 212–230. Oxford: Oxford University Press, 2002.

———. "Parental Responsibilities in an Unjust World." In *Procreation and Parenthood,* edited by David Archard and David Benatar, 128–150. Oxford: Oxford University Press, 2010.

———. "Primary Goods, Capabilities, and Children." In *Measuring Justice,* edited by Ingrid Robeyns and Harry Brighouse, 174–192. Cambridge: Cambridge University Press, 2010.

———. "The Puzzle of Parental Partiality." *Theory and Research in Education* 2, no. 3 (2004): 309–321.

Maier, Anne McDonald. *Mother Love, Deadly Love.* New York: St. Martin's Paperbacks, 1994.

Marks, Loren. "Same-Sex Parenting and Children's Outcomes: A Closer Examination of the American Psychological Association's Brief on Lesbian and Gay Parenting." *Social Science Research* 41, no. 4 (2012): 735–751.

McAvoy, Paula. "There Are No Housewives on *Star Trek*: A Reexamination of Exit Rights for the Children of Insular Fundamentalist Parents." *Educational Theory* 62, no. 5 (2012): 535–552.

McFall, Michael. *Licensing Parents: Family, State, and Child Maltreatment*. Lanham, MD: Rowman and Littlefield, 2009.

McLanahan, Sara and Gary Sandefur. *Growing Up with a Single Parent: What Hurts, What Helps*. Cambridge, MA: Harvard University Press, 1994.

Mill, John Stuart. *On the Subjection of Women*. In *"On Liberty" and Other Writings*, edited by Stefan Collini. Cambridge: Cambridge University Press, 1989.

Miller, David. *On Nationality*. Oxford: Oxford University Press, 1995.

———. *Principles of Social Justice*. Cambridge, MA: Harvard University Press, 2001.

Miller, Richard W. *Globalizing Justice*. Oxford: Oxford University Press, 2010.

Mills, Claudia. "The Child's Right to an Open Future." *Journal of Social Philosophy* 34, no. 4 (2003): 499–509.

———. "Duties to Ageing Parents. " In *Care of the Aged*, edited by James M. Hurber and Robert F. Almeder, pp. 147–166. Totowa, NJ: Human Press, 2003.

Minow, Martha. *Making All the Difference: Inclusion, Exclusion, and American Law*. Ithaca, NY: Cornell University Press, 1990.

Morse, Jennifer Roback. "No Families, No Freedom: Human Flourishing in a Free Society." *Social Philosophy and Policy* 16, no. 1 (1999): 290–314.

Mulhall, Stephen, and Adam Swift. *Liberals and Communitarians*. 2nd ed. Oxford: Blackwell, 1996.

Munoz-Darde, Veronique. "Is the Family to Be Abolished, Then?" *Proceedings of the Aristotelian Society* 99, no. 1 (1999): 37–56.

Nagel, Thomas. "The Problem of Global Justice." *Philosophy & Public Affairs* 33, no. 2 (2005): 113–147.

Noddings, Nel. *Caring: A Feminine Approach to Ethics and Moral Education*. Berkeley: University of California Press, 2003.

Nozick, Robert. *Anarchy, State, and Utopia*. New York: Basic Books, 1974.

———. *The Examined Life: Philosophical Meditations*. New York: Simon and Schuster, 1989.

Nussbaum, Martha. *Women and Human Development: The Capabilities Approach*. Cambridge: Cambridge University Press, 2000.

Nussbaum, Martha, and Amartya Sen, eds. *The Quality of Life*. Oxford: Oxford University Press, 1993.

Oberdiek, John. "Specifying Rights Out of Necessity." *Oxford Journal of Legal Studies* 28, no. 1 (2008): 127–146.

Okin, Susan Moller. *Justice, Gender, and the Family*. New York: Basic Books, 1989.

Olsaretti, Serena. "Children as Public Goods." *Philosophy & Public Affairs* 41, no. 3 (2013): 226–258.

———. "Choice, Circumstance and the Cost of Children." In *Hillel Steiner and the Anatomy of Justice*, edited by Stephen de Wijze, Matthew H. Kramer, and Ian Carter, 70–84. London: Routledge, 2009.

O'Neill, Onora. "Children's Rights and Children's Lives." *Ethics* 98, no. 3 (1988): 445–463.

Overall, Christine. *Why Have Children? The Ethical Debate*. Cambridge, MA: MIT Press, 2012.

Page, Edgar. "Parental Rights." *Journal of Applied Philosophy* 1, no. 2 (1984): 187–203.

Pager, Devah. *Race, Crime and Finding Work in an Era of Mass Incarceration*. Chicago: University of Chicago Press, 2007.

Parfit, Derek. "Equality or Priority?" In *The Idea of Equality*, edited by Matthew Clayton and Andrew Williams, 81–125. Houndmills, Basingstoke: Palgrave Macmillan, 2002.

Pateman, Carole. "Feminist Critiques of the Public/Private Dichotomy." In *The Disorder of Women: Democracy, Feminism, and Political Theory*, 118–140. Stanford, CA: Stanford University Press, 1989.

Patterson, Charlotte J. "Lesbian and Gay Parents and Their Children: Summary of Research Findings." In *Lesbian and Gay Parenting: A Resource for Psychologists*. 2nd ed. Washington, DC: American Psychological Association, 2005.

Plato. *The Republic*. Edited by G.R.F. Ferrari. Cambridge: Cambridge University Press, 2000.

Popenoe, David. "Family Values: A Communitarian Position." In *Macro Socio-Economics: From Theory to Activism*, edited by David Sciulli, 165–183. Armonk, NY: M. E. Sharpe, 1996.

Positively True Adventures of the Alleged Texas Cheerleader-Murdering Mom. Directed by Michael Ritchie. Frederick S. Pierce Company, 1993.

Potter, Daniel. "Same-Sex Parent Families and Children's Academic Achievement." *Journal of Marriage and Family* 74, no. 3 (2012): 556–571.

Purdy, Laura. *In Their Best Interests: The Case against Equal Rights for Children*. Ithaca, NY: Cornell University Press, 1992.

Quong, Jonathan. *Liberalism without Perfection*. Oxford: Oxford University Press, 2011.

Rainwater, Lee, and Timothy Smeeding. *Poor Kids in a Rich Country*. New York: Russell Sage Foundation, 2005.

Rawls, John. *Justice as Fairness: A Restatement*. Cambridge, MA: Harvard University Press, 2001.

———. *Political Liberalism*. New York: Columbia University Press, 1993.

———. "The Sense of Justice." In *Collected Papers*, edited by Samuel Freeman, 96–116. Cambridge, MA: Harvard University Press, 1999. Originally printed in *Philosophical Review* 72, no. 3 (1963): 281–305.

———. *A Theory of Justice*. Cambridge MA: Harvard University Press, 1971.

———. *A Theory of Justice*. Rev. ed. Cambridge, MA: Harvard University Press, 1999.

Raz, Joseph. *The Morality of Freedom*. Oxford: Oxford University Press, 1986.

Rehfeld, Andrew. "The Child as Democratic Citizen." *Annals of the American Academy of Political and Social Science* 633, no. 1 (2011): 141–166.

Reich, Rob. *Bridging Liberalism and Multiculturalism in American Education*. Chicago: University of Chicago Press, 2002.

Report of the Commission on the Measurement of Economic Performance and Social Progress. 2009. www.stiglitz-sen-fitoussi.fr.

Reshef, Yonathan. "Rethinking the Value of Families." *Critical Review of International Social and Political Philosophy* 16, no. 1 (2013): 130–150.

Richards, Norvin. *The Ethics of Parenthood*. New York: Oxford University Press, 2010.

Robertson, John. "The Question of Human Cloning." In *The Human Cloning Debate*, edited by Glenn McGee, 42–57. Berkeley, CA: Berkeley Hills Books, 2002.

Rothstein, Richard. *Class and Schools: Using Social, Economic, and Educational Reform to Close the Black-White Achievement Gap, 2002*. Washington, DC: Economic Policy Institute and Teachers College, 2004.

Sandel, Michael. *The Case against Perfection*. Cambridge, MA: Harvard University Press, 2009.

Scanlon, T. M. *The Difficulty of Tolerance*. Cambridge: Cambridge University Press, 2003.

Schaar, John. "Equality of Opportunity, and Beyond." In *Nomos IX: Equality*, edited by Roland J. Pennock and John Chapman, 228–249. New York: Atherton Press, 1967. Reprinted in *Equality: Selected Readings*, ed. Louis P. Pojman and Robert Westmoreland, 137–147. New York: Oxford University Press, 1997.

Schapiro, Tamar. "What Is a Child?" *Ethics* 109, no. 4 (1999): 715–718.

Scharf, Miri. "A 'Natural Experiment' in Childrearing Ecologies and Adolescents' Attachment and Separation Representations." *Child Development* 72, no. 1 (2001): 236–251.

Scheffler, Samuel. *Boundaries and Allegiances: Problems of Justice and Responsibility in Liberal Thought*. Oxford: Oxford University Press, 2003.

———. "What Is Egalitarianism?" *Philosophy & Public Affairs* 31, no. 1 (2003): 5–39.

Schinkel, Anders. "Filial Obligations: A Contextual, Pluralist Model." *Journal of Ethics* 16, no. 4 (2012): 395–420.

Schoeman, Frederick. "Rights of Children, Rights of Parents, and the Moral Basis of the Family." *Ethics* 91, no. 1 (1980): 6–19.

Schrag, Francis. "Children and Democracy: Theory and Policy." *Politics, Philosophy & Economics* 3, no. 3 (2004): 365–379.

———. "Justice and the Family." *Inquiry* 19, nos. 1–4 (1976): 193–208.

Sclater, Shelley Day, and Candida Yates. "The Psycho-Politics of Post-Divorce Parenting." In *What Is a Parent?*, edited by Andrew Bainham et al., 271–293. Oxford: Hart Publishing, 1999.

Seglow, Jonathan. *Defending Associative Duties*. London: Routledge, 2013.

Shanley, Mary Lyndon. " 'No More Relevance than One's Eye-Color.' " In *Toward a Humane Justice*, edited by Debra Satz and Rob Reich, 113–128. Oxford: Oxford University Press, 2009.

Sher, George. *Desert*. Princeton, NJ: Princeton University Press, 1989.

Shields, Liam. "How Bad Can a Good Enough Parent Be?" Unpublished. Available at http://www.academia.edu/1528782/How_Bad_Can_a_Good_Enough_Parent_Be.

Sommers, Christina. "Filial Morality." *Journal of Philosophy* 83, no. 8 (1986): 439–456.

Steiner, Hillel. *An Essay on Rights*. Oxford: Blackwell, 1994.

Stilz, Anna. *Liberal Loyalty: Freedom, Obligation, and the State*. Princeton, NJ: Princeton University Press, 2008.

Strong, Carson. "Cloning and Infertility." *Cambridge Quarterly of Healthcare Ethics* 7, no. 3 (1998): 279–293. Reprinted in *The Human Cloning Debate*, edited by Glenn McGee, 184–211. Berkeley, CA: Berkeley Hills Books, 2002.

Sumner, L. W. *Welfare, Happiness and Ethics*. Oxford: Oxford University Press, 1999.

Swift, Adam. "Class Analysis from a Normative Perspective." *British Journal of Sociology* 51, no. 4 (2000): 663–679.

———. *How Not to Be a Hypocrite: School Choice for the Morally Perplexed Parent*. Routledge: London, 2003.

———. *Political Philosophy: A Beginners' Guide for Students and Politicians*. 3rd ed. Cambridge: Polity, 2013.

Swift, Adam, and Gordon Marshall. "Meritocratic Equality of Opportunity: Economic Efficiency, Social Justice, or Both?" *Policy Studies* 18, no. 1 (1997): 35–48.

Thomas, Laurence. *The Family and the Political Self.* Cambridge: Cambridge University Press, 2005.

Thomson, Judith Jarvis. "A Defense of Abortion," *Philosophy & Public Affairs* 1, no. 1 (1971): 47–66.

Tomlin, Patrick. "Should Kids Pay Their Own Way?" *Political Studies* (forthcoming 2014).

Tough, Paul. *Whatever It Takes.* New York: Houghton Mifflin, 2009.

Tronto, Joan. *Moral Boundaries: A Political Argument for an Ethic of Care.* London: Routledge, 1993.

UN Convention on the Rights of the Child, 20 November 1989. http://www.ohchr.org/EN/ProfessionalInterest/Pages/CRC.aspx.

UN General Assembly. International Covenant on Economic, Social and Cultural Rights. 16 December 1966. United Nations, Treaty Series. vol. 993, p. 3. http://www.refworld.org/docid/3ae6b36c0.html.

———. Universal Declaration of Human Rights. 10 December 1948. 217 A (III), Article 7. http://www.refworld.org/docid/3ae6b3712c.html.

Velleman, J. David. "Family History." *Philosophical Papers* 34, no. 13 (2005): 357–378.

Waldron, Jeremy. "When Justice Replaces Affection: The Need for Rights." In *Liberal Rights,* 370–391. Cambridge: Cambridge University Press, 1991. First published in *Harvard Journal of Law and Public Policy* 11 (1988): 625–647.

Warnock, Mary. *Making Babies: Is There a Right to Have Children?* Oxford: Oxford University Press, 2002.

Watson, Gary. "Free Agency." *Journal of Philosophy* 72, no. 8 (1975): 205–220.

We Are Fathers 4 Justice: The Campaign Against a Fatherless Society. http://www.fathers-4-justice.org/.

Wellman, Christopher Heath. "On Conflicts between Rights." *Law and Philosophy* 14, nos. 3–4 (1995): 271–295.

Westen, Peter. "The Concept of Equal Opportunity." *Ethics* 95, no. 4 (1985): 837–850.

Whitbeck, Caroline. "The Maternal Instinct." In *Mothering: Essays in Feminist Theory,* edited by Joyce Trebilcot, 185–191. Totowa, NJ: Rowman and Allanheld, 1984.

Winnicott, D. W. *The Family and Individual Development.* London: Tavistock Publications, 1965.

Wolff, Jonathan. "Fairness, Respect, and the Egalitarian Ethos." *Philosophy & Public Affairs* 27, no. 2 (1998): 97–122.

Wollestonecraft, Mary. *A Vindication of the Rights of Woman.* Edited by Sylvana Tomaselli. Cambridge: Cambridge University Press, 1995.

INDEX